CROSS-LINGUISTIC PERSPECTIVES ON LANGUAGE PROCESSING

STUDIES IN THEORETICAL PSYCHOLINGUISTICS

VOLUME 25

The titles published in this series are listed at the end of this volume.

CROSS-LINGUISTIC PERSPECTIVES ON LANGUAGE PROCESSING

edited by

MARICA DE VINCENZI
Università di Chieti and Istituto di Psicologia del CNR-Roma

and

VINCENZO LOMBARDO
Università del Piemonte Orientale 'A. Avogadro', Alessandria

KLUWER ACADEMIC PUBLISHERS
DORDRECHT / BOSTON / LONDON

Library of Congress Cataloging-in-Publication Data

ISBN 0-7923-6146-6

Published by Kluwer Academic Publishers,
P.O. Box 17, 3300 AA Dordrecht, The Netherlands.

Sold and distributed in North, Central and South America
by Kluwer Academic Publishers,
101 Philip Drive, Norwell, MA 02061, U.S.A.

In all other countries, sold and distributed
by Kluwer Academic Publishers,
P.O. Box 322, 3300 AH Dordrecht, The Netherlands.

Printed on acid-free paper

Printed in the Netherlands.

TABLE OF CONTENTS

Marica De Vincenzi and Vincenzo Lombardo

INTRODUCTION

Recent studies in psycholinguistics have ranged through a variety of languages. In this trend, which has no precedent, studies in language processing have followed studies in language acquisition and theoretical linguistics in considering language universals in a broader scope than only in English.

Since the beginning of the century, studies in language acquisition have produced a vast body of data from a number of Indoeuropean languages, and the emphasis on the universal has preceded the emphasis on the particular (see (Slobin 1985) for a review). Nowadays, the research in the field advances by means of a continuous linking between the cross-linguistic uniformities and the individual language influences on development. The level of language universals is continuously refined as the data from a number of languages contribute to the elaboration of a more distinctive picture of the language of children.

The first cross-linguistic studies in theoretical linguistics appeared at the end of the seventies. Within the Chomskian paradigm, the reference to the Romance languages caused a shift from a rule-based toward a principle-based formalism (Chomsky 1981, 1995); within alternative theories, the reduced prominence of the pure phrase structure component in favor of the lexicon and/or the functional relations (see, e.g., Lexical Functional Grammar (Bresnan 1982), Relational Grammar (Perlmutter 1983)) sought empirical support in languages exhibiting deep structural differences with respect to English (e.g. Bantu, Malayalam, Romance and Slavic languages Warlpiri). The

M. De Vincenzi and V. Lombardo (eds.), Cross-linguistic Perspectives on Language Processing, 1–19.

cross-linguistic research tested empirically the universal tenets of a formal theory, both by investigating a single phenomenon available in several languages (e.g. passivization), and by investigating a single phenomenon available in a single language or a group of related languages (e.g. expletives in non pro-drop languages). These two lines of empirical investigation can be reformulated in the recent (cross-linguistic) studies of language processing. The ultimate evidence that one can acquire on narrow aspects of a theory cannot be found within a single language.

The study of the human language processor invokes an obvious comparison with the development of automatic language processors (computational linguistics). A language understanding system is compelled to face the peculiarities of an individual language (see, e.g., the procedural adjustments to face the flexibility of word order, the retrieval of the subject relation in pro-drop languages, and the resolution of ambiguities). Such peculiarities concern both the analyses of the language-specific phenomena in a reference formalism (geared to testing the correctness of the predictions of a theoretical framework) and the strategies for an efficient processing, given a language and a reference framework.. Note the similarity with the second line of investigation above. These requirements have helped both to evaluate the goodness of a linguistic theory, and to formulate linguistic theories oriented towards a computational treatment (e.g., Unification-based grammars (Shieber 1986)). Furthermore, typical cross-linguistic applications, like machine translation, involve the definition of a common representation level for the two target languages (note the similarity with the first line of investigation above).

The cross-linguistic studies in language processing bear on the issue of the universality of the human language processor; that is, whether the components of the processor that have been developed from the study of processing in one (or more) language, can be considered universal. Taking a developmental perspective that evolved from the studies on language acquisition (see above), a pioneering cross-linguistic experience in sentence processing was the research prompted by a general processing framework, the Competition Model of MacWhinney and Bates (1989). The description of the language processor involves, but is not limited to, the definition of the following components:

1. the structural relations which describe the syntactic representation of a sentence and which the processor accesses;

2. the operational primitives which build the syntactic structure;

3. the principles and preferences that guide the processing strategies;

4. the general architecture of the language processor (serial vs. parallel models, autonomy of syntax vs. interactive models, etc.).

The cross-linguistic study of sentence processing addresses the definition and the experimental test of these components, together with an indication of which components or which parts of a component are universal. This goal is far more ambitious than the description of how the sentence processor works for an individual language, since the degrees of freedom for a plausible computational model decrease enormously. The processing primitives and principles proposed for language 1 must hold also for language 2, language 3, etc, and possibly have to account for phenomena that do not occur in language 1.

The definition of a computational model of the language processor results from a compromise between the theoretical elegance of the model and the empirical cross-linguistic coverage. The universality (or reduction) of the entities which form a computational model (i.e. the general architecture, the descriptive relations of the syntactic structure and the processing primitives or principles contribute to the theoretical elegance); however, sometimes only parameterization or language-specific strategies can produce the variations able to cope with multilingual data.. In this latter case, we should question why the proposed strategies are not universal. If the goal of the psycholinguist is to study the human sentence processor, and not "a language" sentence processor, the test of universality serves to establish whether the strategy addresses a level of abstraction sufficient to generalize over different languages and/or constructions (cf. De Vincenzi, in press). With this perspective, a failure to pass such a test can provide fruitful consequences: for example, Frazier and Clifton (1996), prompted by some failures of experimental testing of Late Closure, propose a new parsing principle for a subclass of modifiers (mainly adjuncts).

The definition of the processor components can identify:

5. the relations of the grammatical entities which are responsible cross-linguistically for the characterization of parsing difficulty (see (Frank and Vijay-Schanker, this volume) on c-command, and (Baccino et al., this volume) (Meng and Bader, this volume) on markedness of features);

6. the operational primitives that account cross-linguistically for both parsing and re-analysis (see (Fodor and Inoue, this volume) on Attach and Adjust);

7. the parsing principles governing the initial parsing decisions (see (Meng and Bader, this volume, on Case Preference Principle; Baccino et al. and Frenck-Mestre et al., this volume, on Late Closure vs. Construal, and (Traxler et al., this volume) for an extension to Construal (Frazier and Clifton, 1996));

8. the consequences of the encapsulation of the syntactic information and processing (see (Traxler et al., this volume) on the serial/competitive nature of the processor).

The test of a computational model of the language processor raises a methodological issue: the experimenter can pursue a multilingual or a monolingual approach, a choice which can be roughly related to the two lines of investigation described above for theoretical linguistics.

In the multilingual approach, the experiment tests one or more components of the language processor on a single phenomenon (that is, along one linguistic dimension) which occurs in several languages. Two examples are (a) the studies that compare the attachment of relative clause modifiers to complex noun phrases in several languages (see (Baccino et al., this volume) and (Frenck-Mestre and Pynte, this volume) on French and Italian), and (b) the factors that determine structure priming in sentence production (discourse saliency in (Branigan and Prat-Sala, this volume) and conceptual structure in (Heydel and Murray, this volume)). A crucial point of the experiments is the perfect equivalence of the linguistic materials and its presentation to the participants in both languages. This is in order to ensure that the processing differences found across languages are a true reflection of differences across languages and not of differences across construction. In this latter case, in fact nothing can be claimed about cross-linguistic differences (see Frazier, 1999; Baccino et al., this volume).

In the monolingual approach, the study of some specific aspect of one language (or a group of languages) can carry important implications for the universal aspects of the human sentence processor. The extension of the model of the language processor to account for these language specific phenomena can affect the whole structure of the model, with effects on the universality issues. Examples are the researches that address the processing of the case feature (see (Meng and Bader, this volume) on German) and of the null subject (see (De Vincenzi 1991) on Italian), and the ones that test the plausibility of an architecture (see the discussion on the competition-based model in (Traxler et al., this volume)).

A sort of midway approach occurs when monolingual experiments in one language provide interesting insights about the materials employed in an experiment which tests the same phenomenon in another language. These insights lead to the refinement of the experiment material, which can shed a novel light on the phenomenon at hand. An example is the modifier attachment study conducted on English by Traxler et al. (this volume), which has produced the surprising result of a facilitated processing of ambiguous relative clauses.

In the rest of this introduction, we provide an extensive description of each paper in the volume, by arranging them according to the main focus of each paper.

The two contributions by Fodor and Inoue and by Frank and Vijay-Shanker present general theories of parsing and re-analysis, focussing on the parsing primitives, in terms of basic operations and structural relations respectively.

The main point of Fodor and Inoue's paper is that it is not the case that revision is resorted to only when no more legal attachments exist. The immediate consequence of this point is the abandonment of the RALR (Revision As Last Resort) principle (Fodor and Frazier, 1980) and the coalescence of the Attach and Attach Anyway operations. But let us proceed in order. In previous models, (Lewis, 1993; Fodor and Inoue, 1994, 1998), these two operations referred to the first pass analysis and the re-analysis, respectively. Attach integrates the next input word into the current partial phrase marker, according to the grammar constraints and the parsing preferences; Attach Anyway integrates the next input word into the current partial phrase marker in the location that least severely violates the grammar; a further operation, Adjust, rearranges the items in the current partial phrase marker (or CPPM) in order to satisfy the grammar constraints. In the model proposed in this paper, there is no difference between the two phases, and the revision preferences competes with other preferences in the solution of attachment ambiguity. The collapse of Attach and Attach Anyway into a single operation, Attach (Anyway), makes attachment independent of the grammar check, performed by Adjust. Both in the first-pass analysis and the re-analysis, Attach (Anyway) works by searching the most rapid attachment which least severely violates the grammar (in the extreme case, an attachment is perfectly legal). The race-based model proposed by Fodor and Inoue (cf. McRoy and Hirst 1990; Traxler et al., this volume) selects the most rapid attachment. Since the revision mechanism involves longer and more costly operations, it usually loses the competition against simpler principles. RALR comes out as a by-product of this more general analysis model. The empirical data which justify this model come from the analysis of the Japanese left branching structure, and further recent evidence from English.

Frank and Vijay-Shanker address the type of structural relations which the processor accesses when it updates the syntactic structure. Their claim is that the c-command relation on entities of the syntactic structure is more directly related to parsing difficulty than the dominance relation. In the literature, parsing difficulty is generally related to the type of re-analysis performed. An operational account which is common to several theories of re-analysis is that lowering a constituent is an easy restructuring (cf. Gorrell 1995; Sturt and Crocker 1996). This finding explains, for example, why the re-analysis of an object NP to a subject NP of a subsequent clause is easier in (1) than in (2):

(1) John knows the truth hurts.

(2) Since Joy always jogs a mile seems quite a short distance to him.

In (1), "the truth" moves low in the syntactic structure from the object position of "knows" to the subject position of "hurts"; in (2), "a mile" should move in the syntactic structure from the object position of "jogs" to the subject position of "seems". The first movement is a lowering, the second is not (actually it is not a raising either). The formalization of this account goes back to the D-theory (Marcus et al. 1983): the syntactic structure is an underspecified representation of dominance relations, which grows monotonically. Conscious garden paths require non monotonic retractions of some dominance relations, and the assertion of new dominance relations. Lowering is typically monotonic, because it consists in introducing only new dominance relations. However, there exist some data in the literature (Frank and Vijay-Schanker mention an example from

Japanese) that question the universality of the easiness of lowering. Some authors have solved the puzzle by overtly limiting the application of lowering to some configurations and by introducing parametric variations on the strategy across languages (see e.g. (Sturt and Crocker, 1996)). Frank and Vijay-Schanker offer a radical solution, by changing the relation which the parser refers to for keeping monotonicity. Instead of the dominance relation, they propose the c-command, which is ubiquitous in linguistic theories.

Parametric variations in linguistic primitives and parsing strategies are no longer necessary. The authors show that the known cases of difficult garden-path correspond to violations of the c-command relations in the syntactic structure. This paper provides a radically new perspective on parsing models, which will probably elicit considerable experimental research.

The contributions of Baccino, De Vincenzi and Job, the one of Frenck-Mestre and Pynte, and the one of Traxler, Pickering, Clifton and van Gompel are closely related in that they empirically investigate the parsing of modifiers (such as relative clause, prepositional phrases, adjectival phrases).

The first two papers investigate the attachment of a relative clause to a complex noun phrase in closely related languages, French and Italian; the third paper proposes a new experiment in English on the same topic, with the refinement of the linguistic material that takes into account the insights provided by previous experiments in different languages.

The paper by Baccino et al. gives empirical support to the universality of Late Closure. The study replicates on French subjects the experiment described by De Vincenzi and Job (1995) on Italian. The issue of replication is a fundamental aspect of the study: in fact, the main contribution of this paper is a first step towards the setting of an experimental paradigm that allows the evaluation of parsing preferences across languages. Parallel experiments must be carefully designed in order to avoid external influences that, in a cross-linguistic setting, are much more likely. Specifically, the studies reported here closely matched the experimental procedure, the input segmentation and the linguistic material in the two languages. The material was sentences of the form (3), with the relative clause attachment disambiguated by gender agreement on the participle, and with different prepositions ("of" (3a) and "with" (3b)) within the complex noun phrase:

(3a) The bar-tender was looking at the friend(masc) of the woman who was silent (masc/fem) in front of the pub.

(3b) Nobody invited the movie director with the beautiful girlfriend who remained (masc/fem) to drink.

The results show that there is a similar effect of Late Closure on the reading time of the critical segment, with an immediate facilitation for the attachment of the relative clause to the second noun of the complex noun phrase. However, on the final comprehension measure, there is a difference between French and Italian that the authors attribute to an unavoidable difference between the gender marking on the two languages.

The study by Frenck-Mestre and Pynte investigates the parsing principle influencing the attachment of a relative clause to a complex noun phrase with an eye-movement experiment in French. The material was similar to that used in the Baccino et al. study: namely sentences containing a relative clause that attaches to a complex noun phrase containing the preposition "of" or the preposition "with".

(4) John photographed the daughter of Charles who seemed more disdainful (masc/fem) than usual.

Here, the presentation of the material occurs in two separate blocks, one block containing only the preposition "of", the other containing only the preposition "with". The results show a late closure effect for the preposition "with". However, the attachment preference for the preposition "of" is affected by the order of presentation of the sentences (syntactic priming). The "of" sentences exhibit an attachment preference of the relative clause to the first noun; but, when the block with the preposition "with" is presented first, this preference disappears. The authors call this a syntactic priming effect.

The comparison between these two studies is particularly enlightening with regard to the difficulty of conducting cross-linguistic research in a multilingual approach: both studies conduct a careful consideration of the methodological aspects on the processing of the same construction. The results still show discrepancies that do not permit the confident assessment of the universality of the principle that governs the initial attachment of the relative clause to a complex noun phrase. Nevertheless, there are further methodological aspects to be settled. The internal structure of the relative clause and the presence or absence of experimental fillers may provide interesting cues for the different results of the two studies.

Also in the paper by Traxler et al. the reference phenomenon is modifier attachment. Three eye-tracking experiments evaluate the attachment of prepositional phrases and relative clauses to complex noun phrases. The interesting and novel contribution here is that, contrary to the studies of Baccino et al. and Frenck-Mestre and Pynte, the experiments include three conditions: (a) a condition that disambiguates toward early closure attachment,

(b) a condition that disambiguates toward late closure and (c) a condition which maintains the ambiguity.

(5a) The driver of the car that had the moustache was pretty cool.

(5b) The car of the driver that had the moustache was pretty cool.

(5c) The son of the driver that had the moustache was pretty cool.

The results (expressed in total reading time for the relative clause) reveal an easiness of processing of the ambiguous attachment (condition (c)), with respect to the disambiguated conditions (a) and (b). These data, according to the authors, rule out competitive theories of parsing, such as general constraint-based models. For a constraint-based model, a situation in which two parallel analyses (as in (c)) have to be kept for a longer time, should produce a greater processing load than conditions (a) and (b), in which one analysis can be quickly ruled out by plausibility. According to Traxler et al., Construal seems the most viable theory compatible with the data, although with extensions in the sense of a race-based model.

This research follows the monolingual approach, after the refinements introduced from experiments in other languages. The most relevant finding, namely that an ambiguous structure is parsed faster than an unambiguous one, seems to be in neat contrast with the constraint-based model. This finding should be evaluated on more structures and more languages and with careful attention to the methodology. However, if confirmed, it poses real challenges to either serial or constraint-based processors.

The work of Meng & Bader is another instance of a cross-linguistic study with a monolingual approach, specifically German. The research examines the role of case and number agreement features in the resolution of syntactic ambiguities. The topic of feature processing has often been neglected in theories of sentence processing. In some cases, the reason for this lack of interest is somehow accidental: for example, the case feature is not very rich in the morphology of English, the most studied language from the processing viewpoint. However, case marking is commonly present in German: for example, all articles and all nouns (except proper names and bare nouns) are case marked as nominative, accusative or dative. Therefore, for a scholar of sentence processing in German, the study of case marking processing is inevitable.

Meng and Bader introduce the Case Preference principle, which predicts that, in case of ambiguity, (a) a structural case (such as nominative or accusative) is preferred to a lexical case; (b) the nominative case is preferred to the accusative case.

The first statement of the principle is able to explain why in cases of accusative versus dative object ambiguities, there is a preference for the accusative object analysis. An example is given in (6): in (6) "Personen" has a case marking which is ambiguous between being either accusative or dative. The correct case of "Personen" is determined at the end of the sentence by the argument selection of the verb. The verb "support" in (a) selects an accusative object, while the verb "help" in (b) selects a dative object.

(6a) Personen, die in Not sind, sollte man unterstutzen.

Persons, who are in distress, should one support.

One should support persons who are in distress.

(6b) Personen, die in Not sind, sollte man helfen.
Persons, who are in distress, should one help.
One should help persons who are in distress.

The results show that there is a facilitation for sentences like (6a), as predicted by the Case Preference principle. Furthermore, assuming that the two sentences (6a) and (6b) have similar structural representation, this preference is not easily captured by any phrase structure parsing principle.

Another interesting theoretical question can also be whether parsing decisions based on phrase structural principles can be equally well explained by case preference principles. In a study on wh-questions with a subject/object ambiguity of the wh-element, the authors claim that the well known preference for a subject analysis of the wh-elements can be explained by the second statement of the case preference principle, namely that in cases of ambiguity between a nominative or accusative case marking, nominative is preferred.

The work opens up interesting fields of investigation, namely to see the relative weight of the Case Preference principle and structural parsing principles, and whether such principle interaction holds not only in German but also in other languages that have different systems of Case marking. Definitely, a parsing theory that claims to be universal should address how case marking is processed, at what level of processing it intervenes, and how it interacts with structural factors. The work of Meng and Bader is a first interesting step in this direction.

The contributions by Branigan and Prat-Sala and by Heydel and Murray address the area of language production, largely neglected in the sentence processing literature. Both papers take the multilingual approach, and Heydel and Murray go further in proposing a new cross-linguistic methodology that permits the isolation of conceptual factors in sentence production.

The work of Branigan & Prat-Sala focuses on the influence of discourse context on the productions of syntactic structure, in terms of position prominence (subject versus object – cf. Meng and Bader's work on case preference in processing, this volume) and word order.

Evidence from English (Bock, 1977) has shown that discourse context has an influence on the production of a syntactic structure. In particular, in a recall task, participants tend to repeat the sentence in the format that preserves the order "Given information precedes New information". Branigan and Prat-Sala's paper further refine the influence of discourse context, showing that the relative saliency of two given entities in a discourse, can affect syntactic processing in production. The notion of conceptual accessibility, suggested by Bock & Warren (1985) to explain variations in the production of isolated sentences, provides the interface medium between the discourse saliency and the syntactic structure in the language processor architecture.

The paper describes six experiments conducted in three languages, namely English, Spanish and Catalan. The interesting difference between English on the one hand, and Spanish and Catalan on the other hand, is that English has only one structure in which a patient can be more salient that the agent, namely the passive form, where the patient is the subject. On the contrary, Spanish and Catalan also have the object left dislocated structure, which allows a patient to be more salient (i.e. precedes the agent)

The experiments tested the influence of discourse saliency of participants in short stories on the syntactic structures of utterances produced in describing a picture where the same participants appear. The results showed a significant production of syntactic structures in which the salient element appears earlier than the less salient element. Moreover, active descriptions followed more frequently an agent salient story, while passive descriptions followed a patient-salient story. However, in the latter case, in Spanish and Catalan there was also an increased production of object left dislocated structures.

These results confirm the universality of the influence of discourse structure on the syntactic structure. Cross-linguistic variation in the syntactic structure production is explained through the availability of multiple (language specific) constructions that satisfy the requirements of the discourse structure.

Heydel and Murray's contribution to the investigation of language production addresses what they call the "sentence level priming": the production or perception of a given sentence form, such as active or passive, increases the probability that the speaker will produce another sentence of the same syntactic form. The authors survey the literature on sentence priming: the syntactic repetition is traditionally assumed to depend on a representation or process level that concerns the surface syntactic structure. The authors point out that the data in the literature can fit some alternative explanations to the ones proposed, in particular that this priming effect is due to a conceptual form. The conceptual form here examined refers to the topic/focus articulation of a sentence. In an active sentence, the subject is usually the topic (old) information, while the object is the focus (new) information. In a passive sentence, the opposite is true: the subject (patient) is in focus.

The standard result in sentence priming in English is that production or perception of active sentences increases the production of further active sentences, while production or perception of passive sentences increases the production of other passive sentences. This finding has been usually analyzed as an effect of syntactic form. However, it might well be that the effect is due to the priming of the conceptual form: the distribution of the focus information is what favors the production of form that keeps the agent or the patient in focus. Heydel and Murray observe that in English it is very difficult to test this alternative explanation because there is no alternative word order for passive that allows the patient to be put in focus. In this case, therefore, a monolinguistic methodology is limited, because it cannot discriminate between the various hypotheses of sentence priming.

Therefore the authors propose a cross-linguistic methodology: if subjects are primed across languages and across syntactic structures that keep unaltered the conceptual form, but vary the surface form, then the contribution of the conceptual form to priming is unequivocal.

The authors describe two experiments on German priming in English language production. In German there are two constructions, passive and topicalization of the object, that bring the patient role in focus. However, topicalization of the object has the same surface structure of an active sentence: namely noun phrase (object), verb, noun phrase (subject). The logic here is as follows: active and passive German sentences should prime the productions of active and passive sentences in English as well. However, German object topicalized structure is the critical case: given the surface order of the constituents, it should prime active English sentences, but given its conceptual form it should prime English passives.

The result of the experiment by Heydel and Murray shows that topicalization (in German) primes the production of a passive form (in English), therefore giving a clear indication of the necessary abstraction towards the activation of the conceptual form in sentence priming.

Summing up, the volume provides a perspective on the recent and future research in sentence processing. Cross-linguistic evidence severely constrains the formulation of processing models, and processing models are tested against phenomena in several languages. This trend requires both accurate control of the methodologies for the empirical cross-investigation and more accurate definition of the theoretical primitives of parsing, in order to take into account the uniformities and the differences existing across languages. We believe that this volume offers an in-depth coverage of these themes, proposing also some innovative solutions to many of the issues raised.

REFERENCES

Bock, K. (1977) The effect of a pragmatic presupposition on syntactic structure in sentence answering. Journal of Verbal Learning and Verbal Behaviour, 16, 723-734.

Bresnan, J. (1982), The mental representation of grammatical relations. MIT Press.

Chomsky, N. (1981) Lectures on Government and Binding theory, Foris Publications, Dordrecht.

Chomsky, N. (1995) The minimalist program. Cambridge, MA: MIT Press.

De Vincenzi, M. (1991) Syntactic Parsing Strategies in Italian. Kluwer Academic Publishers, Dordrecht: The Netherlands.

De Vincenzi, M. and Job, R. (1995) An investigation of Late Closure: the role of syntax, thematic structure and pragmatic in initial and final interpretation. Journal of Experimental Psychology: Learning, Memory and Cognition, 21, pp. 1303-1321.

De Vincenzi, M. (in press) Cross-linguistic psycholinguistics. In M. Crocker, M. Pickering and C. Clifton (eds) Architectures and Mechanisms of Language Processing: Cambridge University Press.

Fodor, J.D. and Frazier, L. (1980) Is the human sentence parsing mechanism an ATN? Cognition, 8, 417-459.

Fodor, J.D. and Inoue, A. (1994) The diagnosis and cure of garden paths. Journal of Psycholinguistic Research, 23(5), 407-434.

Fodor, J.D. and Inoue, A. (1998) Attach Anyway. In Ferreira, F. and Fodor, J. D. (eds.) Re-analysis in Sentence Processing, Dordrecht, The Netherlands, Kluwer Academic Publishers.

Frazier, L. (1999) Are Japanese children's parser's parameter's settings the same as the settings of the parameters of the parser of English? APA Review of Books, vol. 44, n. 1.

Frazier, L. and Clifton, C. (1996) Construal. Cambridge, MA: MIT Press.

Frazier, L. and Fodor, J.D. (1978) The sausage machine: A new two-stage parsing model. Cognition, 6, 291-326.

Gorrell, P. (1995). Syntax and Parsing. Cambridge: Cambridge University Press.

Lewis, R. (1993). An Architecturally-based Theory of Human Sentence Comprehension. Unpublished PhD Thesis, Carnegie Mellon University, CMU-CS-93-226.

MacWhinney, B. and Bates, E. (1989). The Cross-Linguistic Study of Sentence Processing. Cambridge, Uk: Cambridge University Press.

Marcus M., Hindle D. and Fleck (1983) D-theory: Talking about talking about trees. In: Proceedings of the 21th Annual Meeting of the Association for Computational Linguistics, 129-136, Cambridge: Ma.

McRoy S.W., and Hirst G. (1990) Race-based parsing and Syntactic disambiguation, Cognitive Science 14, 313-353.

Perlmutter, D. (1983) Studies in Relational Grammar. Chicago, IL: University of Chicago Press.

Shieber, S.M. (1986) An Introduction to Unification-based Approach to Grammar, CSLI Lecture Notes 4, Stanford: CSLI.

Slobin, D. I. (1985) The cross-linguistic study of language acquisition. Volume 1: The data. Hillsdale, N.J.: Lawrence Erlbaum.

Sturt, P. and Crocker, M. (1996) Monotonic Syntactic Processing: a cross-linguistic study of attachment and re-analysis. Language and Cognitive Processes, Vol 11, Number 5, pp.449-494.

Janet Dean Fodor and Atsu Inoue

GARDEN PATH RE-ANALYSIS: ATTACH (ANYWAY) AND REVISION AS LAST RESORT*

ATTACH AND ADJUST

The human sentence processing device sometimes makes errors, and when it does, it can sometimes correct them. This much is generally agreed, though opinions differ with respect to how and why the errors occur. In this paper we are concerned with the process of recovery from garden paths in sentence processing. A garden path occurs when the parser makes an error in assigning structure to the input word string but is nevertheless able to continue integrating some subsequent words into the structure that it has constructed for the sentence so far (the current partial phrase marker, or CPPM). Recognition that a garden path has occurred comes from the subsequent discovery that there is a word in the input string which does not fit into the CPPM. This word is the error signal, or *symptom*, that reveals the existence of the earlier error of analysis. The parser's task is to discover the nature of the problem and put it right if possible. The input may actually be ungrammatical, in which case nothing can be done. But the parser must also consider the possibility that it is the analysis that is at fault: that some aspect of the CPPM prior to the symptom is incorrect. Recovery from a garden path consists in finding an alternative analysis which fits the initial portion of the sentence and also accommodates the symptom and later words.

M. De Vincenzi and V. Lombardo (eds.), Cross-linguistic Perspectives on Language Processing, 21–61.

One way for the processor to find an alternative analysis would be to go back and try parsing the sentence again in a different manner. Another strategy would be to try altering the CPPM to resolve the incompatibility with the symptom word. In previous work (Fodor & Inoue, 1994, 1998) we have argued that the human parsing mechanism does the latter, and specifically that it tackles the problem by fitting the incompatible word into the CPPM as best it can, and then using the grammar to identify what aspect of the CPPM the new word conflicts with. Having discovered where the conflict lies, the parser changes the tree so as to resolve it. That may settle the matter, or it may create a new conflict elsewhere. If it does, the parser sets about eliminating that problem, and so on, until finally — if all goes well — it corrects the original error which sent the analysis astray. At that point the whole CPPM is in a stable state of well-formedness. The conflicting input item has been absorbed, and forward parsing can proceed again.

This parser is defined by three principles. First-pass parsing follows the principle *Attach*. Garden path reanalysis is governed by *Attach Anyway* (see also Lewis, 1993, Ch.3) and *Adjust*.

1. ***Attach***: On receiving a word of the input sentence, connect it to the current partial phrase marker (CPPM) for the sentence in such a way that the resulting CPPM is syntactically well-formed though possibly incomplete at its right edge.

2. ***Attach Anyway***: Having established that there is no legitimate attachment site in the CPPM for the current input word, attach the input word into the CPPM wherever it least severely violates the grammar, and subject to the usual preference principles that govern Attach.

3. ***Adjust***: When a grammatical conflict has been created between two nodes or features X and Y in the CPPM, by either Attach Anyway or Adjust, eliminate the problem by altering minimally (i.e., no more than is necessary for conflict resolution) whichever of X and Y was less recently acted on, without regard for grammatical conflicts thereby created between that node and other elements in the CPPM.

For discussion of various aspects of these principles not touched on here, see Fodor & Inoue (1998). We assume that in case of ambiguity in the first-pass parse, where more than one attachment site for an item exists, Attach chooses between them on the basis of the selection principle *Minimal Everything*. This subsumes more specific principles such as *Minimal Attachment*, *Right Association* (or *Late Closure*), and the *Minimal Chain Principle*, and represents a very general preference for 'least effort' options. We assume that the importance of minimizing effort is ultimately due to the *First Analysis Constraint* (Frazier & Rayner, 1988; see also Frazier & Fodor, 1978), under which the parser adopts whichever attachment of an item is computed most rapidly.[1] This will be relevant to the discussion below. To free the general concept from the details of the Frazier & Rayner wording of it we could reformulate it as *Attach Quickly*:

4. ***Attach Quickly***: On receiving a word of the input sentence, connect it to the CPPM as quickly as possible.

This simply records the fact that under normal circumstances the parser is under pressure to attach each input item as quickly as it can. It entails that the first attachment site that the parser detects is the one it must adopt. Attach Quickly overlaps with the statement of Attach in (1), and holds out the hope that they are one and the same principle. We return to this point at the end of the paper, after we have considered the relation between Attach and Attach Anyway.

The importance of Attach Anyway, which forcibly integrates the garden path symptom into the current analysis, is that the conflict between the CPPM and the garden path symptom is thereby moved into the CPPM, which is a linguistic representation subject to grammatical principles. The grammar can therefore do the diagnostic work of determining the nature of the problem. Since the grammar must constantly be checking well-formedness of the CPPM in the normal course of first-pass parsing, this is not an additional burden. Forcing the incompatible word into the tree is thus more parsimonious than a revision system that first tries to alter the CPPM to provide a legitimate attachment site before integrating the symptom. In the latter case there would have to be some special-purpose device that could reason about how a well-formed CPPM might be altered in such a way that it could accommodate some arbitrary word. The Attach Anyway system needs no additional machinery, except for the operations which effect the tree changes that eliminate grammatical violations: operations such as expelling an item from its current location, stealing a constituent from a nearby site, changing the values of syntactic features. The empirical claim of the model is that these repair operations carry no special penalty. They are no more effortful than first-pass operations, and none of them is significantly more difficult than any other, contrary to the claims of most other models of re-analysis. We propose that only diagnosis carries significant costs. What makes some garden paths harder to recover from than others is that in the difficult ones, Adjust is less successful at identifying which repairs to make.

The adjustment process defined by (3) is linguistically sophisticated because it is guided by the grammar at every step, but still it is not guaranteed to identify the original error in every case. This is because the mistakes made by a 'left-to-right' parsing device operating on the word string result from what the parser knows and does as it encounters the words; they do not necessarily follow a pattern that would be obvious to the parser looking BACK at the tree structure. Adjust does not attempt to reconstruct the actions of the first-pass parser and consider which of them might have been otherwise. It takes no account of where there was ambiguity in the word string and what the parser's alternatives were at those points. Instead, Adjust works on harmonizing the relations within the CPPM, without speculating about how it got to be that way. The relations it considers are those defined by the grammar, relations such as agreement, binding, control, and lexical selection. In Fodor & Inoue (1997, 1998) we show that a number of observed contrasts between easy and difficult garden paths follow from the hypothesis that the path that Adjust follows through the tree from one trouble spot to another is defined by grammatical dependency relations.

In the present paper we consider another area in which this model sheds light on the behavior of the parser. The issue is when and why revision is initiated. This concerns the interplay between first-pass and repair processes, which in this model amounts to the relationship between Attach and Attach Anyway. We will argue here that there is no sharp division between the responsibilities of these two principles, and that they can and should be merged into one. We document the fact that revision is undertaken with less prompting than has been assumed in prior work: it is not the case that revision is resorted to only when no legitimate attachments exist. We conclude that the avoidance of revision is not an absolute goal of the human parser, as would be the case if Attach always applied before Attach Anyway, but is just one desideratum to be weighed in the balance against others. To summarize the argument we develop below: Revision in the diagnosis model begins with Attach Anyway, which is similar to first-pass Attach and naturally coalesces with it. Minimization of revision is then not an absolute rule entailed by a basic fact of parser design, but is just one of the preference principles that guide the operation of the attachment system. So minimization of revision may win or lose against some other preference, depending on what their relative strengths happen to be for a particular construction type. This explains how it is possible for there to be a general tendency to avoid revision and yet exceptions to it, too.

LOW ATTACHMENT VERSUS RALR

Attach and Attach Anyway are similar in both content and function. They differ primarily in the initial clause of Attach Anyway, which presupposes a failed search for legitimate attachments. If this is set aside, then Attach Anyway subsumes Attach. Attach makes only grammatically acceptable attachments, but a grammatically acceptable attachment is the limiting case of an attachment which "least severely violates the grammar". So the two principles could be folded together into a completely general attachment principle governing both first-pass parsing and garden path repair, as in (5):

5. ***Attach (Anyway)***: On receiving a word of the input sentence, connect it to the current partial phrase marker for the sentence wherever it least severely violates the grammar, subject to the preference principles.

There is theoretical elegance to be gained by this unification, but whether it is appropriate is at least in part an empirical matter. Suppose the two principles remain independent. Then it is natural to assume that Attach applies first and searches for fully grammatical attachments for the input word, and that Attach Anyway applies afterwards if none is found. There would be two distinct phases of computation, one making very strict use of the grammar, and then a later one operating with relaxed constraints. By contrast, for the combined Attach (Anyway), legitimate attachments would take priority not because of order of application, but by conformity to the "least severe violation" requirement. We will argue that there is empirical merit in this latter approach. Because of Attach Quickly, the parser's choice of an attachment site is determined by the outcome of a race. The integration of first- and second-pass attachment in (5) implies that there is just ONE race in which attachments involving revision and attachments without revision all participate. It is possible, in that case, that an attachment with revision might in some circumstances win the race. Thus the combined principle Attach (Anyway) offers a natural explanation for the fact that the parser does not always give priority to legitimate attachments.

Avoidance of revision was originally formulated as an absolute principle, the *Revision as Last Resort* (RALR) principle (Fodor & Frazier, 1980).[2] This reflected the empirical generalization, which we believed at the time to be true, that the human parser does not alter structural decisions it has already made, except where it has some specific reason to conclude that they were wrong. The parser's actions at one point in the parse are normally predicated on the decisions it made at earlier points. For example, in *They told the teacher that the children met in the schoolyard*, the minimal attachment of the *that*-clause as a complement rather than a relative clause causes the verb *met* later on to be construed as intransitive (with reciprocal meaning). It is even possible in principle for the parser to end up with a more complex overall analysis, by obeying Minimal

Attachment along the way (though examples are not easy to find).

However, it now appears that this total ban on revision except where absolutely unavoidable was too strong. Some cases have been noted in which it seems that the parser does not obey RALR. In Inoue & Fodor (1995) we observed some shifts in Japanese from left-branching to right-branching structures for no obvious cause; the left-branching structure was well-formed, so this was not a last resort situation. Kamide & Mitchell (1997) have reported a similar effect for relative clause attachment in Japanese. We discuss these examples in sections 6 and 7. First we consider some striking new examples that have been noted in English. In these cases it appears that the tendency towards low attachment (= Late Closure, Right Association, or equivalently: local attachment to the nodes dominating immediately preceding input items)[3] is so strong that the parser prefers to attach low and revise, rather than attach high without revision.

In example (6), there is a height-of-attachment ambiguity for the VP *was biassed against....* Perceivers report a (mild) surprise that the sentence ends as soon as it does.

(6) The lawyer who believed the witness was biassed against repeat offenders.

This suggests that the VP *was biassed against...* is initially attaching low, as the predicate of a complement clause with *the witness* as its subject, rather than attaching high, with *the lawyer who believed the witness* as its subject. On the low attachment analysis the sentence is missing its obligatory matrix VP, so perceivers have the impression that it is incomplete. The preference for the complement clause analysis here is quite surprising, since it is generally regarded as derived by revision of an initial direct object attachment of the postverbal NP (in accord with Minimal Attachment).[4] In the present case such revision is not forced on the parser; it is perfectly avoidable by attaching the VP *was biassed against...* as the predicate of the main clause. Note that the main clause VP is a predictable, obligatory constituent in a prominent tree position, so — even apart from a desire to avoid revision — it could be expected to be a highly favored attachment option. The fact that it is dispreferred suggests that the natural desirability of this attachment site is outweighed by a distaste for high attachment. For the HSPM, low attachment with revision outranks high attachment without revision, at least in this construction.

What we have observed is that the parser's (other) attachment preference principles can override RALR.[5] Another instance of this is found in (7), where intuitive judgments indicate that the VP *irritated the rest of us* tends to attach inside the *that*-clause complement to *fact*, rather than as the VP of the matrix clause. This preference shows up as an expectation for an additional VP (e.g., *spoiled the whole evening*) at the end of (7).

(7) The fact that John didn't like the soprano and the baritone irritated the rest of us...

a. The fact that John didn't like [[the soprano] and the baritone]] irritated the rest of us.

b. The fact that [[John didn't like the soprano] and [the baritone irritated the rest of us]]...

Note that the preferred low attachment of the *irritated* VP involves revision of a first-pass NP-coordination analysis as in (7a) into an IP-coordination analysis as in (7b). The parser could have retained the NP-coordination structure if it had attached the VP high. Also, just as in (6), high attachment of the VP would have had the advantage of filling in the obligatory matrix predicate without which the sentence could not be complete.

Again we can conclude that the preference for low attachment can outweigh other factors, including the avoidance of revision.

Phillips (1996) presents examples of other constructions which display this ability of low attachment to overpower RALR. This is the case in (8), at least if adding a relative clause into a noun phrase counts as revision.[6]

(8) Because the conference organizers liked the caterers they hired them for the banquet in honor of the former president.

The clause beginning *they hired...* tends at first to attach as a relative clause modifying *the caterers*. Phillips' self-paced reading data confirm this relative clause preference. Elevated reading times for the pronoun *them* in (8) (relative to an unambiguous baseline sentence) indicate that it comes as a surprise, as it would if the parser were anticipating a relative clause 'gap' at that position. As in the previous examples, an apparently optimal alternative attachment is overlooked. There is an obligatory site in (8) for a finite clause at the matrix level, a site that the parser could anticipate well in advance, and that requires no revision; yet (until the disambiguation by *them*) the parser is oblivious to it.

To sum up: English offers a number of examples in which revision of the first-pass analysis is not treated by the parser as if it were a last resort option. It appears that what is paramount for the parser, at least in these contexts, is low attachment; to achieve it, the parser is prepared to undo its earlier work and re-attach prior material. We suppose (though the explanation is not central to our point here) that the low attachment preference is due to the way in which the parser searches for possible attachment sites (see Fodor & Inoue, 1998). We assume that appropriate nodes are projected upward over the input word (with any obligatory sister nodes represented also), and that the parser compares this stack of potential nodes with those along the right edge of the CPPM, looking for a match that will permit unification of the two partial structures. A preference for both low and minimal attachment is predicted on the assumption that this search for matching nonterminals starts at the bottom of the two structures. This would be for 'least effort' reasons, to minimize the number of nodes that need to be examined and to establish the shortest path linking the new input item with the previous one. That is, the hunt for an attachment site is governed by Attach Quickly, which favors Late Closure and Minimal Attachment.

DOES RALR EXIST?

We have suggested that Late Closure (low or local attachment, Right Association) is such a powerful tendency that it outweighs RALR. But this is plausible only if there is reason to believe that Late Closure is a powerful tendency. In fact there has been considerable discussion recently to the effect that LC is weak or nonexistent, or at least considerably more limited than early work on English suggested (e.g., Kimball, 1973). High attachment has been observed in Spanish, Italian, French, Dutch, German, Afrikaans, and possibly other languages (Cuetos & Mitchell, 1988; Frazier & Clifton, 1996; Mitchell & Brysbaert, 1998). This would seem to undermine our proposed explanation of RALR violations. If RALR is defeasible by a very weak Late Closure tendency, then RALR can't be very forceful either, in which case exceptions to RALR are of little interest. We will argue now that this is not the appropriate conclusion to draw from examples like (6) - (8).

Across all languages, only one case of ambiguity resolution by high attachment has been reported (for ambiguities involving two sites of the same category differing only with respect to their height in the CPPM).[7, 8] This involves attachment of a relative clause to either a higher or a lower NP node, where the two sites are separated by one PP node, as in (9a). And this construction (9b) shows only a marginal LC bias for English as well.

(9a) Alguien disparó contra [NP la criada [pp de [np la actriz + REL CL (que estaba en el balcón)
Someone shot against the maid of the actress who was on the balcony

(9b) Someone shot [NP the servant [PP of [NP the actress + REL CL (who was on the balcony)

The high attachment bias seems to be weakened if the adjunct to be attached is a non-clausal constituent such as a PP, as in (10).

(10a) Alguien disparó contra [$_{NP}$ la criada [$_{PP}$ de [$_{NP}$ la actriz + PP (con el pelo negro)
Someone shot against the maid of the actress with black hair

(10b) Someone shot [$_{NP}$ the servant [$_{PP}$ of [$_{NP}$ the actress + PP (with black hair)

Also, Igoa (1995) presents experimental data for examples like (11a), showing that a lower clause location is preferred for a PP argument in Spanish where the choice is between attachment as a VP argument in the matrix or in a relative clause. The same seems to be true of English, as in (11b).

(11a) Raúl vendió el libro que habia robada a su amigo.
Raúl sold the book which had stolen to/from his friend.
'Raúl sold the book which he had stolen to/from his friend.'

(11b) John grabbed the book that he had borrowed from his friend.

The classic Right Association example from Kimball (1973) also works in both languages. The examples in (12) are globally ambiguous but the interpretation in which the adverb modifies the lower clause is strongly preferred.

(12a) Juan dijo que Bill se fue ayer.
Juan said that Bill clitic left yesterday

(12b) John said Bill left yesterday.

These examples of low attachment could easily be multiplied. As indicated, they seem to obtain in Spanish as well as English, even though Spanish is one of the languages which favors high relative clause attachment to N1 in the *N1 - P - N2 - Rel* construction in (9). If, as we claim, low attachment is the norm, some explanation is needed for the maverick construction (9), which not only differs across languages but also contrasts with other constructions in the same language; we return to this in section 7 below. Whether or not the explanation of the cross-construction difference that we give there is correct, we believe there is ample evidence that low attachment is indeed a powerful universal tendency for most constructions in natural language. From this we can conclude that its dominance over RALR in examples like (6) - (8) does not show that there is no reluctance at all to re-analyze. It indicates only that avoiding revision is not the HSPM's absolutely highest priority.

LOW ATTACHMENT WITHIN THE REVISION SYSTEM

Examples (10) - (12) show low attachment in normal first-pass parsing. Examples (6) - (8) show low attachment overriding a prior first-pass parsing preference. The preference for low attachment is apparently even more pervasive than this. Sturt & Crocker (1996) have observed a preference for low attachment within the revision process itself. Their examples are shown in (13). There is a height-of-attachment ambiguity for the final VP.

(13) I know the man who believes the countess killed...

a. I know the man who believes the countess killed herself.

b. I know the man who believes the countess killed himself.

Both potential attachments involve revision of an NP from direct object of the preceding verb to subject of its clausal complement. (This does not constitute a revision in all models; see note 4. But we will not discuss this here.) The first-pass analysis of (13) makes the NP [*the man who...*] the direct object of *know*, and the NP *the countess* the direct object of *believes.* When *killed* is encountered, one of these assumptions must give way. In the preferred revision, the verb *killed* attaches as sister to the lower NP (*the countess*) rather than to the higher one (*the man who believes the countess*). This makes the feminine anaphor in the completion (13a) more natural than the masculine anaphor in (13b).

More kinds of examples are needed, of course. But if it holds up on further investigation, it is of considerable interest that the parser exhibits similar preferences in the Attach operation of first-pass parsing and the Attach Anyway operation that initiates revision, because it is compatible with the idea that there is no real dividing line between the two.

DOES LOW ATTACHMENT ALWAYS DEFEAT RALR?

Though low attachment sometimes defeats RALR, there are limits to its supremacy; it does not always win. In (14) there is a height-of-attachment ambiguity for the VP *annoyed his wife*, which is quite similar to the ambiguities in (6) - (8) above. But the preferred resolution of it is different.

(14) The fact that the old man shaved in bed annoyed his wife.

The VP *annoyed his wife* could in principle take as its subject the NP *the old man shaved in bed* with *shaved in bed* as a reduced relative modifying *the old man*. This is not the first-pass analysis of such a string, but would result from revision of *shaved in bed* from a main clause to a relative. In that case, another VP would be needed, such as *was very obvious*. In fact, perceivers do not feel the lack of another VP in this example. The VP *annoyed his wife* clearly prefers to attach at the matrix level, and the word string is analyzed without difficulty as a complete sentence. Thus in this case the parser chooses high attachment with no revision, rather than low attachment with revision, in contrast to examples like (6) - (8). What is the relevant difference between the two kinds of case? It seems likely that in (14) the revision needed for the low attachment is too difficult. It is well known that the conversion of a main clause into a reduced relative clause (as in *The horse raced past the barn fell*) tends to be overlooked by the parser, creating a severe garden path.

A less extreme example is (15).

(15) The bullies pushed the boy who put the candy in his mouth into the trashcan.

Compare this with (16) (based on examples in Gibson, 1991):

(16) The boy put the candy in his mouth into the trashcan.

It is clear from (16) that when necessary the parser can lower the PP *in his mouth* from first-pass VP attachment to within-NP attachment, in order to make place for the directional PP *into the trashcan* beneath the VP. In (15) this same re-analysis would permit the directional *into the trashcan* to attach in the lower clause. But at least for some perceivers the directional PP prefers to attach in the main clause, modifying *pushed* rather than *put*. This construction seems to sit approximately on the borderline, where the costs of revision and of high attachment balance out.

The contrast between (6) - (8) and (14), (15) indicates that only easy low-attachment revisions take precedence over revision avoidance. We know of no examples in which RALR is violated by a revision of a kind that is independently known to be difficult. It would be satisfactory to be able to claim, also, that there are no examples in which RALR is violated other than under pressure from an independently known preference principle. In the case of (6) - (8), the pressure is provided by Late Closure, a familiar instance of Minimal Everything. But there are other cases where the force that counters RALR is not so easy to recognize. We illustrate with adjunct attachment in Japanese, a left-branching language.

HIGH ATTACHMENT VERSUS RALR?

The Japanese examples that shift from a left-branching to a right-branching structure are particularly interesting because the revision can be seen as the RAISING of a constituent to a higher tree position, once that position becomes available. The change appears to be spontaneous, unmotivated by any other pressure from the attachment system. It seems, therefore, that a preference for the high attachment site is itself the driving force behind this violation of RALR. Given the framework we have developed so far, a revision can occur just in case it is MOTIVATED. Thus a raising revision in violation of RALR would be understandable if the tree revision is slight, and if the pressure to attach high is strong and exists independently of RALR violations. So now we must ask three questions. Does the revision in question genuinely constitute a raising revision? Is there any pressure in natural language toward high attachment? If so, does this pressure fall under Minimal Everything, ultimately due to Attach

Quickly? We consider below some different answers to these questions. Though it is too early to be sure, we think there is reason to believe that high attachment is favored in some contexts by a preference for balanced tree structures in which sister constituents are of roughly equal 'weight', and that this taste for balanced phrases is due to the needs of prosodic phrasing rather than to any syntactic preference principle. But whether the Japanese examples actually involve a raising revision is debatable, as we show below.

The examples in question are all NPs consisting of an adjunct followed by a noun with genitive case marking (*-no* in Japanese, *'s* in the English examples below), followed by another noun. The input sequence is thus *adjunct - N1+GEN - N2*, which could in principle be assigned either a left-branching or right-branching structure. This is illustrated by (17), from Inoue & Fodor (1995). Intuitive judgments indicate that (17) is generally parsed as left-branching, unlike the examples we discuss below. The relationship between the adjective and the noun in (17) is NOT altered between the initial attachment, when only one noun has been encountered, and the final preferred structure once both noun sites are available.

(17)	shinsetsuna	gakusei-no	imooto
	kind	student-GEN	(younger) sister

ON-LINE: [shinsetsuna gakusei]
"kind student"

FINAL PREFERENCE: LEFT-BRANCHING
[[shinsetsuna gakusei]-no imooto]
"sister of kind student"

LESS PREFERRED: RIGHT-BRANCHING
[shinsetsuna [gakusei-no imooto]]
"kind sister of student"

It should be noted that the less preferred right-branching analysis for (17) is also fully grammatical and acceptable in Japanese. The corresponding phrase in English, *a kind student's sister*, has only the left-branching structure (meaning 'sister of the kind student') because on the right-branching analysis the adjective precedes a genitive that modifies the same noun, which the grammar of English does not allow. In English, unlike Japanese, when a genitive and an adjectival adjunct modify the same noun, the genitive must precede the adjective phrase (*a student's kind sister*). Apparent exceptions to this, such as *an empty dog's bowl*, can be shown to contain lexical noun-noun compounds: the adjective modifies the whole compound noun (*dog's bowl*) which contains an INTERNAL genitive. This grammatical difference between Japanese and English is of interest, but we cannot consider it further here.

Though this is easily overlooked, BOTH ways of extending the initial tree for *shinsetsuna gakusei-no* can be regarded as involving some revision. The right-branching analysis alters the modification dependency established on-line between the adjunct and the first noun. The left-branching analysis leaves that intact but alters the external relations of the NP containing the adjective, if the parser is a full-attachment system which anticipates NP attachment into a clausal structure while the NP is being built (see Inoue & Fodor, 1995). On the left-branching analysis, the NP that contains *shinsetsuna* is demoted from presumed argument (e.g., subject, if sentence-initial), to being a lower genitive modifier within that argument, losing the relationship it had to the main predicate of the sentence. However, though it involves some revision, the left-branching structure has been argued to be the MINIMAL way of revising the initial tree (see Frazier & Clifton, 1998). If this is correct, then the preference in (17) is as expected if RALR is generalized, as has been proposed, to a *Minimal Revision* principle (Frazier, 1990a; Inoue, 1991). In that case a shift to the right-branching structure would need to be motivated by some other influence on parsing.

One example in which such a shift occurs is (18) (from Inoue & Fodor, 1995, fn. 20), where the adjunct is phrasal, consisting of an adjective with a preceding adverbial modifying it.

(18) kyokutanni shinsetsuna gakusei-no imooto
extremely kind student -GEN (younger) sister

ON-LINE: [[kyokutanni shinsetsuna] gakusei]
"extremely kind student"

FINAL PREFERENCE (SOME SPEAKERS):
LEFT-BRANCHING
[[[kyokutanni shinsetsuna] gakusei]-no imooto]
"sister of extremely kind student"

FINAL PREFERENCE (SOME SPEAKERS):
RIGHT-BRANCHING
[[kyokutanni shinsetsuna] [gakusei-no imooto]]
"extremely kind sister of student"

We noted that some speakers, though not all, show a tendency to adopt the right-branching analysis on encountering the second noun. This right-branching tendency is of interest because it appears to be unprovoked by any grammatical problem in continuing the original analysis; both the left- and the right-branching structure are well-formed, just as for (17) above. The only difference between (17) and (18) is the complexity of the initial adjective phrase. In some way this facilitates recognition of the right-branching structure and encourages its adoption even at the cost of unnecessary revision.

Kamide & Mitchell (1997) have reported a similar tendency toward an eventual right-branching analysis for an adjunct preceding a *N1+GEN - N2* sequence, when the adjunct is a relative clause as in (19).

(19) Dareka-ga barukonii-ni iru joyuu-no mesitukai-o utta.
Someone-NOM balcony-LOC is actress-GEN servant-ACC shot
"Someone shot the servant of the actress who was on the balcony."

ON-LINE: [Rel. Cl + actress]
(= the actress was on the balcony)

FINAL PREFERENCE: RIGHT-BRANCHING
[Rel. Cl. [joyuu-no mesitukai]]
(= the servant was on the balcony)

FINAL NON-PREFERRED: LEFT-BRANCHING
[[Rel. Cl + joyuu]-no mesitukai]
(= the actress was on the balcony)

In a questionnaire study, answers to questions (e.g., *Who was on the balcony?*) indicated that subjects most often preferred the right-branching structure. Branigan, Sturt & Matsumoto-Sturt (1996) have confirmed this questionnaire result (and extended the investigation to other modified noun-noun constructions in Japanese). Kamide & Mitchell also conducted an on-line reading task with similar materials (in which pragmatic plausibility of the two analyses was manipulated). The sentence version whose meaning required left-branching structure was easier to read at the first noun (with which the relative clause was compatible) and still at the second noun (with which the relative was not compatible), but by the sentence-final matrix verb the left-branching version was read more slowly than the right-branching version. Kamide & Mitchell interpret this as showing that Japanese parsing is non-deterministic, and imply that during the processing of the sentence the relative clause is detached from the lower noun and reattached as modifier of the higher second noun.

For examples with simple adjuncts like (17) and with phrasal adjuncts like (18), the contrast in final preference is supported by experimental data reported by Hirose, Inoue, Fodor & Bradley (1998). Though there are no comparable experimental data for the examples with clausal versus non-clausal adjuncts, intuitive judgments suggest that the eventual right-branching preference may be stronger in the relative clause examples than in the Adjective Phrase examples.[9] Thus, any account of the right-branching tendency in these complex NP constructions should also explain this apparent dependence on the length of the adjunct: long (or heavy) adjuncts show the greatest tendency to rise to the higher site.[10]

We now review, very briefly, three possible approaches to this phenomenon, highlighting just the major points for and against each one. We hope to present more extensive discussion and justification for these claims in future work. Our conclusion will be that in fact no raising is involved in these examples. We suggest that adjunct raising on the left is an illusion created by the low attachment of N2 on the right.

RIGHT ASSOCIATION IN A LEFT-BRANCHING LANGUAGE

Raising the adjunct

What is the reason for the instability of the [*adjunct + N1*] structure? Why does the prenominal adjunct raise when N2 is encountered? Kamide & Mitchell (op. cit.), and Branigan et al. (op. cit.) suggest that the motivation for raising a prenominal adjunct in Japanese is the same as the motivation for high attachment of the postnominal relative clause in Spanish and other languages (except English) as in (9a) above. This account has the merit of reducing two puzzles to one, but there are some points that count against it.

High attachment of post-nominal relatives has been attributed to the *Relativized Relevance* principle of Frazier (1990b), or the *Predicate Proximity* principle of Gibson, Pearlmutter, Canseco-Gonzalez & Hickok (1996). These principles attribute high attachment tendencies to a general preference for nearness to a verb or to the sentence root; more precise details are not important here. As noted, English is an exception. These principles would seem to predict, incorrectly, a high attachment bias for a relative clause in a complex NP in English. For Predicate Proximity the reason given for low attachment in English is that this principle is parameterized and is weak in English, though strong in Spanish and other languages. For Relativized Relevance, it is proposed by Frazier & Clifton (1996) that there is a countervailing principle, Grice's *Maxim of Clarity*, which favors the use of unambiguous forms where possible. Since English has the form *the actress' servant who was on the balcony*, in which the relative clause unambiguously modifies *servant*, perceivers are entitled to assume that the use of the ambiguous form *the servant of the actress who was on the balcony* is reserved for cases where the relative modifies *actress*.

Languages which lack this alternation between the Saxon genitive (with *'s*) and the Norman genitive (with *of*) lack this reason for attaching the relative low, so Relativized Relevance applies unopposed. (But see Mitchell & Brysbaert, 1988, on Afrikaans, which is reported to have both genitive forms but to attach high.)

The Gricean argument, if correct, should apply equally to prenominal adjuncts. Let us for the moment adopt Frazier & Clifton's proposal that Relativized Relevance applies in all languages and is offset by the Maxim of Clarity in languages with alternative forms that are unambiguous. This predicts a preference for high adjunct attachment in Japanese, which lacks a Norman-type genitive, but a preference for low prenominal adjunct attachment in English. Prenominal adjuncts occur in English, though they are restricted to APs and other right-headed adjuncts such as *rudely shouting* or *obviously unprepared*; full relative clauses (which are left-headed) are not allowed before the noun. The 'adjunct raising phenomenon' observed in Japanese occurs also in English examples such as (20).

(20) the recently divorced bishop's daughter

ON-LINE: [[recently divorced] bishop]

FINAL PREFERENCE: RIGHT-BRANCHING
[[recently divorced] [bishop's daughter]]

FINAL LESS PREFERRED: LEFT-BRANCHING
[[[recently divorced] bishop]'s daughter]

Perceivers' judgments indicate that at the point of processing *bishop*, it is understood that the bishop is recently divorced; but once *daughter* is encountered, there is a preference for the right-branching structure in which *recently divorced* modifies the higher noun *daughter*.[11] Now note that the alternative Norman genitive form *the recently divorced daughter of a/the bishop* is unambiguous; the adjunct can modify *daughter* only. Hence the Maxim of Clarity implies that the use of the ambiguous Saxon genitive form (20) should be reserved for cases where the intended meaning is that it is the bishop who is divorced; so perceivers should attribute that meaning to it. But this is not so.

This is a reason for doubting that the prenominal adjunct examples exhibit raising of the adjunct under the influence of Relativized Relevance: it predicts incorrectly that English should differ from Japanese by resisting the tendency to high attachment of prenominal adjuncts, just as it resists for postnominal adjuncts. Predicate Proximity faces an exactly comparable counterargument, but it is quicker to state. The Predicate Proximity parameter must be set to WEAK for English to account for (9b); but if it is, there is no explanation of high adjunct attachment in (20). The only way out would be to suppose that there are two unrelated parameters, one for prenominal and one for postnominal adjuncts. But then the explanatory content of the model is seriously weakened.[12]

We note that both Predicate Proximity, and Relativized Relevance with the Maxim of Clarity, could be said to make the correct prediction for SHORT adjuncts in English. We observed in section 6 that a single-word prenominal adjunct in Japanese prefers to modify N1, and the same is true in English. For (21), many perceivers favor modification of *bishop*, or at least are neutral between the two analyses in contrast to (20).

(21) the divorced bishop's daughter

Thus BOTH languages tend toward high multi-word adjuncts and low single-word adjuncts in prenominal position. The prediction of Relativized Relevance and Predicate Proximity that English adjuncts attach low is thus compatible with this example — the inability of these models to account for high attachment of the adjunct in (20) translates into apparent success in accounting for low attachment of the adjunct in (21). But of course, what this amounts to is a failure to address the influence of adjunct length at all. No assumptions about parameter settings or ambiguity avoidance could account for all the examples, long and short, in either English or Japanese. This is a further reason for doubting that height of adjunct attachment has to do with nearness to verbs or to the sentence root. These have no obvious connection with constituent length, and they offer no explanation for why length is a relevant factor.[13]

Finally, if the revision in (18), (19) and (20) is effected by raising the adjunct, as Kamide & Mitchell and Branigan et al. suggest, then it would appear that two raising operations are needed in an example like (22).

(22) this obviously incompetent plumber's assistant

FIRST PASS:
[this obviously incompetent plumber]

FINAL PREFERRED: RIGHT-BRANCHING
[this obviously incompetent [plumber's assistant]]

NON-PREFERRED: LEFT-BRANCHING
[this obviously incompetent plumber]'s assistant]

As shown, this is ambiguous between a right-branching *N1's N2* sequence in which the adjunct *obviously incompetent* applies to *assistant*, and a left-branching analysis in which this adjunct applies to *plumber*. In either case, the demonstrative determiner *this* is required by the grammar to apply to the same noun as the adjunct. (For example, in *this obviously incompetent plumber's assistants*, number agreement forces the determiner to apply to N1, and only the plumber can be understood as incompetent; in *these obviously worthless child's mittens*, the plural determiner must apply to the plural N2, not the singular N1, and here only N2 can be understood as modified by the adjunct.) However, the determiner and the adjunct do not constitute a single phrase. Thus, to achieve the final preferred analysis by means of raising the left side of the structure would require the raising of two independent constituents. It could reasonably be expected that this would be more work than raising just one constituent, and yet the high attachment of the adjunct seems to occur just as spontaneously and naturally here as in (20). That is, the right-branching structure does not appear to be any harder to arrive at — or any easier to avoid — where two constituents raise than where only one does.

Low attachment of N2

A plausible explanation for the easiness of two-constituent examples is that the revision does not involve raising of the left part of the structure, but is due to low attachment of the right part of the structure: if N2 is attached at a height between the adjunct and N1, rather than above them both, the same eventual effect would be achieved, but without any operations on non-constituents. However many separate items there are to the left, one noun attaching low on the right would make them all appear to rise. This is diagrammed in (23b).

(23) a. Raising the adjunct (7.1)

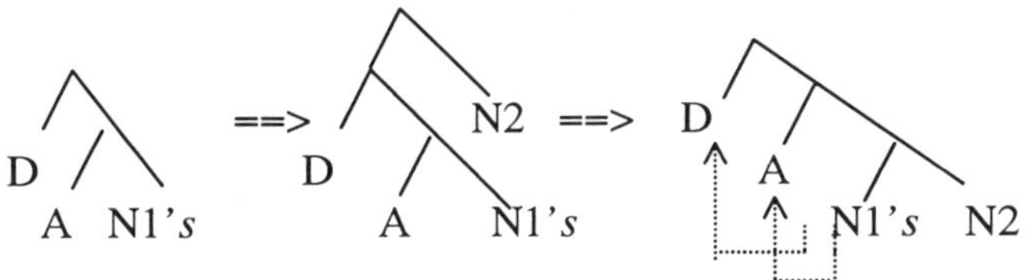

ON-LINE ATTACH N2 HIGH RAISE D AND A ON LEFT

b. Low attachment of N2 (7.2)

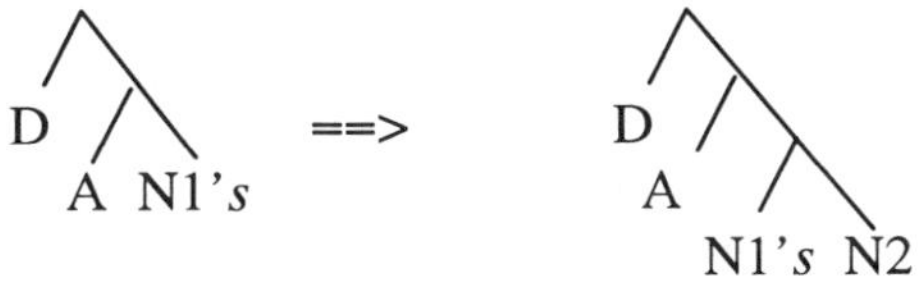

ON-LINE ATTACH N2 LOW OVER N1

NOTES:
D = Determiner, A = Adjunct (simple or complex)
'*s* is shown as cliticized to N1 (but see discussion below)

There is no evidence for (23a). For instance, as Kamide & Mitchell point out, the initial interpretation of the adjunct as modifying N1 could be due to step one, when only N1 is present, so it does not demonstrate the existence of the intermediate stage with N2 attached above the adjunct. Perhaps all that (23a) has to recommend it is an approximate analogy with post-nominal modifiers in right-branching languages. It has been claimed, for example, by Baccino, De Vincenzi & Job (this volume) that adjunct raising does occur in Italian and French. They interpret their findings as showing that a relative clause initially attaches (by Late Closure) to the second (lower) noun and then rises (for thematic reasons) to the higher N1 by the time of post-sentential semantic integration. However, the analogy is imperfect. In Japanese the relative clause doesn't attach, in the technical sense, to either noun; the relative is processed first, and the nouns are attached to it. From that perspective the two steps of (23a) have no obvious motivation.

In short, it seems likely that prenominal adjunct raising is the wrong picture. Though a (long) prenominal adjunct ends up attached high, associated with N2, it probably does not do so as a result of being detached from the lower site and reattached at the higher one. The fact that it starts low and ends high does NOT entail that it moved up. More plausibly, N2 subsequently attached lower than the adjunct.

Low N2 attachment is straightforward. It does not involve retroactive alteration of structure that is no longer at the active right edge of the tree. The explanation assumes only the usual incremental attachment of incoming items into the right edge.[14] Also, low N2 attachment is in accord with Late Closure, so we need look no further for the pressure that encourages the parser to disrupt the relation between the adjunct and N1 by interjecting N2 into it. Examples (18) - (20) thus fall together with (6) - (8) in which it is the desire for low attachment on the right that outweighs RALR. It may seem surprising that Japanese, a "left-branching language", favors Right Association, i.e., low attachment on the right. But this is exactly what a universal model of the human parsing mechanism would predict: that the structural preference is universal even though the range of structures it applies to differs from one language to another. In very many constructions of Japanese, there is a rigid series of lexical heads leading up the right edge of the tree, which offers no opportunity for low right attachment. But as noted in Inoue & Fodor (1995), a right-headed language also contains right-branching structures when the head is phrasal and recursive, as when an adjunct modifies the head. In such constructions the grammar permits low right attachment, and the parser's preference for it becomes apparent, even in an otherwise left-branching language.

There are, however, a few thistles on this explanatory path also. First, the adjunct heaviness factor is not accounted for. It would have to be claimed that N2 attaches low only if the adjunct is fairly long. Furthermore, sentence completion preferences suggest that the *'s* in English and the *-no* in Japanese attach high, at the top of the whole [*(D)* + *A* + *N1*], prior to receipt of N2. If so, it must be assumed that when N2 attaches low, it pulls the genitive morpheme down, as shown in (24).

(24)

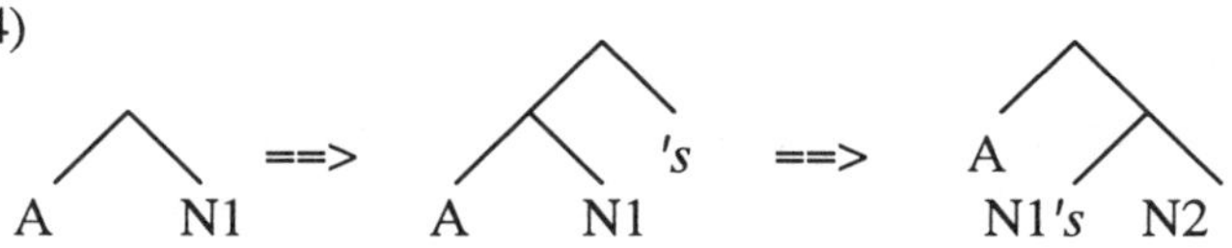

This would constitute another violation of RALR. And though not out of the question, it seems a little odd to suppose that the genitive marker is content to attach high but the noun that follows has a strong need to attach low.

Prosodic balance

We turn now to a very different account of this collection of phenomena. Our suggestion is that a heavy adjunct likes to be high because that allows the complex NP construction to divide evenly into two parts of roughly equal weight, which is prosodically preferred. This was Inoue's hunch, reported in our earlier paper for example (18) above, and it appears to explain the data in both languages presented here. For instance, in (19) a prosodic balance principle would favor division into */ barukonii-ni iru /* and */ joyuu-no mesitukai-o /* rather than into the less balanced */ barukonii-ni iru joyuu-no /* and */ mesitukai-o /*. Similarly, in English the balanced division */ the recently divorced / bishop's daughter /* would be preferred over */ the recently divorced bishop's / daughter /*. With a short adjunct, however, there are only three prosodic elements in the complex NP, and no strong preference about whether to divide them into two and one, or one and two; the former may prevail just because it entails the least revision, resulting in association of the adjunct with the lower noun. Thus the effect of adjunct weight is accounted for.

The fact that a three-element structure becomes prosodically unstable when a fourth item is added to it has been observed before. Kubozono (1993) discusses complex NPs (both lexical compounds and phrasal) in Japanese and reports that a sequence of three words whose meaning calls for a left-branching structure exhibits the prosody appropriate to that structure, but when a fourth word is added the prosodic pattern changes to that appropriate to a double binary structure [[- -][- -]], even though this runs counter to the meaning. For instance, he notes that the left-branching (25a) exhibits a prosodic contour virtually indistinguishable from that of (25b), which has a double binary syntactic structure; both show a "metrical boost" (a rise in F0) at the third item.

(25) a. [[[mariko-ga nonda] wain-no] nioi]
Mariko-NOM drank wine-GEN smell
"the smell of the wine that Mariko drank"

b. [[aiko-no neesan-no] [uuru-no erimaki]]
Aiko-GEN sister-GEN wool-GEN muffler
"Aiko's sister's woollen muffler"

Kubozono attributes this departure from the expected syntax-conditioned contour for (25a) to the *Rhythmic Structure Principle* of Selkirk (1984). He emphasizes that the preference for even rhythms is a very general property of prosodic patterning in natural language. Note that (25a) contains a relative clause and has essentially the same structure as the NP in

Kamide & Mitchell's (19) above, though unlike (19) it is semantically/pragmatically unambiguous. Our proposal is that the balanced prosodic contour is assigned by readers to both ambiguous and unambiguous instances, and that for the ambiguous ones it sways the structural preference of the syntactic parser.

The same prosodic considerations could account for the high attachment preference of a relative clause in construction (9a) in Spanish and other right-branching languages except English. It would also explain the low attachment preference for a shorter attachee such as a PP in (10) in all languages. Regardless of whether the adjunct precedes or follows the sequence of two nouns, a long adjunct will need to be balanced by the two nouns together, while a short adjunct can be balanced by a single noun as its sister. (The peculiarity of English with respect to (9b) needs some different explanation. Fodor, 1998, offers the suggestion that the relative pronoun is grouped with N2 in a single prosodic phrase, and that this precludes the high attachment motivated by prosodic balance.) For constructions where the host constituent is long and the attachee is short, such as (11) and (12), the balance is best achieved if the attachee takes only half of the host construction as its sister (e.g., only the lower clause of a two-clause construction).

The prosodic balance explanation accounts for the final preferred structure in examples (18) - (20) but is not committed to any particular means for arriving at it. So it is compatible in principle with either raising of a prenominal adjunct as in 7.1, or low attachment of the second noun as in 7.2. Of the two, low N2 attachment is more satisfactory. The only counts we have observed against it are now covered by the influence of prosodic phrasing. That is, the effect of adjunct weight is now explained, and so is the odd behavior of the genitive marker. The genitive morpheme forms a prosodic word with the word that precedes it.

Rather than assuming that it attaches high, as in the middle diagram of (24), we may assume that it attaches into the CPPM as part and parcel of the preceding word, though its syntactic and semantic scope may be broader (e.g., in *the man next door's dog*). In *the recently divorced bishop's*, which is assigned left-branching structure, (and similarly for *kyokutanni shinsetsuna gakusei-no* in (18)), the genitive morpheme is part of the word *bishop's*, but its scope encompasses the whole phrase built so far. But when the N2 *daughter* is encountered, as the fourth stressed word in the sequence, the sequence splits into *the recently divorced* and *bishop's daughter*, and the genitive case is now associated only with *bishop*. Thus the low attachment of the second noun changes the scope of the genitive *'s* without actually reattaching it in the tree.

In sum: There is a violation of RALR in (18) - (20), but the revision is slight, and the prosodic balance principle provides the motivation for it. Hence it fits our general theory of possible RALR violations.

CONCLUSIONS

Though the evidence is slender as yet, it begins to suggest two interesting conclusions: (i) that the same attachment preference principles (e.g., Late Closure or prosodic balance) govern both first- and second-pass parsing; and (ii) that when an attachment preference runs counter to RALR, the preference can win if it is strong enough. Obviously, we need to work harder on the question of how strong is strong enough. But already some implications emerge. Conclusion (i) is in keeping with the merger of Attach and Attach Anyway. It is at least a necessary condition on their being one and the same principle. And conclusion (ii) provides some positive (albeit indirect) support for the merger, in that it suggests that the avoidance of revision is just one preference factor among others. It appears that in all cases where revision occurs other than in a genuine last resort situation, it is because a powerful attachment tendency is pitted against an easy revision. It seems reasonable to surmise that RALR violations occur because there can be a trade-off for the parser between avoiding revision and conforming to its (other) preference principles.

This is exactly as would be expected from a parser governed by Attach Quickly. In the diagnosis model, a revision begins with the attachment of an input item in a way that is not compatible with the current analysis, which in most cases means an ungrammatical attachment (see note 4). Hence, avoiding revision would amount to avoiding illegal attachments. If so, RALR would amount to the principle that legitimate attachments should always take precedence over illegitimate ones. However, it is easy to see that this might not be the case. If a legitimate attachment exists but is very dispreferred, it will be slow to compute. Because of Attach Quickly, the parser may be tempted to adopt instead an attachment at a more preferred site because it is computed sooner — even if it is grammatically defective and will require Adjust to step in afterwards to patch up the problem. Revision represents extra work and to that extent would be undesirable; but we see that it may in some cases allow the parser to act more quickly than if it were to wait for a perfectly correct attachment site to present itself.

The fact that attachment-with-revision sometimes wins the race rules out the picture of two distinct processes - Attach operating to strict standards in the first pass, followed by Attach Anyway which imposes much looser standards on potential sites and applies only if Attach fails. If that were the case, RALR would be an absolute restriction on human parsing. The fact that RALR is not exceptionless indicates that there is in fact no hard and fast line between so-called first-pass and second-pass operations. (See also Stevenson, 1994, 1998.) The distinction is not lost altogether, since Adjust retains its own individuality; it is a follow-up process that occurs only after revision has been initiated by the choice of attachment. But the initiation of revision is continuous with normal forward parsing. In all cases, an item is attached at the first place in the CPPM that suggests itself. We conclude that there is just one attachment principle which governs all stages of parsing (including also, though we have not discussed it here, the re-attachment operation for any items expelled or ousted from their original positions by Adjust; see also Lewis, 1993.) It seems, then, that the combined Attach (Anyway) principle in (5) is indeed more appropriate than the separate principles (1) and (2). It instructs the parser to do the best it can in the circumstances. Attachment without revision is just one instance of that, sometimes achievable without sacrifice of other goals, but not set apart as a different mode of parsing.

SPECULATION

The considerations raised above suggest that Attach (Anyway), as formulated in (5), may overestimate the extent to which the parser even AIMS at making well-formed attachments. Quite possibly, all the facts can be accounted for on the assumption that the parser does not care whether attachments are grammatical or ungrammatical. This suggestion goes beyond the mere reduction of RALR violations to Minimal Everything and ultimately Attach Quickly. In previous work we have always assumed that the parser's primary goal is to obey the grammar. In the case of Adjust, this is apparently still a necessary assumption: why else would the parser undertake its conflict resolution work except to satisfy grammatical constraints? In the attachment system, however, we might suppose that economy of effort and speed of response to the input are the parser's ONLY priority. Whatever contributes to efficiency is favored. There is no parsing principle that defines fully grammatical attachment as a goal. Suppose ungrammatical attachments are generally a little slower to compute than grammatical ones, for whatever reason (e.g., because an imperfect match between the nodes projected over the input and the CPPM is harder to spot than an exact match, or because well-formed attachment routes are somehow facilitated by being generable by the grammar). Then all the phenomena above would still follow. On this assumption, ungrammatical attachments would usually arrive for consideration later than grammatical ones and would lose the race. But an ungrammatical attachment site could win the race if the speed differential due to the position or minimality of attachment gave it a sufficient headstart over its grammatical competitors. Then Adjust would be called in to reconcile the conflict in the CPPM created by this attachment. Such cases would look like 'RALR violations', but there would be no RALR — not even as a preference principle — and no violation.

If later work should support this conjecture, it would permit the coalescence of Attach (Anyway) and Attach Quickly. The two conditions at the end of the statement of Attach (Anyway) would fall out as consequences of Attach Quickly. That is: both the avoidance of grammatical violations, to the extent that it occurs, and the standard preferences for minimal structure and low attachment, would result from the pressure to work fast, as would the interactions between them that we have been concerned with in this paper. In that case, these conditions would be satisfied without needing to be explicitly stated. So the attachment system would be governed by the single, simple principle (4) Attach Quickly: On receiving a word of the input sentence, connect it to the CPPM as quickly as possible.

Whether this further simplification can be carried through depends on whether the relative timing advantages of all the various factors that can contribute to the attractiveness of an attachment can be worked out in detail so that they succeed in predicting exactly the trade-offs that are observed to occur. We must leave much of this task for further work, and until then, this suggestion remains tentative. However, the more specific proposal that revision-avoidance, though indeed a desideratum for the parser, can be outweighed by its other fundamental inclinations, is an empirical hypothesis which can be tested and refined, by seeking out cases of apparently spontaneous revision and looking to see whether they contain, after all, some sufficient motivation for the parser's meddling with the existing CPPM. Our proposal here has been that prosodic phrasing may provide such motivation even when purely syntactic structural preferences do not.

NOTES

* We thank the members of the Max-Planck-Institute of Cognitive Neuroscience in Leipzig for their comments on this work. Special thanks are due to Paul Gorrell for his insightful comments on an earlier draft, and to Yuki Kamide and Patrick Sturt for interesting discussion of the Japanese examples.

[1] In Frazier & Rayner's (1988, p.263) wording: "First Analysis Constraint: At choice points the processor adopts the first syntactic analysis available (specifically the analysis that follows from Minimal Attachment, Late Closure and the Most Recent Filler Strategy) rather than pursuing multiple syntactic analyses or delaying analysis of the input". The simpler wording in (4) separates the general principle (of taking the first analysis computed) from particular strategies (such as the Most Recent Filler Strategy).

[2] A more recent extension of RALR is the *Minimal Revisions Principle* of Frazier (1990a); see also the *Minimal Revision Principle* of Inoue (1991). These become relevant in section 6 below.

[3] Though we will often refer to LOW attachment in this paper, we believe the correct formulation is in terms of LOCAL attachment. There is clearly no tendency, for example, for the parser to sacrifice Minimal Attachment by attaching a word very low at the bottom of a long downward chain of left-branching nodes (e.g., to attach a sentence-initial *John's* very low in English,

or to attach the second word of *Taro-ga shinsetsuna* ("Taro-NOM kind") as the beginning of an object complement clause in Japanese).

[4] It should be noted that this does not constitute revision in all models, e.g., description-theoretic models (Marcus, Hindle & Fleck, 1983; Gorrell, 1995) in which domination statements can be freely added to the current description of the CPPM. Clearly, RALR differs in its scope depending on what counts as a revision. When RALR was first proposed, some subtle distinctions concerning revision processes had not yet been drawn, so its intended scope is not certain. In our current model there are two potential definitions of what constitutes revision for purposes of RALR: (a) if an item is attached into the CPPM in such a way that it alters some existing grammatical dependency, or (b) if an item is attached into the CPPM in such a way that it creates an illicit grammatical dependency which Adjust must then modify. In principle there could be an attachment that is a case of (a) but not (b). In fact we know of no really clear instances of this. (In particular, the revision in (6) from direct object NP to subject of a complement clause (a) alters the dependency between the NP and the preceding verb, and (b) also creates ungrammaticalities of argument selection and case assignment which must then be adjusted.) For present purposes it is not important which definition is assumed.

[5] See Frazier & Clifton (1998) for a somewhat similar idea. They propose a trade-off between their *Minimal Revisions Principle* and a *Visibility Principle* which generally favors low attachment (replacing Late Closure in their theory).

[6] Phillips does not discuss RALR in connection with examples like (8), but attributes the parser's choice to a competition between low attachment and minimal attachment. If (8) does involve revision, this would mean that low attachment is strong enough here to defeat the combined force of RALR and MA.

[7] Frazier & Fodor (1978) noted that high attachment in accord with Minimal Attachment wins over low attachment in constructions like *John carried the books for Susan* where both are quite local. See Clifton, Speer & Abney (1991) for more recent discussion and experimental data for English, and Igoa (1995) for related data for Spanish. In this case, however, the two potential sites differ in category and other properties, not just in their height in the CPPM. We will not discuss such examples here.

[8] According to the Construal model of Frazier & Clifton (1996), adjuncts are not attached into the tree but are associated with a thematic domain. But this distinction will not be relevant to our discussion.

[9] Though in general, greater heaviness of the adjunct seems roughly correlated with a greater tendency for it to modify the higher noun, it may be that a relative clause shows more resistance to reinterpretation than an equally heavy AP does, because of reluctance to tamper with the binding relation between the relative clause 'gap' (empty category) and the head noun (or its associated operator). More empirical data are needed before further claims can be made concerning the relative strengths of these various factors.

[10] We assume that heaviness, in the relevant sense, is a function of both length and grammatical category (e.g., a clause is heavier than a phrase even if they contain the same number of words). But this distinction is not central to our argument, and we will refer freely to either length or heaviness in what follows.

[11] We emphasize that the English examples contain *N's N* lexical compounds. This does not greatly alter the argument we make here, however.

[12] This argument presumes that other parsing preferences in the system favor a low prenominal adjunct, and that a high adjunct could only be due to Predicate Proximity. But we are hesitant about the premise here. The analogue to Late Closure in Gibson et al.'s model is called *Recency*. It is clear that for an *N1 - N2 - adjunct* sequence Recency favors right-branching, i.e., a low adjunct. But it is not clear what it implies for an *adjunct - N1 - N2* sequence. If parsing is left-to-right, then the nouns are attached to the adjunct rather than vice versa. We discuss this way of looking at the prenominal adjunct construction below.

[13] There is a possible grammatical explanation for the adjunct length effect in Japanese. The sequence *adjunct + N1 [+GEN]* modifying the same following N2 is probably not base-generated but derived by transformational preposing of the adjunct. This movement (like extraposition in English) is less acceptable for a short adjunct than for a long ('heavy') one. Thus for a short adjunct, attachment to N2 would be less acceptable than attachment to N1. This explanation of the length facts would be compatible with the Relativized Relevance and Predicate Proximity approaches (given a background

preference for N2 attachment). However, it does not apply to English examples like (20) and (21).

[14] The data reported by Kamide & Mitchell (op. cit.) show the shift to high attachment occurring only two constituents later than N2. However, in the data of Hirose et al. (1998), there was significant high attachment (relative to a baseline condition) at the N2 position. This is consistent with direct low attachment of N2 as in (23b).

REFERENCES

Baccino, T., De Vincenzi, M. and Job, R. (this volume) Cross-linguistic studies of the Late Closure strategy: French and Italian.

Branigan, H., Sturt, P. and Matsumoto Sturt, Y. (1996) Left branching attachment and thematic domains. Poster presented at AMLaP-96 Conference, Torino, September 1996.

Clifton, C., Jr., Speer, S. and Abney, S. (1991) Parsing arguments: Phrase structure and argument structure as determinants of initial parsing decisions. *Journal of Memory and Language* 30, 251-271.

Cuetos, F. and Mitchell, D. C. (1988) Cross-linguistic differences in parsing: Restrictions on the use of the late closure strategy in Spanish. *Cognition* 30, 73-105.

Fodor, J. D. (1998) Learning to parse? *Journal of Psycholinguistic Research* 27, 285-319.

Fodor, J. D. and Ferreira, F. (eds.) (1998) *Re-analysis in Sentence Processing*. Kluwer Academic Publishers, Dordrecht, The Netherlands.

Fodor, J. D. and Frazier, L. (1980) Is the human sentence parsing mechanism an ATN? *Cognition* 8, 417-459.

Fodor, J. D. and Inoue, A. (1994) The diagnosis and cure of garden paths. *Journal of Psycholinguistic Research* 23.5, 407-434.

Fodor, J. D. and Inoue, A. (1997) Garden path diagnosis: The Grammatical Dependency Principle. Manuscript, CUNY Graduate Center. To appear in M. Ryan (ed.) *CUNYForum* 20.

Fodor, J. D. and Inoue, A. (1998) Attach Anyway. In J. D. Fodor and F. Ferreira (eds.).

Frazier, L. (1990a) Identifying Structure under X^0. In A. Jongman and A. Lahiri (eds.) *Yearbook of Morphology*, 3, 87-109.

Frazier, L. (1990b) Parsing modifiers: Special purpose routines in the human sentence processing mechanism? In D. A. Balota, G. B. Flores d'Arcais and K. Rayner (eds.) *Comprehension processes in reading*. Erlbaum, Hillsdale, NJ.

Frazier, L. and Clifton, C. (1996) *Construal*. MIT Press, Cambridge, MA.

Frazier, L. and Clifton, C. (1998) Sentence re-analysis and visibility. In J. D. Fodor and F. Ferreira (eds.).

Frazier, L. and Fodor, J. D. (1978) The Sausage Machine: A new two-stage parsing model. *Cognition* 6, 1-34.

Frazier, L. and Rayner, K. (1988) Parameterizing the language processing system: Left- vs. right-branching within and across languages. In J. A. Hawkins (ed.) *Explaining Language Universals*. Basil Blackwell, Oxford, UK.

Gibson, E., Pearlmutter, N., Canseco-Gonzalez, E. and Hickok, G. (1996) Recency preference in the human sentence processing mechanism. *Cognition* 59, 23-59.

Gorrell, P. (1995) *Syntax and Parsing*. Cambridge University Press, Cambridge, UK.

Hirose, Y., Inoue, A., Fodor, J. D. and Bradley, D. C. (1998) Adjunct attachment ambiguity in Japanese: The role of constituent weight. Poster presented at the 11th Annual CUNY Conference on Human Sentence Processing, New Brunswick, NJ, March 1998.

Igoa, J. M. (1995) Parsing decisions and the Construal hypothesis: Attachment preferences in primary phrases. Paper presented at the Second Symposium on Psycholinguistics, Tarragona, Spain, April 1995.

Inoue, A. (1991) *A Comparative Study of Parsing in English and Japanese*. Unpublished Ph.D. dissertation, University of Connecticut, Storrs, CT.

Inoue, A. and Fodor, J. D. (1995) Information-paced parsing of Japanese. In R. Mazuka and N. Nagai (eds.) *Japanese Sentence Processing*. Lawrence Erlbaum Associates, Hillsdale, NJ.

Kamide, Y. and Mitchell, D. C. (1997) Relative clause attachment: Non-determinism in Japanese parsing. *Journal of Psycholinguistic Research* 26, 247-254.

Kimball, J. (1973) Seven principles of surface structure parsing in natural language. *Cognition* 2, 15-47.

Kubozono, H. (1993) *The Organization of Japanese Prosody*. Kurosio Publishers, Tokyo.

Lewis, R. L. (1993) *An Architecturally-based Theory of Human Sentence Comprehension*. Unpublished Ph.D. dissertation, Carnegie Mellon University, Pittsburgh, PA.

Marcus, M. P., Hindle, D. and Fleck, M. M. (1983) D-theory: Talking about talking about trees. *Association for Computational Linguistics*, 21, 129-136.

Mitchell, D. C. and Brysbaert, M. (1998) Challenges to recent theories of cross-linguistic variation in parsing: Evidence from Dutch. In D. Hillert (ed.) *Sentence Processing: A Cross-Linguistic Perspective*. Academic Press, San Diego.

Phillips, C. (1996) *Order and Structure*. Unpublished Ph.D. dissertation, MIT, Cambridge, MA.

Selkirk, E. (1984) *Phonology and Syntax: The Relation between Sound and Structure*. MIT Press, Cambridge, MA.

Stevenson, S. (1994) Competition and recency in a hybrid network model of syntactic disambiguation. *Journal of Psycholinguistic Research* 23, 295-322.

Stevenson, S. (1998) Parsing as incremental restructuring. In J. D. Fodor and F. Ferreira (eds.).

Sturt, P. and Crocker, M. W. (1996) Monotonic syntactic processing: A cross-linguistic study of attachment and re-analysis. *Language and Cognitive Processes* 11.5, 449-494.

Robert Frank and K. Vijay-Shanker

LOWERING ACROSS LANGUAGES*

The contrast in processing difficulty among different cases of local ambiguity has often been captured in terms of the type of re-analysis that is required. Of particular importance has been the distinction between lowering and raising of a constituent from the position in which it is attached originally, raising being the more costly operation and therefore producing conscious garden path effects. Unfortunately, this simple dichotomy has proven insufficient to capture the ease of resolving a range of cases of local ambiguity: many cases, which ought to be resolvable by lowering, yield garden path effects. In this paper, we focus on an apparent contrast in lowering possibilities between English and Japanese. We show how by adopting the structural relation of c-command as the primitive used by the parser to characterize structural relations, we can account for these contrasts without resorting to positing distinct parsing strategies in the two languages. Instead, the use of c-command enables us to derive the apparent parsing differences from independently necessary grammatical differences. Finally, the use of c-command as a parsing primitive provides, we believe, a way to bring together two strands of work on parsing models, those rooted in structure and those rooted in lexical and thematic relations.

LOCAL AMBIGUITY AND LOWERING

It is well-known that local syntactic ambiguities are rampant in natural language. In processing a sentence, there are likely to be

M. De Vincenzi and V. Lombardo (eds.), Cross-linguistic Perspectives on Language Processing, 63–87.

multiple analyses compatible with the prefix seen or heard, although only one of these might turn out to be consistent with the rest of the sentence. In general, however, processing seems effortless, and the presence of such ambiguity apparently does not give rise to difficulties in processing. This might be attributed to the fact that we do not necessarily pursue all analyses. As long as the appropriate analysis is not discarded, processing could be continued without difficulty. There is, however, a contrast in processing difficulty among different types of local syntactic ambiguities. In some cases, we seem compelled to select one of the possible analyses prior to hearing the disambiguating context, an analysis which then turns out to be incompatible with subsequent input. When this is discovered, we experience some confusion or difficulty, what has been called a "garden path" effect. A well-known example of such a case is

(1) While she was mending the sock fell off her lap.

Prior to hearing the word *fell*, the sequence *she was mending the sock* could be treated as a single sentence. Such an analysis of this sequence is in fact appropriate for completions like that in (2).

(2) While she was mending the sock the phone rang.

Alternatively, the noun phrase *the sock* can be taken to be the subject of the matrix sentence to which the *while* adverbial clause is adjoined. This is the analysis that is necessary for (1). To explain the anomaly of (1) and acceptability of (2), it has been proposed that the parser pursues only the single sentence analysis immediately upon hearing *the sock*, without waiting for disambiguating context. If we assume that revising this analysis is difficult for the parser, this explains why cases like (1) that are incompatible with the selected analysis pose difficulty, while those like (2) which are compatible do not.

Many cases of local ambiguity do not, however, seem to trigger this kind of premature decision that leads to subsequent difficulty. For such cases, any number of possible completions are parseable by the listener without significant difficulty. For example, the initial sequence of words in (3) can be grammatically followed by any of the completions in (4).

(3) I saw the ...

(4) a. ... student yesterday.

b. ... student's mother yesterday.

c. ... the student leave the room yesterday.

In each of these completions, the structural position of the noun phrase initiated by the determiner *the* differs. In the first completion, this noun phrase is attached as the object, whereas in the second, the object of *saw* is a different NP, namely *the student's mother* (headed by *mother*) and not *the student.* In the final completions, the correct analysis requires that the verb *see* take a sentential complement. Nonetheless, speakers do not appear to experience significant difficulty in any of these cases. The ease in processing these different completions suggests that the initial sequence triggers neither a premature commitment to attach the noun phrase projected by the determiner *the* as the object NP nor to fix a specific sense for the verb *saw* (corresponding to its subcategorizations); decisions that would need to be retracted for the different completions. This is in apparent contradiction with what we hypothesized above concerning examples (1) and (2) above, namely that we did in fact make an immediate commitment to one analysis over the other.

There is however a way to reconcile these cases. Suppose that in both sets of examples we do make an immediate commitment that the NP–V–NP sequence corresponds to a simple SVO sentence. This will necessitate re-analysis both in completions that cause difficulty and some that do not. However, there is a significant difference between these classes of cases. In the situations in (4), the NP *the student* is consistently re-analyzed to a position which is "lower" in the tree than that in which is originally resides (see Figure 1). That is, in every case of "easy" re-analysis, the NP continues to be a member of every constituent that it was originally hypothesized to be a member of. In contrast, the re-analysis that is necessary for an example like (1) involves raising of the NP out of the constituent (object of the verb *mending*) into which it is originally attached (see Figure 2).

Thus, we might hypothesize that re-analyses requiring the use of lowering are less costly than those requiring raising (Abney 1989, Pritchett 1987).[1] This difference in types of re-analysis turns out not to be an idiosyncratic property of the English parsing mechanism, but applies to languages that are rather structurally distinct, such as Japanese, as we shall soon see.

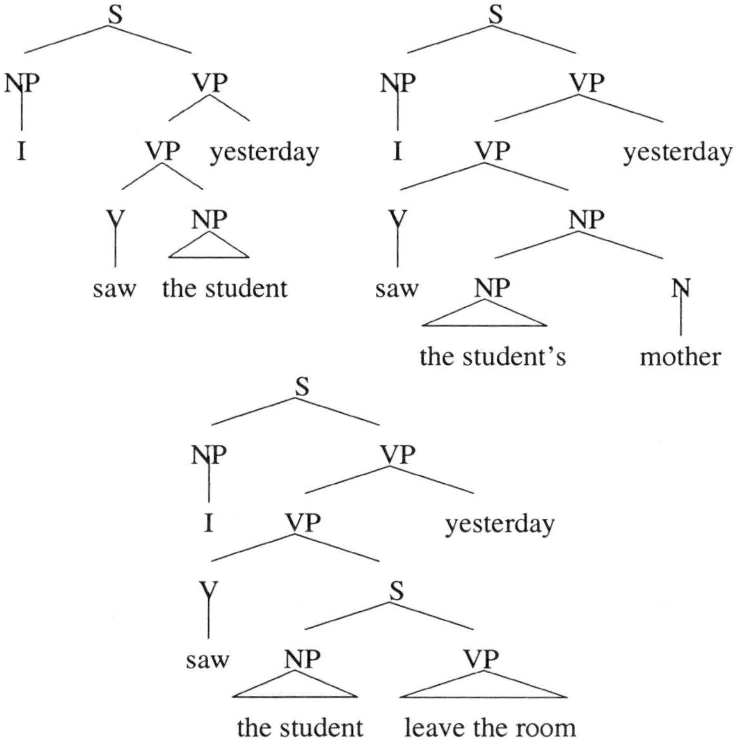

Figure 1: Analyses for (4)a-c

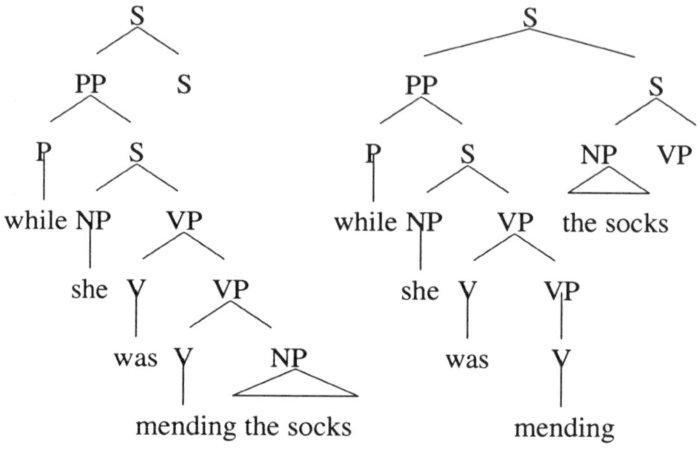

Figure 2: Possible analyses for initial sequence in (1) and (2)

D-THEORY PARSING

Since the work of Marcus, Hindle and Fleck (1983), there have been a number of proposed parsing models that manipulate descriptions of trees rather than trees themselves (Weinberg 1993, Gorrell 1995, Sturt and Crocker 1996). The main benefit of such *D-Theory* models is that they provide a simple characterization of those cases of local ambiguity that give rise to conscious processing difficulty and those that do not. When more than one analysis is possible, such parsers make assertions about phrase structure that are common to these analyses. Such underspecification is exploited so that no commitment is made to any one particular analysis, but rather to a set of analyses assumed to be appropriate for the prefix of the input uttered. As processing proceeds and more input words are encountered, additional assertions would reduce this set of possible analyses.

However, for some completions, it is possible that some property of an initial description must be withdrawn; that is, the parser does not behave monotonically. If we take retraction of assertions to be difficult for the parser, this allows us to characterize those cases of local ambiguity that give rise to conscious processing difficulty as those whose parsing descriptions grow non-monotonically during the course of the sentence. Though these models differ from one another in precisely how and when they make use of underspecification, they all exploit *dominance* (as opposed to immediate dominance) as a primitive in (under)specifying structures.

Given our previous discussion on lowering versus raising, one can understand why D-Theory parsers make assertions of dominance. The use of domination instead of immediate domination allows the model to represent "easy" cases of local ambiguity because this representation is compatible with more than one phrase structure tree whose nodes are connected by immediate domination links: any domination link can be "stretched" to an unbounded length to accommodate additional as yet unspecified structure. That is, when a parser asserts that a node *X* dominates a node *Y*, additional statements (say based upon the words in remainder of the sentence) affecting the relation between these two nodes can only serve to "lower" *Y* to any position within the tree rooted by *X*. Thus, for instance, when the prefix *I saw the student* is encountered, rather than attaching the phrase *the student* as being immediately dominated by the verb phrase headed by *saw* (which roughly states that this noun phrase is to be considered as the object of the verb), the assertion of the verb phrase dominating the noun phrase could be made by the parser. For any of the completions given in (4) above, this domination assertion would hold in the final analysis.

While the assertion that *X* dominates *Y* enables us to predict relative processing ease for cases where *Y* needs to be "lowered" within the constituent given by *X*, this domination assertion also predicts difficulty in processing a completion for which the appropriate analysis would have node *Y* raised out of the constituent *X*, as this calls for retraction of the domination assertion. Thus, for an example like 0, if we assume that the parser initially asserts that the VP headed by *mend* dominates the NP *the sock*, parsing the remainder of the sentence will necessitate retraction of this dominance link and therefore will cause difficulty.

LOWERING IN JAPANESE

There have been a number of attempts to apply the distinction between local ambiguities whose resolution requires lowering and those that demand raising to examples from Japanese. Consider, for example, the following easily processed sentences (from Inoue 1991 and Mazuka and Itoh 1995):

(5) a. [$_{Rel}$ Mary-ga sinseihin-wo t_i kaihatusita] kaisya-ga$_I$ tubureta
Mary-nom new product-acc developed company-nom went bankrupt
"The company where Mary developed the new product went bankrupt."

b. Yamasita-ga [$_{Rel}$ t_i yuuzin-wo houmonsita] siriai-ni$_i$ tegami-o kaita
Yamasita-nom friend-acc visited acquaintance-dat letter-acc wrote
"Yamasita wrote a letter to an acquaintance who visited his friend."

In each of these sentences, the initial sequence consists of a nominative NP followed by an accusative NP in turn followed by a transitive verb. Since Japanese is a verb-final language, let us assume that the parser asserts that these comprise a simple matrix sentence. In both cases, the verb is followed by an NP, a sign that the previously encountered material cannot be the matrix clause, but instead must, at least in part, make up a relative clause modifier to the following NP. In example (5)a, it is the entire NP–NP–V sequence that comprises the relative clause. In the second case, only the second, accusative NP *yuuzin-wo* and the verb reside within the relative.

In both cases, the re-analysis required by the completions can be accomplished by lowering, or its D-theory analog. In (5)a above, no domination link needs to be retracted and we need only to add further domination links to embed the previously constructed sentence within the NP. In (5)b, we can assert a domination link between the NP *siriai-ni* and the previously constructed VP, so as to embed it within the relative clause modifier. This can be done without retracting any domination links, as the subject NP and this new NP remain dominated by the originally constructed matrix S (see Figure 3).

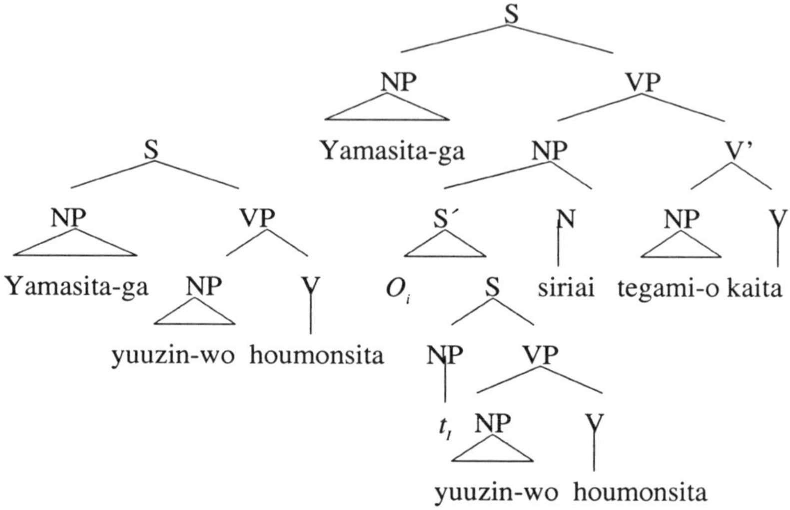

Figure 3: initial and subsequent analyses for (5)b above

The previous examples contrast in ease of processing with the following garden path sentence (from Mazuka and Itoh 1995):

(6) Yamasita-ga yuuzin-wo [$_{Rel}$ PRO t_i houmonsita] kaisya-de$_i$ mikaketa
Yamasita-nom friend-acc visited company-loc saw
"Yamasita saw his friend at the company he visited."

This example begins with precisely the same NP–NP–V sequence as (5)b. Note that in Japanese, subject and object noun phrases need not be overt. Thus, one possible resolution of the relative clause structure, and the one that is necessary here, retains neither of the first two NPs as arguments of the verb *houmonsita* within the relative modifier of *kaisya-de*. Instead, the subject NP of the relative clause is filled by a null pronoun (represented as PRO in (6)), and the head NP *kaisya-de* is interpreted as the object (see Figure 4).

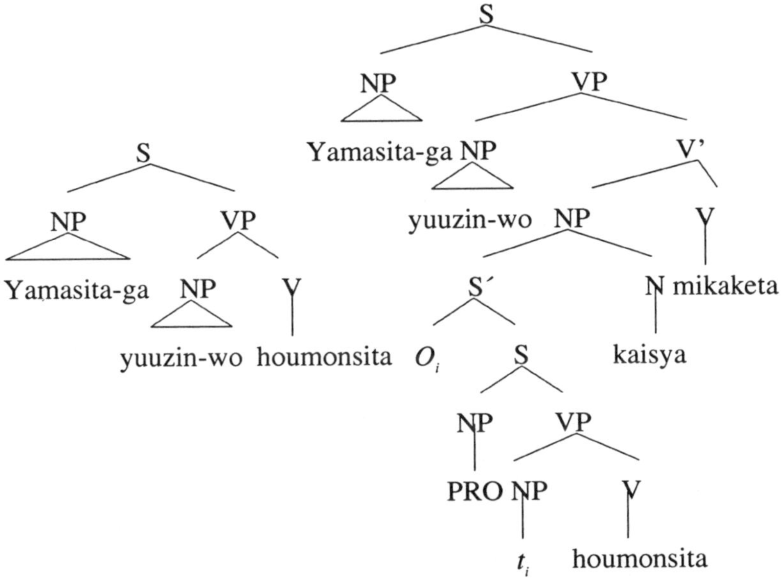

Figure 4: initial and subsequent analyses for (6)

Note that if we allow cost-free lowering, this re-analysis should be possible (contra Gorrell 1995): we need only lower the verb *hoomonsita* inside the relative clause, in D-theory terms stretching the previously asserted dominance relation between VP and V (cf. also Sturt and Crocker 1996). This case therefore poses a serious puzzle for the D-theory/lowering account of "easy" local ambiguities.

A number of proposals have been made to reconcile the difficulty of examples like (6) with the D-theory view of parsing. Weinberg (1993) suggests that a link between a VP and the verb must be understood as one of direct domination rather than simple domination. Her justification for this derives from the need for nodes in a structure to be licensed, and it is only in virtue of the VP immediately dominating the V from which it projects (and with which it shares features) that it is (internally) licensed. While sufficient to distinguish (6) from the cases in (5), this proposal suffers from the need to introduce a new structural relation, immediate domination, into the vocabulary of the parser. Furthermore, it is unclear why, in contrast to V and VP, VP must not be directly dominated by S (or I′ and VP under Weinberg's structural assumptions), given that S is typically taken to be a projection of the verb in some sense and hence should share many of its features (Grimshaw 1991).

Sturt and Crocker (1996) suggest an alternative, which does not necessitate the introduction of new descriptive vocabulary. They note that under the D-theory view of parsing, there are no restrictions whatsoever on the set of dominance relations that can be added at each point during the parse, i.e., the set of constituents that can be lowered. What is crucial is that none are retracted. Sturt and Crocker suggest that in order to produce a feasible parsing model a particular set of parsing operations (each of which adds a particular set of dominance relations) must be specified along with a control structure to determine which operation should be applied when. Though we will not need to elaborate in detail the parsing operations they propose (see their paper for description), the essential insight behind their choice of operations is that additional dominance relations may only be asserted (or alternatively "attachments" made) between nodes on the right edge of the previously built structure and the left edge of the projection of the most recently encountered word or vice versa. Crucially, this prevents re-analysis internal to constituents that have already been established. Sturt and Crocker also specify an ordering in which the parser searches for possible "attachments" from among this restricted set of loci for new dominance statements until an attachment is found that is both grammatical and semantically plausible. In the case of English, Sturt and Crocker suggest that the parser considers the possibilities in a bottom-up fashion. This proposal mirrors a wealth of proposals in the psycholinguistics literature about preference for low over high attachment (Kimball 1973, Frazier 1979). For Japanese, however, Sturt and Crocker propose that attachment sites are considered in a top-down fashion. Example (5)a is rendered unproblematic since the assertion of dominance between the NP *kaisya* 'company' heading the relative clause and the previously constructed S is a grammatically and semantically possible attachment, as 'company' can be interpreted as a locative modifier of the transitive clause. In example (5)b, such an adverbial construal of the head NP *siriai* 'acquaintance' is impossible, blocking the assertion of a statement of dominance of S by NP. Next, attachment at the VP level is attempted, and is successful, as *siriai* is a possible subject of the clause *yuuzin-wo houmonsita* 'visited his friend'. Thus, the parser asserts that the NP headed by *siriai* dominates this VP, thereby lowering the VP within the relative clause. For the problematic example (6), the same sequence of attachments is attempted. Because the NP *kaisya* 'company' can be construed as a locative modifier, the parser posits that this NP dominates the previously constructed S (with an interpretation *the company where Yamasita visited his friend*), ignoring the possibility of lowering only the verb *houmonsita* 'saw'. This will have the effect that the two initial NPs will not be able to escape from the relative clause to serve as arguments to the main verb, blocking the necessary analysis.

This proposal is intriguing in that it avoids the need to resort to additional vocabulary in the parser's structural description. The parser posits only relations of dominance. As dominance relations alone are insufficient to block lowering of the verb alone, Sturt and Crocker exploit a specific ordering among re-analysis possibilities to prevent this case of re-analysis from occurring. Though Sturt and Crocker provide a potential explanation for why English and Japanese should differ in the orderings in which they consider alternative re-analyses, stated in terms of Frazier's (1994) Minimal Revisions Principle, there is little independent empirical support for the proposal that the Japanese parser searches in a top-down fashion.[2] This is in contrast to the wealth of parsing evidence for low attachment preferences. Further, to the degree that it can account for the same range of data, a proposal which unifies the actions of the parser across languages is clearly to be preferred to one which posits divergent parsing behavior, as it avoids a potential learning problem. In the next section, we will make just such a proposal, one that maintains the advantage of Sturt and Crocker's approach in using a single structural relation in the parser's representation, while avoiding the need to parameterize the behavior of the parser across languages.

A NEW PARSING PRIMITIVE: C-COMMAND

All of the parsing models we have discussed in the D-theory line of research have shared the property of using assertions of dominance to (under)specify hypothesized structure. It is worth noting, however, that the dominance relation, while almost universally adopted for describing trees, is rarely used directly in stating linguistic principles and characterizing the relations that underlie structure building. Consider, for example, the relation of selection of a complement by a head. Stated in terms of dominance, a head *H* selects the phrase that is dominated by the node that (directly) dominates *H*. This rather indirect characterization is rarely used, however. Instead, alternative structural relations are typically exploited. Thus, we often say that a head selects a phrase under the configuration of *c-command.* Roughly speaking, a node *X* c-commands another node *Y* if it is the case that *X* precedes *Y* or vice-versa and the parent of *X*, say *Z*, dominates *Y*. Thus, while *Z* dominates both *X* and *Y*, the precedence requirement ensures that *X* can not dominate *Y* (or vice-versa). In contrast to dominance, the use of the c-command relation in linguistic theory is ubiquitous. It is this structural relation that has been implicated in phenomena such as binding, negative polarity item licensing, quantifier scope, movement, among others. With this conceptual motivation, we suggest that the parser builds representations using the relation of c-command rather than dominance. We will see that the use of c-command by a D-theory style parser enables it to mimic much of the behavior of dominance-based parsers, particularly in the range of examples that have motivated the use of dominance. Further, two simple strategies to determine when a parser asserts c-command explains not only the lowering possibilities seen in domination-based parsers but also explain why the range of phrases that can be lowered can be constrained.

To illustrate the use of c-command, consider the situation where the parser encounters the initial sequence in (3), focusing especially on the relation between the verb *saw* and the NP *the student.* If we were to assume that the NP was the object of the verb, it would follow these two should c-command one another. Furthermore, the verb would c-command any word or phrase that appears with the NP, but any proper subphrase within NP would not c-command the verb. The verb *saw* allows for two distinct types of complements, however: a noun phrase or a sentence. Since *the student* would fit as an initial sequence for either of these, the parser can safely assert that the verb c-commands the NP. This assertion can be seen, in terms of dominance, as the assertion that the verb phrase headed by this verb dominates the NP. Thus, any lowering of the NP will not force a retraction of the assertion of c-command. Once there is evidence that the subcategorized complement is finished, then can we assert that the NP c-commands the verb, thereby "closing" the VP constituent. It is only the assertion of the second c-command relation that effectively completes the combination of a head and a complement it subcategorizes.[3]

It is not difficult to see that a parser using c-command can mimic the behavior of dominance-based parsers. For those examples where a constituent was attached to the right of some selecting lexical head as an argument (cf. (4)), lowering is compatible with assertions of a (unidirectional) c-command relation from the attachment site to the attached element. Raising of elements attached in the same fashion, as in 0 vs. 0, will similarly be blocked: in a higher position, it will no longer be c-commanded by the selecting head, the verb *mending* in these cases.

EXPLAINING THE CROSS-LINGUISTIC CONTRAST

The important point in our proposed use of c-command in parsing is that it is more than a simple notational variant on dominance. In particular, when we state that a verb c-commands an NP, the structural relation between the verb and its parent is not underspecified. Thus, a c-command based parser posits that while the noun phrase can be lowered, the verb alone can not. In this respect, the structure a c-command-based parser posits is less flexible than that of a dominance-based parser. In fact, we believe that there is empirical support for precisely this restriction, support which stems from the Japanese cases discussed above.

Consider the behavior of the c-command-based parser on an NP–NP–V sequence such as those which begin examples (5)a, (5)b, and (6). Let us assume as before that the parser initially hypothesizes that this sequence constitutes a simple SOV clause. In c-command terms, this will mean (at least) that the first (nominative) NP c-commands the second (accusative) NP as well as the verb, and also that the verb c-commands the accusative NP, as a result of the hypothesized thematic dependency (more on this below). This allows us to explain why lowering of the entire S is possible in (5)a, as no c-command relations are disturbed, and also why the VP can be lowered in (5)b, as the c-command relations between the nominative NP and elements of the VP are preserved under lowering. In contrast, the lowering of the verb alone (without the lowering of the initial NPs) that would be necessary to re-analyze the initial sequence in (6) to produce a globally well-formed analysis would violate the c-command relation of the accusative NP by the verb. Thus, the use of c-command allow us to directly capture the differences among the different cases of lowering, indicating why re-analyses that require lowering of the verb alone give rise to garden paths.

Recall that the definition of c-command requires that the parent of the c-commander must dominate the c-commandee. Thus if a verb c-commands an NP, it has as an immediate consequence that the verb must remain immediately dominated by its VP (which must also dominate the NP): lowering of the verb would mean that the parent of the verb no longer dominated the NP. This use of immediate domination is extremely reminiscent of Weinberg's proposal discussed above. What is novel here, though, is that the requirement of direct domination follows in our case directly from the use of c-command, and does not require any further stipulations.

In the cases we have discussed thus far, we have been implicitly assuming the parser uses some sort of strategy to posit c-command on the basis of identified thematic relations to structural relations. Let us now make this explicit. For the purposes of this paper, we focus on the head-complement relation:

(7) Head-Complement Strategy: when an element *Y* is recognized as the complement of a head *X*, assert that *X* c-commands *Y*.

As noted above, when *Y* remains the complement in the final structure, it will also c-command *X*, the head. We assume that this is filled in by some other process, perhaps waiting until the delivery of the syntactic structure to a interpretive level of processing (see footnote 3).

The Head-Complement Strategy allows us to account for the apparent counter-examples to the distinction between the types of Japanese examples we have discussed above. Mazuka and Itoh (1995) point out the following example whose structure is identical to that in (6), but which they report is considerably easier to process:

(8) Hirosi-ga aidoru kasyu-wo [$_{Rel}$ PRO t_i kakusita] kamera-de totta
Hirosi-nom popular singer-acc hid camera-with photographed
"Hiroshi photographed the popular singer with the camera he was hiding."

Mazuka and Itoh observe that the difference between this example and structurally similar garden paths "can probably be accounted for by factors including the meaning of the individual verb, the strength of the relation between the NP and the verb, and other pragmatic knowledge. For example, hiding a popular singer ... is probably not as likely an event as ... visiting a friend ..." (p. 308). We can make use of these observations directly in our explanation of the ease of processing this case: the parser does not recognize a head-complement relation between the verb *kakusita* 'hid' and the preceding NP *aidoru kasyu-wo* 'popular singer'. Thus the Head-Complement Strategy does not apply, and consequently there is no assertion of c-command of the NP by the verb which blocks lowering of the verb alone.

There will be situations in which we will want to integrate structural elements in the absence of any hypothesized thematic dependencies. To do this, we could assume the existence of a default mapping between ordering and c-command (Kayne 1994, Weinberg 1997, Phillips 1996, Phillips and Gibson 1997).

(9) Default Order Mapping Strategy: In the absence of conflicting information, assert that *X* c-commands *Y* for successive elements in the input *X* and *Y*.

The simplest interpretation of this strategy involves successive words in the input. If *X* is the rightmost (overt) word in a recently closed constituent, a natural generalization will assert that the closed constituent containing *X* c-commands *Y*. Of course, such a strategy cannot apply generally, as grammars allow structures that are not strictly right branching. We envision sources of information such as prosodic (or punctuation) boundaries, thematic completeness of a constituent, and certain aspects of discourse context to constitute the type of evidence the parser might utilize to block application of this strategy , as well as to determine closure of constituents.

The combination of the Head-Complement and Default Order Mapping strategies has interestingly divergent implications for SVO and SOV languages.[4] For an SVO language, the two strategies will result in the assertion of an identical c-command relation in the case of identified V–O sequences, i.e., the verb will c-command the object NP. As discussed above, this relation gives the familiar pattern of cost-free re-analysis via lowering of the hypothesized object. However, for an SOV language, the application of the two strategies will yield a relation of mutual c-command between the verb and object: the object c-commands the verb because of the precedence relation between them, while the verb c-commands the object because of the hypothesized head-complement relation. Consequently, no lowering of the either the object or verb alone is possible, explaining the Japanese behavior. The difference in lowering possibilities between Japanese and English thus follows from the independently necessary word order difference between the two languages, and we do not need to posit distinct parsing strategies for the two languages.

FURTHER IMPLICATIONS

The use of c-command as a primitive for the parser has a number of other beneficial effects on explaining cases where lowering appears to be blocked. Recall the following classic garden path sentence:

(10) The horse raced past the barn fell.

Consider the behavior of parsers that utilize only domination statements. Under the standard assumption that the VP headed by *raced* is initially parsed as that of the main clause and therefore dominated by the root S, there is nothing to block lowering of this VP into the relative clause modifying the NP *the horse*. Unfortunately, this would predict that (10) is as easily processed as (11).

(11) The horse raced past the barn a few minutes ago.

Gorrell (1995) argues that such an example motivates the need to add the relation of precedence to the parser's vocabulary. By saying that the subject NP precedes the VP headed by *raced*, the re-analysis required in (10) is blocked since this precedence relation could no longer hold if the VP were within the NP, as precedence and dominance are mutually exclusive. C-command allows us to avoid this use precedence entirely. By the Default Order Mapping Strategy, the NP *the horse* will be taken to c-command the verb *raced*. Since a node cannot c-command something that it contains, the verb cannot be lowered within this NP. In contrast, (11) can be processed without the retraction of this c-command relation.

An additional example that Gorrell uses to motivate the need for precedence to block cases of lowering is:

(12) I gave the man the report criticized a demotion.

If the parser asserts only that the VP headed by *gave* dominates the two NPs *the man* and *the report*, there is nothing to prevent the noun phrase *the report* from being lowered into a relative clause modifying *man*. To render such lowering non-monotonic, Gorrell proposes that the parser should additionally assert a statement of precedence between the two NPs. The explanation for the impossibility of lowering goes through just as in the previous case. Suppose, though, the parser posits a c-command relation between the two NPs, i.e., the first one c-commands the second (Larson 1988). This will have a similar effect of blocking the possibility of lowering without resorting to precedence.

CONCLUSION

In this paper, we have investigated the processing of locally ambiguous sentences whose non-preferred analyses differ from the preferred one in terms that can be characterized as lowering. We have found that not all instances of lowering are equally easy for the human sentence processor, in contrast to what would be expected under the D-theory proposal of Marcus, Hindle and Fleck (1983), where structures are (under)specified through the use of a dominance, rather than immediate dominance, relation. We have attempted to show how the use of c-command as the primitive relation for specifying the parser's hypothesized structure enables us to distinguish between those cases of lowering that are unproblematic and those that give rise to conscious garden path effects. In particular, we have seen how differences between the word order of Japanese and English explains why lowering along the right frontier is possible in English, though not in Japanese.

We believe that c-command is a far more natural choice than dominance as the primitive for the parser's description as it allows us to link the parser's operations more directly to the selectional relations that are presumably driving much of its action.[5] The use of a relation between the verb and the NP is reminiscent of the use of thematic selection as a parsing primitive (Pritchett 1987, inter alia), unsurprisingly as (local) c-command is the structural analog of selection. Yet, since c-command is a structural relation, it need not be retracted in many situations that would necessitate thematic re-analysis. We believe that the use of c-command as a primitive in description-based parsing provides a way of bringing together two divergent strands of work on parsing models, those rooted in structure and those rooted in lexical and thematic relations.

NOTES

* We thank John Chen, Colin Phillips and the audience at the 1996 AMLaP conference in Torino for helpful comments. This work was partially supported by NSF grants SBR-97-01247 and SBR-97-10411.

[1] For an alternative way of distinguishing difficult from easy cases of re-analysis, see Fodor and Inoue (this volume).

[2] Indeed, one of the two cases that Sturt and Crocker bring up in support of their proposal does not seem to follow (about the other case, see below). The relevant example is the following (their example 23):

Yamasita-wa yuuzin-wo [$_{Rel}$ PRO t_i houmonsita] kaisya-de mikaketa

Yamasita-top friend-acc visited company-loc saw
"As for Yamasita, he saw his friend at the company he visited."

This sentence is identical to the garden path example with the single difference that the initial NP is morphologically marked as topic rather than as nominative case. They observe that speakers find this sentence considerably easier to process than 0. Since topic marked NPs must not appear within an embedded clause, the possibility of lowering the entire S within the relative clause is ruled out. They conclude, therefore, that nothing blocks the possibility of the V lowering analysis, hence its relative acceptability. However, they neglect to consider the possibility of the VP lowering analysis in which *kaisya* 'company' is construed as a locative adverbial for a null-subject relative, i.e., the company where (he) visited his friend. Following a top-down strategy, this ought to be considered prior to V-lowering, and hence should block it, yielding a garden path.

[3] This is not to say that interpretation of the structure will be impossible until the assertion of this final relation. Rather, during the course of the parse, an interpretation can be derived by extracting the so-called "standard referent" of the description (Marcus, Hindle and Fleck 1983, Rogers and Vijay-Shanker 1996). If the verb is asserted to c-command an NP and further assertions are made, the standard referent of this set of assertions will have the NP c-commanding the verb as well, as this corresponds to the minimal well-formed tree structure satisfying all of the assertions. Of course, the parser's behavior will not be monotonic over the representations that are extracted as standard referents at each point during the parse.

[4] Note that so long as specifiers occur to the left of the head, the existence of this default strategy obviates the need for a mapping between the spec-head relation and c-command. The default mapping will always give the desired result: that the specifier c-commands the head.

[5] From the perspective of the text, where c-command is defined in terms of domination, it is somewhat surprising that the parser should choose to manipulate this more abstract relation. In other work (Frank and Vijay-Shanker 1995, 1998), we have argued that c-command should not be viewed as a relation derivative from dominance, but rather that it should be taken to be the primitive relation in terms of which phrase structures are defined. From this perspective, it is of course natural, and indeed virtually necessary, to take c-command as the basic relation that the parser manipulates. For the

purposes of this paper, we leave open the issue of whether c-command is a primitive or derivative relation, keeping in mind that the former is the more attractive possibility.

REFERENCES

Abney, Steven. 1989. A computational model of human parsing. *Journal of Psycholinguistic Research* 18:129–144.

Barton, G. Edward and Robert C. Berwick. 1985. Parsing with assertion sets and informational monotonicity. In *Proceedings of the 9th International Joint Conference on Artificial Intelligence*, 769–771.

Frank, Robert and K. Vijay-Shanker. 1995. C-command and grammatical primitives. *GLOW Newsletter* 34:24–25. Paper presented at the 18th GLOW Colloquium.

Frank, Robert and K. Vijay-Shanker. 1998. Primitive C-Command. Manuscript, Johns Hopkins University and University of Delaware.

Frazier, Lyn. 1994a. *On Comprehending Sentences: Syntactic Parsing Strategies*. PhD thesis, University of Connecticut, Storrs, CT.

Frazier, Lyn. 1994b. Sentence (re-)analysis. Talk presented at the 9th Annual CUNY Conference on Human Sentence Processing.

Gorrell, Paul. 1995. *Syntax and Parsing*. Cambridge: Cambridge University Press.

Grimshaw, Jane. 1991. Extended projection. Manuscript, Brandeis University.

Inoue, Atsu. 1991. *A Comparative Study of Parsing in English and Japanese*. PhD thesis, University of Connecticut, Storrs, CT.

Kayne, Richard. 1994. *The Antisymmetry of Syntax*. Cambridge, MA: {MIT} Press.

Kimball, John. 1973. Seven principles of surface structure parsing in natural language. *Cognition* 2:15–47.

Larson, Richard. 1988. On the double object construction. *Linguistic Inquiry* 19:335–391.

Marcus, Mitchell, Donald Hindle, and Margaret Fleck. 1983. D-theory: Talking about talking about trees. *In Proceedings of the 21st Annual Meeting of the Association for Computational Linguistics*, 129–136, Cambridge, MA.

Mazuka, Reiko and Kenji Itoh. 1995. Can Japanese speakers be led down the garden path? In Reiko Mazuka and Norika Nagai (Eds.), *Japanese*

Sentence Processing, 295–329. Hillsdale, NJ: Lawrence Erlbaum Associates.

Phillips, Colin. 1996. *Order and Structure*. PhD thesis, MIT, Cambridge, MA.

Phillips, Colin and Edward Gibson. 1997. On the strength of the local attachment preference. *Journal of Psycholinguistic Research* 26(3):323–347.

Pritchett, Bradley. 1987. Garden path phenomena and the grammatical basis of language processing. *Language* 64(3):539–576.

Rogers, James and K. Vijay-Shanker. 1996. Towards a formal understanding of the determinism hypothesis in D-theory parsers. In Harry Bunt and Masaru Tomita (Eds.), *Recent Advances in Parsing Technology*, 59–78. Dordrecht: Kluwer.

Sturt, Patrick and Matthew Crocker. 1996. Monotonic syntactic processing: A cross-linguistic study of attachment and re-analysis. *Language and Cognitive Processes* 11(5):449–494.

Weinberg, Amy. 1993. Parameters in the theory of sentence processing: Minimal commitment theory goes east. *Journal of Psycholinguistic Research* 22(3):339–364.

Weinberg, Amy. 1997. Local optimization and economy in a minimalist parser. Talk presented at the Hopkins Optimality Theory Workshop.

Thierry Baccino, Marica De Vincenzi and Remo Job

CROSS-LINGUISTIC STUDIES OF THE LATE CLOSURE STRATEGY: FRENCH AND ITALIAN

INTRODUCTION

The issue of the universality of parsing strategies is a central one in a theory of sentence processing, and addressing this issue crucially requires cross-linguistic data. While the need for cross-linguistic research has been argued about for a long time, and pioneering work has been done in this field (e.g. MacWhinney, Bates and Kliegl 1984), recently there has been increasing awareness that in order to yield significant and productive generalizations it is necessary to identify and clearly specify the level at which the comparison among language structures is to be performed.

A domain in which this has been particularly evident is that of parsing preferences concerning the attachment of modifiers to complex noun phrases. For several years the uncontroversial view has been that constituents such as relative clause modifiers are attached to the last constituent that has been parsed. This view was expressed by a principle of syntactic attachment, called either Right Attachment (Kimball, 1973) or Late Closure (Frazier and Fodor, 1978). However, in recent years there have been contrasting results in different languages, some showing a Late Closure preferences, others showing an Early Closure preference and still some others no preferences at all. Such a situation has motivated several authors to propose alternative hypotheses about parsing strategies. On the one hand, Cuetos

M. De Vincenzi and V. Lombardo (eds.), Cross-linguistic Perspectives on Language Processing, 89–118.

and Mitchell (1988) argue for the existence of language-specific strategies. On the other hand, Frazier and Clifton (1996) propose that different parsing strategies are applied to different types of linguistic constituents (the Construal hypothesis), in particular that relative clause modifiers are not immediately attached to constituents consulting only syntactic information, but rather that their attachment will be determined by a variety of linguistic factors that vary cross-linguistically.

However, a third position is possible: in particular, we believe that the abandonment of Late Closure in favor of a principle of association, or the existence of language-specific strategies may be questioned (see also Gibson, Perlmutter, Canseco-Gonzalez, Hickock, 1996 for a similar idea). In our opinion, in fact, the studies done in different languages have not always adhered to the requirement for the compared structures to be "equivalent" at the level of relevant features.

Let us take the case of the studies on the attachment of relative clauses to a complex noun phrase, as in (1), where the relative clause "that came yesterday" can either refer to the daughter (NP1) or to the woman (NP2).

(1) John met the daughter of the woman that came yesterday.

There are several dimensions along which a cross-linguistic research should be matched in order to provide productive generalizations about what are the initial and/or final preferences of interpretation of the relative clause.

The first obvious dimension is that the type of structure should be the same in the two languages: e.g. either subject or object relative clauses, with the complex noun phrase in either subject or object position. It is a well known fact (Sheldon, 1974) that relative clauses in which the head noun has the same role in the main and the relative clause are earlier acquired and faster comprehended. Imagine then a cross-linguistic study whose goal is to establish whether there is a universal attachment preference of relative clauses to complex noun phrases. Imagine that the research compares the attachment preference of a complex noun phrase in subject position, using a subject relative clause in L1 and an object relative clause in L2. It is likely that the outcome would show a preference for an early closure attachment of the relative clause stronger in L1 than in L2, simply because in L1 the head noun of the complex noun phrase has the same (subject) role in the main clause and in the relative clause. In other words, in would be still entirely possible that the attachment preferences are the same in the two languages, if the grammatical roles of the complex noun and of the relative clause were systematically controlled. Therefore, a cross-linguistic comparison that did not keep the studies parallel along this dimension could give rise to differences in the preference of the relative clause attachment that are not due to language specific effect, but rather to the application of some other principle (such as the parallel function) favoring one structure over the other.

The second dimension along which to match a cross-linguistic comparison is that the linguistic means of disambiguation of the attachment should be the same in the two languages: either grammatical[1] or pragmatic. For example, if L1 has morphological agreement between the relative clause and the head noun and L2 does not, any difference found between the two languages cannot be attributed to different strategies in processing relative clauses, but rather it could be attributed to the parsing differences in the use of pragmatic and grammatical information. For example, within a modular processor, the two types of information are used at different processing stages and therefore an initial attachment preference cannot be picked up by the time pragmatic information comes into play. Evidence for such a difference can be found comparing Clifton (1988) and Carreiras and Clifton (1993); see also Igoa and Carreiras (personal communication).

A third important dimension is the methodological one, in at least two aspects. The first aspect is that the point of disambiguation has to be *comparable* in both languages. If, by hypothesis, in L1 the point of disambiguation is shortly after the attachment point and in L2 the disambiguation comes some constituents afterward, then different attachment preferences cannot be attributed to language specific difference, but to the timing operation of the language processor (cf. De Vincenzi and Job, 1993).

A second methodological aspect concerns the presentation procedure used in the experiments: whenever there are different segmentation, presentation procedures, or dependent measures, the results cannot be directly compared, but they have to be evaluated in terms of what parsing stages the different segmentation, presentations or dependent measures reflect (cf. Ferreira and Henderson 1990; De Vincenzi and Job, 1996; Gilboy and Sopena, 1996; Henstra, 1996; Brysbaert and Mitchell, 1996).

COMPARING FRENCH AND ITALIAN

The present work focuses on the attachment of relative clause modifiers comparing French and Italian with respect to immediate and final interpretation, in order to collect empirical data on the universality of the Late Closure strategy. There are several reasons for this comparison. The first one is that in French, in sentences similar to (1), there seems to be an extremely high preference for an Early closure interpretation of a relative clause (Zagar et al., 1997). Sentence fragments like (2) were completed with an adjective agreeing with the first NP (the barrister) 96% of the time:

(2) Un journaliste aborda l'avocat de la chanteuse qui semblait plus...

(A journalist approached the barrister(masc) of the singer(fem) who seemed more....)

This very high preference is at odds with the results obtained in other languages (cf. data from Spanish and English in Frazier and Clifton, 1996; data from Italian in De Vincenzi and Job, 1993), where the percentage of Early Closure interpretation in similar structures (such as (1)) varies from 50% to 67%. The first question then is: is there something really language specific about French, or is the difference due to the linguistic material used? In other words, are the structures in (1) and (2) really comparable? To answer this question, we tested final interpretation in French using exactly the same structures tested in American-English and Italian, namely sentences as (1).

The second reason to perform an accurate comparison between French and Italian is that there are differences in the *on-line* reading studies results. In Italian, De Vincenzi and Job (1993; 1995) have shown that there is an initial preference to attach the relative clause low (to NP2) with prepositions such as "de" ("of") and with thematic assigner prepositions (such as "with", "avec"). In French, however, Frenck Mestre and Pynte (this volume) and Zagar et al. (1997) have shown that an initial preference to attach the relative clause low is detectable only with a thematic assigner preposition ("avec"); when the preposition is "de" ("of"), there is an initial preference to attach the relative clause high (to NP1).

This difference found in French in the *initial* attachment between the two types of prepositions is compatible with the Construal hypothesis, which claims that relative clause modifiers are initially associated with the last thematic domain and a variety of factors determines initial interpretation. For example, Frazier (1990) has shown that there is a pragmatic preference (the Relevance Principle) to interpret a relative clause as relevant to the main assertion of the sentence. In sentences like (1) the main assertion is the main clause "John met the daughter". The relevance principle then predicts that the preference should be to interpret the relative clause as referring to "the daughter", rather than to "the woman". However, when the complex noun phrase contains a thematic assigner, such as the preposition "with" (cf (3)), then the last thematic domain to which the relative clause is associated contains only NP2.

(3) John knew the boy with the strange girl-friend who was sitting in the kitchen.

The availability of only NP2 in the last thematic domain predicts then a preference for NP2 attachment of the relative clause.

The Late Closure theory predicts the same final preferences as Construal. However, the critical difference is in the initial attachment. Late Closure predicts that initial attachment is performed by a syntactic parser which is blind to the thematic properties of the sentence, and therefore it predicts an INITIAL attachment to NP2 for either type of preposition. When the pragmatic parser comes into play, the Relevance principle will favor an Early Closure interpretation. If at the level of the discourse representation NP1 is available, then the parser may re-analyze the structure as an Early Closure structure in order to get a more pragmatically plausible analysis. However, NP1 is available to be construed with the relative clause only when NP1 and the relative clause are *within the same thematic domain*. In cases like (3), NP1 is not in the same thematic domain as the relative clause, and therefore the re-analysis of the attachment from NP2 to NP1 will not be performed because to reinterpret a constituent as outside of its current thematic domain is costly (cf. Pritchett, 1988; De Vincenzi and Job, 1995, p. 1309; Frazier and Clifton, 1996).

The Late closure hypothesis, then, at least in the version proposed by De Vincenzi and Job (1995), predicts the same off-line preferences as Construal, namely an Early Closure preference for the preposition "OF", but a Late Closure preference for the preposition "WITH". However, crucially, the INITIAL attachment preferences should always be Late closure for the different types of prepositions, and, other things being equal, for different languages. The precise assessment of the initial attachment preference for the preposition "de" is therefore crucial to discriminate between parsing models, both within a single language and across different languages.

In this French-Italian comparison, the linguistic material was chosen matching all the factors that are relevant for drawing a cross-linguistic comparison, and actively controlling the inevitable differences (i.e. word phonology). We chose French constructions parallel to the Italian one that we have already studied (De Vincenzi and Job, 1993; 1995 experiment 1) and whose disambiguation was performed in an analogous way in the two languages. In the on-line study also the presentation procedures, the segmentation of the sentences and the dependent variables recorded were closely matched in the French and Italian studies.

MATERIAL

Sentences containing a complex NP of the form (definite article -Noun1 -Preposition -definite article -Noun2) were used, followed by a subject Relative Clause (RC). They were originally used by Clifton (1988) in English, by De Vincenzi & Job (1993, 1995 Experiment 1) in Italian and were translated into French.

The complex noun phrase was always in the object position of the main clause. The relative clauses were subject relatives, i.e. the head of the clause was the subject of the clause. This was done in order to permit (gender) agreement of the verb to disambiguate the attachment of the relative clause in both languages. With respect to this aspect, French and Italian are similar in that they have a morphological system with gender marking on the determiner, on the noun, on the adjective and on the past participle.

However, some differences exist. In Italian, in singular forms, gender marking on the past participle is always "a" for agreement with a feminine noun and "o" for agreement with a masculine noun. Gender marking on the noun is more variable. For animate/human nouns, the most productive class uses "a" for feminine and "o" for masculine marking, but several exceptions exist. For example, several masculine and feminine nouns end in "e": "leone" (lion, Masculine); "pulce" (flea, Feminine)[2].

In French, for most animate human nouns and for past participles the feminine form is obtained by addition of the inflection "e" at the end of the masculine form (see examples in (4a)). However, also in this case several exceptions exist, including invariable forms ("pianiste", the pianiste).

(4a)	Italian:	maestr-o	maestr-a
		teacher-M	teacher-F
	French:	avocat	avocat-e
		lawyer-M	lawyer-F

A noteworthy difference between French and Italian is that in French gender marking is generally apparent only in written language, and there is no distinction at the phonological level. In Italian, instead, the gender suffix is always pronounced. See examples in (4b).

(4b)	Italian:	ferito	ferita
		/ferito/	/ferita/
		hurt(M)	hurt(F)
	French:	blesse	blessee

/blesse/ /blesse/
hurt(M) hurt(F)

In the two studies to be reported below, sentences containing the preposition "de" (of) or the preposition "avec" (with) were used. This manipulation was introduced in order to test the role of thematic structure in attachment preferences. The two prepositions differ in their thematic properties. In particular, only "avec" is a thematic assigner. As noted earlier, several theories (Pritchett, 1988, De Vincenzi and Job, 1995, Frazier and Clifton, 1996) predict that analysis or re-analysis of a constituent outside a thematic domain is dispreferred. This means that there should be a stronger preference for low attachment with "avec" than with "de".

Further, this manipulation allows us to directly test Late Closure (or any recency/proximity preference model, cf. Gibson et al., 1996) against Construal. In fact, Late Closure predicts an INITIAL preference to attach the RC low for all prepositions, while Construal predicts that the initial association should be already open to a variety of factors, thematic domain included. Therefore, Construal predicts an initial lack of Late Closure effect for the preposition "de".

STUDY 1

The first study was a questionnaire study in which university students were asked the preferred interpretation of the relative clause attachment by marking one of the two possible answers.

Materials and procedure

Eight sentences contained the preposition "de" (of), and 8 sentences contained the preposition "avec" (with). The NP1 and NP2 concerned always human protagonists of the same gender. In order to introduce an ambiguity into the relative clause attachment, the gender was balanced having half of the sentences containing male protagonists and the other half female protagonists (see examples 5 and 6 with the corresponding English translation).

(5) NP-Verb-[NP1-de-NP2-Relative Clause].
Le docteur appelait la fille de la dame qui s'etait blessee a' la main.
Qui se blessa? fille dame
(The doctor called the daughter of the woman who hurt herself in one hand)
Who hurt -self? daughter woman

(6) NP-Verb-[NP1-avec-NP2-Relative Clause].
Le cuisinier observait la cliente avec la dame qui s'etait plainte des plats.
Qui se plaignit? cliente dame
(The cook observed the client(F) with the woman who complained for the food)
Who complained? client(f) woman

Sentences were randomized in the questionnaire as was the order of the nouns in the question (NP1/NP2 and NP2/NP1) but every subject received the same order of sentences. The experimental sentences were mixed with 20 filler sentences of a variety of syntactic structures, containing no complex noun phrases.

Participants
91 students of the University of Nice took part in the study.

Results
Percentages of Late Closure preferences are reported in Table 1, along with the American English data (Clifton, 1988) and the Italian data (De Vincenzi and Job, 1993). The results show a similar pattern across languages: there is a strong preference for the Late Closure interpretation with the preposition WITH while

with the preposition OF there is a small preference for the Early Closure interpretation.

	French	American English	Italian
de (of)	44.5	45	49
avec (with)	76.3	64	70

Table 1: Percentage of Late Closure preferences in the questionnaire studies

These results are important because they show that similar off-line preferences are found across languages that differ at the typological level. French and Italian, contrary to English, have a rich morphological system and a relatively free word-order. While this result is at odds with the 96% Early Closure preference reported for French by Zagar et al. (1997), also quoted in Mitchell, Cuetos and Zagar, 1990), it is entirely consistent with the result of a frequency count reported by Charolles who analyzed a corpus derived from the newspaper Le Monde (quoted in Mitchell, Cuetos, Corley, & Brysbaert, 1995). For the structure NP1 de NP2, Charolles found 53,4% attachments of the RC to NP2 (i.e, a slight Late Closure Attachment preference).

The inconsistency between the questionnaire data reported by Zagar et al. (1997) for French and the present data illustrates the problem of the comparability of structures not only across languages, but even within a language. We shall address this point in the final discussion.

STUDY 2

A reading time experiment was performed using the same material as Study 1. We varied the gender of one of the noun of the complex noun phrase, so that the two nouns had different gender and the relative clause attachment could be disambiguated by the gender marking of the relative clause verb (see examples in Table 2). The purpose of the experiment was to investigate whether the initial Relative Clause attachment preferences are the same as the final ones, or whether, as found in Italian (De Vincenzi and Job, 1995, Experiment 1), there is an initial preferred attachment determined by the application of the Late Closure principle.

Material and Procedure

The sentences used in the Questionnaire study were presented one at a time on a computer screen. Each sentence was divided in five segments as shown in Table 2. They were presented using a moving-window, non-cumulative self-paced presentation. Each sentence was followed by a comprehension question that queried the attachment of the relative clause. The question appeared all at once on the screen, with the two nouns referring to the two alternatives appearing underneath it. The question never carried any gender marking (which would immediately disambiguate what the correct answer was) and this was ensured by using the simple past form of the verb. The reciprocal order of the two nouns in the question was counterbalanced, to avoid order biases. The subjects had to answer by pressing a left or a right button, corresponding to whether the correct noun appeared to the left or to the right side of the screen. Examples of the experimental material are given in Table 2. A full list of the experimental sentences is in the Appendix .

Type of Preposition: DE

L'avocat suspectait\le pere\de la fille\qui s'etait trahi(e)\au proces.
Qui se trahit? Fille - Pere

L'avvocato diffida\ del padre\ della ragazza\ che si e` tradita -o\ al processo.
Chi si tradi`? Ragazza - Padre

The lawyer suspects\the father\ of the girl\ who betrayed her -himself\ at the trial.
Who betrayed -self? Girl - Father

Type of Preposition: AVEC

Personne n'invitait\le directeur\avec la belle amie\qui etait reste(e)\pour boire.
Qui resta pour boire? Amie - Regisseur

Nessuno invito`\ il regista\ con la bella amica\ che era rimasta -o\ a bere.
Chi rimase a bere? Amica - Regista

Nobody invited\ the movie director\ with the beautiful girdlfriend\ who remained+F -+M\ to drink.
Who stayed to drink? Girlfriend - Movie director

Table 2. Example Sentences used in the Experiment. The Italian version and the literal English translation are given after the French version. Slashes (/) indicate segmentation, double slashes indicate the critical disambiguation segment.

The reading time on each segment of the sentence, the time to answer the comprehension question and the answer to the question were recorded. A repeated measures design was used, incorporating a Latin Square. Each subject saw one version from each sentence pair, and each subject was exposed to all conditions. This means that each subject saw a total of 76 sentences: 16 experimental sentences plus 60 filler sentences of a variety of syntactic forms. Order of presentation of the sentences was randomized for each subject.

Participants
Forty students of the University of Nice participated in the experiment. They were all French native speakers.

Results
Data are summarized in Table 3. The mean reading times were computed for each segment. Analyses of variance with repeated measures were conducted on the reading times with both Subjects (F1) and Items (F2) as random factors. Two variables with two levels each were considered: Closure (Late vs Early) and Preposition ("de" vs "avec").

Experimental condition	SEGMENT NUMBER					Question RT	% correct
	1	2	3	4	5		
Argument							
Early Closure	1254	1104	1216	1438	1331	3082	89
Late Closure	1351	1066	1178	1380	1287	3310	55
Adjunct							
Early Closure	1259	1101	1316	1583	1523	4432	47
Late Closure	1202	1073	1376	1380	1288	3371	89

Table 3. Average Reading Time by Different Experimental Conditions in Experiment 1, with Question-Answering Reaction Time (RT) and Percentage Correct

There were no significant effects on the 1st and 2nd segment. On the third segment, where the preposition appeared, there was a significant effect of preposition ($F1(1,39) = 7.301$, $p < .01$, $F2(1,12) = 5.097$, $p < .05$). Reading time was slower with sentences containing the preposition "avec" than with sentences containing the preposition "de". Anovas performed on the 4th segment showed a significant effect of Closure ($F1(1,39)=4.35$ $p<.05$, $F2(1,12)=3.58$, $p=.08$) where sentences in the Late Closure Conditions (1380ms) were read faster than in the Early Closure Conditions (1510ms). On the last segment (5th segment) which might show some kind of 'wrap-up' processes, there was a significant effect of Preposition ($F1(1,39)=4.521$ $p<.05$, $F2(1,12)=8.592$, $p<.01$) and a significant effect of Closure, ($F1(1,39)=6.304$, $p=.02$; $F2(1,12)=18.202$, $p<.001$). As in segment 4, Late Closure sentences (1288ms) were read faster than Early Closure sentences (1427ms). The interaction Closure and Preposition was not significant in the subject analysis ($F1(1,39)=2.733$) but was significant in the items analysis, ($F2(1,12)=8.523$ $p<.01$).

In the comprehension task, times to answer the question were shorter for sentences with the preposition "de" than with the preposition "avec" ($F1(1,39)=7.01$ $p<.01$, $F2(1,12)=6.731$, $p<.025$). There was also an effect of Closure significant only by Subjects ($F1(1,39)$ $=4.727$ $p<.05$, $F2(1,12)=2.884$). The interaction Closure x Preposition was significant ($F1(1,39)=6.347$, $p<.025$, $F2(1,12)= 6.456$, $p<.025$). Times to answer were longest for sentences with the preposition 'avec' in Early Closure condition, the comparison between this condition and the three others yielding a significant effect ($F(1,39)=9.475$ $p<.01$).

As far as comprehension accuracy is concerned, there was an interaction between Preposition and Closure, $F1(1,39) = 112.795$ $p<.001$, $F2(1,12) = 56.103$ $p<.001$. This was due to the fact that sentences with the preposition OF were better comprehended in the Early Closure condition, while sentences containing WITH were better comprehended in the Late Closure condition.

DISCUSSION

The reading time data show an initial preference for a Late Closure attachment of the relative clause regardless of the preposition type. This result confirms the validity of the Late closure preference cross-linguistically since parallel results are obtained with closely matched material in Italian (De Vincenzi and Job, 1995, Experiment 1).

Also the response time and accuracy on the comprehension questions parallel the Italian data, showing a preference for sentences with the preposition "de" to take the Relative Clause as modifier of the first NP and for sentences with the preposition "avec" to take the Relative Clause preferentially interpreted as modifier of the second NP[3].

However, these results show an interesting effect. Unlike Italian, the French material gives rise to very low accuracy data and to rather long response times in the thematically dispreferred conditions: With the preposition "de" readers clearly disprefer the Late Closure attachment and conversely with the preposition "avec" they disprefer the Early Closure attachment. In other words, French readers seem to show the same final preferences as if the sentences were not grammatically disambiguated. These results are surprising given the gender marking, and introduce a difference with the Italian data.

However, there is no necessity to invoke any language specific strategy here. Gender agreement in French is marked in the written form, not in the oral form. In order to explain this pattern, it is sufficient to postulate that phonological recoding strategies are used by the subjects to hold information in short term memory. Such strategies are essential for sentence comprehension, as shown by Kleiman (1975): A sentence acceptability judgment was impaired by continuous digits repetition, by about the same amount as a phonemic judgments. Vallar and Baddeley (1984) have reported analogous effects with a neurological patient with a phonological working memory impairment.

Given that phonological recoding seems necessary in sentence comprehension and that the French past participle is phonologically ambiguous regarding gender information, it is likely that the information about gender agreement on the past participle is not fully available when the comprehension task is performed.

SOME DIFFERENCES WITH OTHER FRENCH STUDIES ON RELATIVE CLAUSE ATTACHMENT

As previously mentioned, researches on French by Frenck-Mestre and Pynte (this volume) and by Zagar et al. (1997) show an initial preference for Early closure attachment of the relative clauses to complex noun containing the preposition "de". What could be the reasons for these differences?

One hypothesis suggested by Frenck-Mestre and Pynte (this volume) is that the difference is due to a methodological variable: our material contained an equal number of experimental sentences with the prepositions "avec" and "de", and this mixture possibly biased the preference of the preposition "de" for a Late Closure attachment: "..prepositions which have lexical content, such as "with", clearly influence processing. Specifically, they uniformly lead to an N2 preference across languages."(Frenck-Mestre et al., this volume). However, as also noted by Frenck-Mestre and Pynte, this hypothesis is hardly sustainable given the high proportion of filler sentences we used. Further, we think that we can discard this hypothesis considering that, contrary to what Frenck-Mestre and Pynte suggest, there are studies that used ONLY the preposition "de" and still show an initial Late Closure (NP2) attachment preference: these are the cases of Henstra (1996) in English and Kamide and Mitchell (1997) in Japanese. Therefore, there is independent experimental evidence which excludes the idea that an initial Late closure effect for the preposition "de" is due to a lexical priming of other prepositions in the experimental material.

Our hypothesis for the difference among the studies on French is that the studies above mentioned, and ours, despite superficial similarities, really tested different linguistic constructions. In particular, there are two linguistic dimensions (i.e. types of noun phrases and types of relative clauses) in which the sentences used in the French studies of Frenck-Mestre and Pynte (this volume) and Zagar et al, (1997) are quite different from ours and in a way that we think biases an early closure attachment.

Frenck-Mestre and Pynte material used a complex noun phrase containing two different types of nouns: N! was always a definite NP, while N2 was always a proper noun, as shown in (7):

(7) John photographed the daughter of Charles who seems more disdainful....

First of all, why to have a systematic difference among the two NPs? The different referentiality character influences RC attachment. Relative clauses can attach to a proper noun only if they are appositive, not as restrictive. Appositive relative clauses generally serve as "parenthetical comments" or "afterthoughts". They are always introduced by a wh-pronoun, never by the complementizer THAT or by an empty complementizer (see 8 a,b,c):

(8) a. John - who you met last week- is a good teacher.
b. * John - that you met last week- is a good teacher.
c. * John - you met last week- is a good teacher.

Appositive relative clauses are set off in a separate intonative contour by the rest of the sentences. They usually have a pause after their antecedent or a descending tone on the relative clause. In writing, a comma usually separates the appositive relative clause from its antecedent. Given that there was no comma in the experiments, a restrictive interpretation of the relative clause is forced. This means that in sentences like (7) the reader cannot attach the relative clause to the second NP, because, being a proper noun, the attachment would be ungrammatical. To put it simply, in the restrictive reading the attachment of the relative clause in (7) is not even ambiguous, it can attach only to NP1; only in the appositive reading can the relative clause attach to either noun. Therefore, to perform a Late Closure attachment to a proper noun, the reader would have to reinterpret the relative clause as appositive. However, this reinterpretation would be quite hard for at least two reasons: one reason is that an appositive relative clause requires a different intonation pattern, and re-analysis is more costly as it involves stress reassignments, as demonstrated and discussed by Bader (1998) and by Fodor (1998). Second, it is not obvious that appositive relative clauses have the same type of attachment as restrictive relative clauses: for example Cinque (1981/2) suggests that they are to be considered as dislocated structure or even coordinate structures. In this latter hypothesis, an appositive relative clause has a more complex syntactic attachment than a restrictive one. Therefore, it is entirely likely that an initial Late closure preference for the "de" sentences in the Frenck-Mestre and Pynte research, is obscured by the re-analysis due to the revision from the restrictive to the appositive reading. This should not hold for the preposition "avec" where both initial and final preferences favor a Late closure reading.

Another important linguistic aspect is the type of relative clause used by Frenck-Mestre and Pynte (this volume) and

Zagar et al, 1997. We (and almost all of the literature on RC attachment) have used a complex NP followed by a relative clause; the disambiguation was on the verb of the relative clause. They used a more complex structure, namely a complex NP followed by a relative clause with the impersonal verb SEEM and containing a comparative clause; the disambiguation was on the adjective of the comparative clause, as illustrated in (9):

(9) Jean photographie la fille de Charles qui semble plus dedaigneux/se que d'habitude.

The verb SEEM has always a non-thematic subject filled with an expletive or with a raised subject. In (9) the subject of SEEM is a raised subject and the underlying structure of the sentence is (10b), derived from (10a):

(10) a. that T seem [the girl be more disdainful..]
b. the girl [CP wh [that [T-wh seems [T1 more disdainful..]

There is also another possibility, namely that the subject of SEEM is coindexed with an entire clause, as shown in (11):

(11) Jean photographie la femme sur le point de mourir, ce que semble une mauvaise ideé.
Jean photographed the dying woman, which seems a bad idea.

The general point we want to make here is that using a verb which takes non-thematic subjects, such as SEEM, can bias the results because it introduces an extra syntactic chain and, consequently, it invalidates the comparison across languages, if the same structure is not used in both languages.

In fact, in Frenck-Mestre et al. material (cf (9)), at the verb SEEM the subject position cannot be immediately filled, but the reader/listener has to wait for the comparative clause. The actual assignment of the extraction site of the Relative Clause head is therefore delayed. The initial locality preference that subsumes Late Closure can be overcome by the intervening constituents in those cases where initial and final preferences diverge, i.e. for the preposition "de". Further, we predict that such constructions should show a higher preference for an Early Closure interpretation, in that the temporary assignment of an interpretation to the relative pronoun presumably obeys principles of pronoun interpretation, based on discourse factors (see Hemforth, Konieczny and Scheepers, in press), and not on principles of syntactic attachment. This hypothesis would explain the very high 96% percent of early closure preference interpretation, reported by Zagar et al. (1997) with such structures.

Notice that the use of these different linguistic constructions can give us some interesting information about what affects parsing decisions: for example, we predict that the very same Early Closure should be found in Italian for constructions as (7), with a proper noun as NP2, and for constructions as (9), with an impersonal verb and a comparative clause. In any case, parsing of an appositive versus a restrictive relative clause is a topic that is worth serious investigation, because it could reveal some interesting facts, not only about syntactic parsing, but also about principles of sentence interpretation (cf. Frazier, 1998). Also, the process of non-thematic subjects is worth further investigation.

The point here is how to use this new information. If the goal of these manipulations is to test the universality of parsing decisions and strategies across languages, then the question is ill formed. In our view, a study whose goal is to assess whether a construction is parsed by similar principles in two different languages, should ensure that the same linguistic construction is tested in the two languages (cf. also Frazier, 1999 for a discussion of this topic).

CONCLUDING REMARKS

The two studies here reported have shown that the final interpretation in both the questionnaire and the on-line experiment is affected by the thematic properties of the complex Noun Phrase. Initial interpretation, instead, is driven by a syntactic principle, namely a preference to attach to the last constituent. These two results support models of sentence parsing that postulate an initial preference to attach modifiers to the most recent constituent such as the model of Kimball (1973), Frazier and Fodor (1978), De Vincenzi and Job (1995), and Gibson et al. (1996).

The data do not support the Construal hypothesis (Frazier and Clifton, 1996) since it predicts an initial attachment preference modulated by the argument structure of the complex noun phrase. In particular, it would predict no initial Late Closure preference for the preposition "de", a result clearly not found in our data.

Finally, our data support a view of the human sentence processor that uses universal parsing strategies, not language specific strategies, as proposed by Cuetos and Mitchell (1988). The comparison here performed shows a remarkably similar pattern across different languages. Also, the apparently different findings between the two languages were accounted for by the unavoidable difference in phonology between French and Italian. Once this difference was explained at the proper level of analysis, we demonstrated that a similar pattern emerges between the two languages. Admittedly, before asserting that a parsing strategy such as Late Closure is universal, many more languages should be tested and there should be falsifications at the appropriate level of analysis. However, we hope that this work demonstrates, at least, that very careful analysis of the differences and similarities across the linguistic material used in psycholinguistic studies should be carried out before drawing any conclusion across languages.

NOTES

[1.] Within grammatical disambiguation, the two languages should be matched also in the type of morphological disambiguation. For example, if L1 has been studied using gender disambiguation and L2 with number agreement disambiguation, we could expect different results based on the representational and processing difference between gender and number (cf. Nicol, 1988, De Vincenzi and Di Domenico, 1996)

[2.] In almost all cases, gender marking is unambiguously given by the noun article: "il", "lo" for masculine nouns, "la" for feminine nouns. However the article is ambiguous if there is elision in cases such as: "l'ape" (the bee, feminine); "l'alce" (the moose, masculine)).

[3.] The accuracy rates reported here for French and in the De Vincenzi and Job (1995) for Italian refer to the comprehension questions to all and only the experimental sentences. These rates would be higher if we had counted only accuracy to questions probing filler sentences, as done by Brysbaert and Mitchell (1996).

REFERENCES

Bader, M. (1998) Prosodic influences on reading syntactically ambiguous sentences. In F. Ferreira e J. D. Fodor (Eds.) *Re-analysis in Sentence Processing*. Kluwer Academic Publishers: Dordrecht, the Netherlands, 1-46.

Brysbaert, M. and Mitchell, D. C. (1996) Modifier attachment in sentence parsing: Evidence from Dutch. *The Quarterly Journal of Experimental Psychology*, 49A, 664-695.

Carreiras, M. and Clifton, C. (1993) Relative clause interpretation preferences in Spanish and English. *Language and Speech*, 36(4), 353-372.

Cinque, G. (1981/2) On the theory of relative clauses and markedness. *The Linguistic Review*, 1, pp. 247-294.

Clifton, C. (1988) Restrictions on Late Closure: Appearance and Reality. Paper presented at the 6th Australian Language and Speech Conference, University of New South Wales, August 19-21.

Cuetos, F. and Mitchell, D. C. (1988) Cross-linguistic differences in parsing: Restrictions on the use of the Late Closure strategy in Spanish. *Cognition*, 30, p. 73-105.

De Vincenzi, M. & Di Domenico, E. (1996) Gender and Number: Differences in use and representation. In L. Nash e A. Zribi-Hertz (Eds.) *Actes du deuxieme colloque LANGUES et GRAMMAIRE*. Universite' Paris-8, Department des Sciences du Language, pp. 95-109.

De Vincenzi, M. and Job, R. (1993) Some observations on the universality of the Late Closure strategy: evidences from Italian. *Journal of Psycholinguistic Research*, 22, 189-206.

De Vincenzi, M. & Job, R. (1995) An investigation of Late Closure: the role of syntax, thematic structure and pragmatics in initial and final interpretation. *Journal of_Experimental Psychology: Learning, Memory and Cognition*, 21, pp. 1303-1321.

De Vincenzi, M. and Job, R. (1996) On the conditions of applicability and detection of the Late Closure strategy. Poster presented at the *9th CUNY Annual Conference on_Human Sentence Processing*, City University of New York, New York, March 21-23.

Ferreira, F. and Henderson, J. (1990) The use of verb information in syntactic parsing: A comparison of evidence from eye-movements and segment-by-segment self-paced reading. *Journal of Experimental Psychology: Learning, Memory and Cognition*, 16, 555-568.

Fodor, J. D. (1998) Learning to Parse? *Journal of Psycholinguistic Research*, 27, 2, 285-319.

Frazier, L. (1998) Getting There (Slowly). *Journal of Psycholinguistic Research*, 27, 2, 123-146.

Frazier, L. (1999) Are Japanese children's parser's parameter's settings the same as the settings of the parameters of the parser of English? *APA Review of Books*, vol. 44, no1, 57-59.

Frazier, L. and Clifton, C. (1996) *Construal*. Cambridge, MA: MIT Press.

Frazier, L. and Fodor, J.D. (1978) The sausage machine: A new two-stage parsing model. *Cognition*, 6, 291-326.

Gibson, E., Pearlmutter, N., Canseco-Gonzalez, E., Hickock, G. (1996) Recency preference in the human sentence processing mechanism. *Cognition*, 59, 23-59.

Gilboy, E. and Sopena, J. (1996) Segmentation studies of Late Closure in Spanish. In M. Carreiras, J. Garcia-Albea & N. Sebastian Galles (Eds) *Language Processing in Spanish*, Hillsdale, N.J.: Erlbaum.

Hemforth, B. ,Konieczny, L. and Scheepers, C. (in press) Syntactic attachment and anaphor resolution: two sides of relative clause attachment. In M. Crocker, M. Pickering and C. Clifton, jr. (Eds) *Architecture and Mechanisms for Language Processing*. Cambridge: Cambridge University Press.

Henstra, J. (1996) Relative Clause attachment in English: Eye-tracking versus self-paced reading. Poster presented at AMLaP-96, Torino, Italy, September 20-21.

Kamide, Y., Mitchell, D. C. (1997) Relative clause attachment: nondeterminism in Japanese parsing. *Journal of Psycholinguistic Research*, vol. 26, 2, 247-254.

Kimball, J. (1973) Seven principles of surface structure parsing in natural language, *Cognition*, 2, pp. 15-47.

Kleiman, G. M. (1975) Speech recoding in reading. *Journal of Verbal Learning and Verbal Behavior*, 14, 323-339.

MacWhinney, B., Bates, E. and Kliegl, R., (1984) Cue validity and sentence interpretation in English, German,and Italian. *Journal of Verbal Learning and Verbal Behavior*, 23, 127-150.

Mitchell, D. C., Cuetos, F., Corley, M. M. B and Brysbaert, M. (1995) Exposure-based models of human parsing: Evidence for the use of coarse-grained (non-lexical) statistical records. *Journal of Psycholinguistic Research*, 24, 469-488.

Mitchell, D. C., and Cuetos, F., Zagar, D. (1990) Reading in different languages: Is there a universal mechanism for parsing sentences? In D. Balota, G.B. Flores D'Arcais & K. Rayner (a cura di) *Comprehension Processes in Reading*. Hillsdale, NJ: Lawrence Erlbaum Associates, Inc., pp. 265-284.

Nicol, J. (1988) *Coreference processing during sentence comprehension*. Unpublished Doctoral Dissertation, Massachussetts Institute of Technology, Cambridge, Ma.

Pritchett, B. (1988) Garden path phenomena and the grammatical basis of linguistic performance. *Language* 64, 539-576.

Pynte, J. and Frenck-Mestre, C. (this volume) Resolving syntactic ambiguities: Cross-linguistic differences?

Sheldon, A. (1974) The role of parallel function in the acquisition of relative clauses in English. *Journal of Verbal Learning and Verbal Behavior*, 13, 272-281.

Vallar, G. and Baddeley, A. D. (1984) Phonological short-term store, phonological processing and sentence comprehension: A neuropsychological case study. *Cognitive Neuropsychology*, 1, 121-141.

Zagar, D., Pynte, J. and Rativeau (1997) Evidence for early closure attachment in first-pass reading times in French. *The Quarterly Journal of Experimental Psychology.*

APPENDIX

French Sentences (and their English translation) used in Study 2: Relative Clauses with Gender Disambiguation. On the verbs, the Late Closure version is indicated first, then the Early Closure version.

1. Le docteur appelait le fils de la dame qui s'etait blesse(e) a la main.
Qui se blessa? Fils - Dame

The doctor called\ the son\ of the lady\ who hurt her -himself\ in one hand.
Who hurt self? Son - Lady

2. Le cafetier regardait l'ami de la femme qui etait emu(e) devant le bar.
Qui s'emut? Ami - Femme

The bar -tender was looking at\ the friend+M\ of the woman\ who was silent+F -+M\ in front of the pub.
Who was silent? Friend+M - Woman

3. L'avocat suspectait le pere de la fille qui s'etait trahi(e) au proces.
Qui se trahit? Fille - Pere

The lawyer suspects of\ the father\ of the girl\ who betrayed her - himself\ at the trial.
Who betrayed -self? Girl - Father

4. Le journaliste interrogeait l'amie du senateur qui s'etait suicide(e) hier soir.
Qui se suicida? Senateur - Amie

The reporter interviewed\ the girlfriend\ of the senator\ who killed him -herself\ yesterday night.
Who killed -self? Senator - Girlfriend

5. Le duc aidait le fils de la couturiere qui s'etait eventre(e) a cause des dettes.
Qui s'eventra? Fils - Couturiere

The duke had helped\ the son\ of the dressmaker\ who shot her - himself\ for the debts.
Who shot -self? Son - Dressmaker

6. Julie reconnaissait la collegue du dirigeant qui etait parti(e) depuis peu.
Qui partit? Collegue - Dirigeant

Tina recognized\ the colleague+F\ of the boss+M\ who escaped+M -+F\ long ago.
Who ran away? Colleague - Boss

7. Paul connaissait la secretaire du directeur qui etait tomb(e) a la fete.
Qui tomba? Secretaire - Directeur

Ezio knew\ the secretary+F\ of the boss+M\ who had fainted+M - +F\ at the party.
Who fainted? Boss - Secretary

8. Jean flirtait avec la niece du danseur qui s'etait assis(e) dans le jardin.
Qui s'assit? Danseur - Niece

Gianni was flirting with\ the niece\ of the dancer+M\ who was seated+M -+F\ in the garden.
Who was seated? Dancer - Niece

9. Antoine haissait le garcon avec l'amie qui s'etait exhibe(e) a la fete.
Qui s'exhiba? Garcon - Amie

Antonio hates\ the boy\ with the girlfriend\ who performed her - himself\ at the party.
Who performed -self? Boy - Girlfriend

10. Tous admirait l'homme avec la fille qui s'etait mis(e) a chanter un opera.
Qui chanta? Homme - Fille

Everybody admires\ the man\ with the daughter\ who started her - himself\ to sing an opera.
Who sang? Man - Daughter

11. Personne n'invitait le directeur avec la belle amie qui etait reste(e) pour boire.
Qui resta pour boire? Amie - Directeur

Nobody invited\ the movie director\ with the beautiful girdlfriend\ who remained+F -+M\ to drink.
Who stayed to drink? Girlfriend - Movie director

12. L'oncle rencontrait le president avec la collegue qui etait invite(e) par nous.
Qui fut notre invite'? Collegue - President

The uncle met\ the headmaster\ with the colleague+F\ who had been+F -+M\ our guest.
Who had been our guest? Colleague - Headmaster

13. Lucie observait la bonne avec l'ami qui s'etait brule(e) a un bras.
Qui se brula? Bonne - Ami

Luca was watching at\ the waitress\ with the boyfriend\ who burned him -herself\ on the arm.
Who burned -self? Waitress - Boyfriend

14. Laure enviait la cousine avec le fiance qui s'etait enrichi(e) par la drogue.
Qui s'enrichit? Cousine - Fiance

Pina envyied\ the cousin+F\ with the boyfriend\ who enriched him -herself\ with drug.
Who enriched -self? Cousin+F - Boyfriend

15. Le cuisinier connaissait le client avec la dame qui s'etait plaint(e) des plats.
Qui se plaignit? Dame - Client

The cook knew\ the client\ with the woman\ who complained+F - +M\ about the food.
Who complained? Woman - Client

16. Le pretre invitait la fille avec l'ami qui s'etait sauve(e) de l'accident.
Qui se sauva? Ami - Fille

The priest hosted\ the girl\ with the boyfriend\ who saved him - herself\ in the crash.
Who saved -self? Boyfriend - Girl

Cheryl Frenck-Mestre and Joel Pynte

RESOLVING SYNTACTIC AMBIGUITIES: CROSS-LINGUISTIC DIFFERENCES?

The present study is an attempt to discover some of the factors which influence readers' comprehension when faced with several possible interpretations of a sentence, and whether any universal account can be postulated for this process across, if not all, at least closely related languages. This issue has indeed been the object of considerable debate (cf. Cuetos, Mitchell & Corely, 1996; Frazier & Clifton, 1996; Gibson, Pearlmutter, Canseco-Gonzales & Hickok, 1996, MacDonald, Pearlmutter & Seidenberg, 1994; for recent discussions).

One unquestionable fact is that the human language processor (HLP) is rapid, so rapid that, more often than not, the reader is not cognizant of the ambiguity inherent in many common structures, as exemplified in the English sentence "John said he took the trash out yesterday." This fact has led to the supposition that the HLP has at its disposal immediate procedures which allow it to make decisions based on "minimal" information and without necessary recourse to semantic or pragmatic factors. Moreover, in the specific instance of local syntactic ambiguities, decisions may be made in the absence of this extra-structural information.

Given this capacity, the immediate question is, what are the procedures that allow such efficiency? By one account, the AHLP obeys heuristic structural principles in order to analyse incoming information quickly (Frazier & Clifton, 1996; Frazier, 1987; 1989; 1990). The proposal is far reaching in that these

M. De Vincenzi and V. Lombardo (eds.), Cross-linguistic Perspectives on Language Processing, 119–148.

structural principles are assumed to be operant in all languages, with only the "vocabulary", i.e. the lexical items and specific grammar, differing across languages. In this model, structures are preferred or disfavored based on their relative syntactic simplicity alone. A quite different proposal has been put forward by advocates of a frequency-based parser, where particular analyses would be adopted by the adult reader due to his/her prior exposure to a given language and its idiosyncrasies. Two distinct frequency models have been proposed. The one is corpus-based, taking into account the number of occurrences of particular syntactic structures in written corpuses and proposing an immediate effect of this factor on parsing (Brysbaert & Mitchell, 1996; Cuetos & Mitchell, 1988; Mitchell, 1994). The other focuses on lexical statistics, under the assumption that syntactic and lexical ambiguity are tightly linked (MacDonald et al., 1994). As stated by MacDonald et al. (1994, p. 682) "To the extent that information required by the syntactic component is stored with individual lexical items, it will be difficult to find a boundary between the two systems." These frequency-based approaches resemble the structural approach in that they assume a common underlying mechanism across languages. However, this assumption is based on statistical properties of the language rather than on syntactic complexity, and these statistics--concerning the frequency of structures and/or of lexical properties--are by definition variable across languages (and within a language if one heeds individual differences or maturational changes). The strength of the frequency-based account lies indeed in its ability to accommodate cross-language differences, even for structures which are identical across very similar languages.

The corpus-based, or "linguistic tuning" hypothesis has been disdained by some on the grounds that it does not specify how frequency counts should be tallied on the one hand, and that it offers a descriptive rather than a truly explanatory account on the other. The model does not in fact offer an explanation for how differences in the frequencies of structures originate. As stated by Corely et al. (1996, p. 181), however, "The function of the statistically driven parser is to explain the rapid mechanisms employed in real-time parsing and not to go beyond that to account for the prevalence of different structures in the language." Furthermore, the authors question the validity of the assumption that models which aspire to explain the distribution of structures within a given language are necessarily superior to an account which makes use of the available statistics to generate testable predictions.

The lexical, or constraint-satisfaction, approach assumes that multiple factors convene to determine which structure is the most probable of the possible alternatives. For example, the decision to interpret a PP as modifying the preceding NP or VP, in a sentence such as "Brutus hit the gladiator with the shield" will depend upon the frequencies of different usage of the noun, the verb and the preposition. Two studies which specifically investigated the role of the verb in this particular ambiguity revealed that PP attachment is strongly affected by the argument structure of the verb (Frenck-Mestre & Pynte, 1997) and by its semantic class (Sedivy & Spivey-Knowlton, 1994). Longer reading times were incurred when PP attachment was not coherent with the attachment most frequently found with the particular class of verb than when it was. Based on these types of examples across numerous studies and various syntactic ambiguities, MacDonald et al. (1994) build a compelling argument for the involvement of lexical statistics in syntactic analysis. Akin to the tuning hypothesis, however, the model fails to specify *how* the differences in lexical frequency initially arise, e.g. how it came to be that an English verb such as "review" is used more often as a past participle NP modifier than as a transitive verb, whereas the inverse is true for a verb such as "race". Whereas this may seem to be a somewhat vacuous question as concerns lexical ambiguity (i.e. why "blue" more frequently connotes color than emotion), it may be less trivial as concerns syntactic ambiguities (see also Frazier, 1989; Steedman, 1989; Tanenhaus & Carlson, 1989; for further comments on this type of model).

Both the structural, rule-based approach and frequency-based models of syntactic parsing have received their share of experimental support and criticism. One structure, in particular, has proved to be a stringent test of these models, such being a relative clause preceded by a complex NP[1], as illustrated in (1). The ambiguity of this structure is due to there being more than one potential host site for the attachment of the RC. In (1), the RC "who seemed more confident..." can be attached either to the head of the complex noun phrase (i.e. the barrister seemed confident) or to the second NP (i.e. the singer did).

(1) A journalist approached the barrister of the singer who seemed more confident than usual

This particular structure triggered quite a large number of studies, following the seminal work by Cuetos and Mitchell (1988) in which they clearly demonstrated that Spanish and English speaking subjects resolve it differently in their respective native languages. The results of these studies, summed up nicely in two recent reviews of the question (Cuetos, Mitchell & Corley, 1996; Frazier & Clifton, 1996, chapter 4) show a considerable disparity across languages. Restricting ourselves, however, to three romance languages, we note that the data is not unequivocal even for these three. Questionnaire experiments (in which subjects are asked to choose off-line between the two interpretations) have produced similar results for Spanish (Carreiras & Clifton, 1993; Cuetos & Mitchell,

1991; Gilboy, Sopena, Clifton & Frazier, 1995) Italian (De Vincenzi & Job, 1993; 1995), and French (Baccino, De Vincenzi & Job, this volume; Zagar, Pynte & Rativeau, 1997). In NP PP RC structures including the preposition "of", there is a clear advantage for the head of the complex NP (N1) to be assigned the role of subject of the RC[2]. However, while subjects' off-line preferences clearly converge for these three languages, the on-line data for this structure in fact vary across the three. Whereas a clear "N1" preference is found in French (Frenck-Mestre, 1997; Zagar et al., 1997, but see Baccino et al., this volume) and in Spanish (Carreiras & Clifton, 1993; Cuetos & Mitchell, 1988; Gilboy et al., 1995; but see Gilboy & Sopena, 1996), an "N2" preference has been reported for Italian (De Vincenzi & Job, 1993; 1995). Our aim is to show that the apparent discrepancy of the Italian on-line data (and the French data presented by Baccion et al, this volume) may prove to be less of an enigma than originally thought. Prior to introducing our own explanation for the apparent cross-language differences, however, it is worthwhile to examine whether existing models can account for the data.

In their review of the question, Frazier and Clifton (1996) suggest that indeed some caution may be warranted before concluding that a clear "N2" or "late closure" preference has been shown for this structure in Italian. The Italian on-line data (as well as French data presented by Baccino et al, this volume) are in fact rather difficult to reconcile with the Construal Hypothesis forwarded by Frazier and Clifton, which postulates that Frazier's (1987) late closure principle (which predicts an N2 preference for all languages for this particular structure) does not apply for "non-primary relationships" such as relative clauses. Attachment would be the result, in this case, of "late" discourse-level dependent processes. Roughly speaking, unless N2 is theta-marked in some manner (for example by the preceding preposition), N1 will be the last discourse entity in focus and hence should be construed as the host of the RC (cf. Clifton & Frazier, 1996; Gilboy et al., 1995, for further restrictions). This holds, at least, for languages such as Italian, Spanish and French which possess only one means of expressing genitive or possessive relationships. This account neatly explains readers' consistent off-line N1 preference across Spanish, French and Italian for the structure NP "of" NP RC, but it does not predict a difference between on-line and off-line preferences in these languages, nor does it predict an on-line N2 preference in Italian. The construal hypothesis, in and of itself, cannot thus account for the pattern of data which has been reported in the literature.

Does the frequency-based approach provide a more parsimonious account of the data? The response is rather equivocal. As outlined above, the model readily accomodates individual differences as well as cross-language differences given that both are the product of variations in the linguistic input. Nonetheless, it is not immediately apparent how the model can account for the reported difference between on and off-line preferences in Italian. One might suggest, as Frazier and Clifton indeed have, and as we will later, that there is something at work in the Italian study which renders it different from previous studies. Even so, quite recent evidence, presented by Mitchell and colleagues (Mitchell, Brysbaert and Grondelaers, 1997; Mitchell & Brysbaert, in press) deals a life-threatening blow to the notion that readers' preferences and thus ease of syntactic processing can be determined by statistical properties of the language in question. In a nutshell, when on-line RC attachment preferences were examined for materials which were modelled closely on corpora based sentences, it was found that these preferences were quite the *opposite* that which would be predicted by the corpora. This result poses a serious problem for any frequency-based model of parsing.

Can any current model of parsing account for the data at hand? The last "surviving" candidate is Gibson and colleagues "Recency/Predicate Proximity" model (Gibson et al., 1996), which is somewhat of a hybrid between a structural and a frequency-based approach. The model assumes that the human language processor obeys structural principles, but that the weight of these principles varies across languages. As concerns RC attachment, two principles--*predicate proximity*, calling for attachment as close as possible to the main predicate, and *recency*, favoring attachment to more recent hosts--compete. The model can account for cross-language differences by positing that for some languages, say Spanish and French, predicate proximity outweighs recency, whereas for others, say Italian, precedence is given to the recency principle. However, it is not clear how the model can account for differences *within* a language, i.e. as concerns on-line and off-line preferences (Baccino et al., this volume; De Vincenzi & Job, 1995), or individual differences (cf. Corley & Caldwell, 1996). Another limitation of this model, highlighted by Cuetos et al. (1996) is its failure to account for the differences incurred by a change in preposition in the structure NP PP RC. It has been demonstrated in English (Gilboy et al., 1995; Frazier, 1990), Spanish (Gilboy et al. 1995; Cuetos et al., 1996) Italian (De Vincenzi & Job, 1993; 1995) and French (Baccino et al., this volume) that changing the preposition from "of" (or its equivalent) to a preposition which has lexical content, such as "with" or "near", radically influences readers' interpretation--measured both on- and off-line--for this structure. Neither of the structural principles included in the Gibson et al. model can readily account for this lexical effect.

The fact that prepositional changes influence the interpretation of the NP PP RC structure may provide an important clue, in fact, as to why immediate attachment preferences in Italian have been found to differ from those found in Spanish and French. In both of the studies that showed an initial "late closure", i.e. N2, preference in Italian (De Vincenzi & Job, 1993; 1995), the set of experimental sentences included a mixture of prepositions. In the 1993 study, subjects read an equal number of NP PP RC sentences including the preposition "di" (i.e."of") and sentences including contentful prepositions, namely "con", "nel" or "sul" (with, in the, on the), whereas in the 1995 study, there were an equal number of N1-di-N2 sentences and of N1-con-N2 sentences. The study reported by Baccino et al. (this volume), in French, also used an equal ratio of the two prepositions ("avec" and "de"). As just stated, prepositions which have lexical content, such as "with", clearly influence processing. Specifically, they uniformly lead to an N2 preference across languages. While the materials in the studies by De Vincenzi and Job (and by Baccino et al.) also included a large number of fillers (the ratio of NP PP RC sentences to fillers was roughly 1:4), it is nonetheless possible that this mixing of contentful prepositions and "of" affected readers' interpretations. It is noteworthy that in the French and Spanish studies where a clear and immediate N1 preference has been found for this structure, the preposition included in the complex NP was either systematically "de" (Clifton & Carreiras, 1993; Cuetos & Mitchell, 1988; Frenck-Mestre, 1997; Zagar et al., 1997) or was "de" in the large majority of cases (Gilboy et al., 1995). The 50/50 ratio of preposition types introduced in the Italian studies may possibly have introduced an "N2" bias, and thus caused readers to abandon an otherwise present N1 preference for N1-*of*-N2 sentences, at least momentarily as the off-line preference for these sentences was in fact N1.

In view of the above, we ran an eye-movement study, in French, to ascertain whether the normally observed N1 preference in this language for the N1-*of*-N2-RC structure could be perturbed by the processing of NP-PP-RC sentences in which the preposition had lexical content, namely "with". French subjects' on-line attachment preference for this structure, both when the preposition was "de" (i.e. "of") and "avec" (i.e. "with"), were examined by means of eye-movement recordings. This technique provides a sensitive on-line measure of linguistic processing, and presents the additional advantage of avoiding any biases introduced by segmentation. Most importantly, our study allowed us to investigate the influence of one preposition on the other. This was accomplished by having subjects read *blocks* of sentences of this structure (NP-P-NP-RC), in which the preposition was "de" in one block, and "avec" in the other.

Below we report in detail the specifics of our eye-movement study in French.

EXPERIMENT

Methods

Subjects. Sixteen native speakers of French, enrolled at the University of Provence, who were naive as regards the purpose of the experiment voluntarily participated in a single session which lasted approximately thirty minutes.

Materials. All materials were presented in French. Thirty-two experimental sentences were presented. Sentences were of the structure: N VERB NP PP RC (see example 2). All sentences were seen in eight conditions, defined by the factors Attachment of the RC (N1 versus N2), Preposition ("de" versus "avec") and Order (the "de" block first versus the "avec" block first). A given subject saw each sentence in only one condition.

(2) Jean photographie la fille de (avec) Charles qui semble plus dédaigneux(se) que d'habitude.

(John photographed (the daughter of) (the girl with) Charles who seemed more disdainful (masc/fem) than usual.)

Subjects saw two blocks of 20 sentences, each containing 16 experimental sentences preceded by 4 practice trials of completely different structures. In one block, the 16 experimental sentences all contained the preposition "de" (i.e. "la fille de Charles"). In the other block, the preposition was always "avec" (i.e. "la fille avec Charles"). The order of blocks was counterbalanced across subjects, with half of the subjects seeing the "de" block first, and half seeing the "avec" block first. In each block, half of the sentences required N1 attachment of the RC, and half required N2 attachment. Attachment of the RC was determined by gender marking on the adjective, underlined in the example sentence. The two nouns of the complex NP were always opposite in gender. For both N1 and N2 attachment of the relative, half were feminine disambiguations and half were masculine disambiguations. There was thus no difference in length of the adjective region (note, also, that the masculine and feminine forms generally varied by only one letter).

Results

The results are reported independently for the two blocks of sentences. First, we report the results obtained for the block of sentences including the preposition "de" (of) in the complex NP preceding the relative clause ("la fille de Charles", i.e. "the daughter of Charles"). The results are then reported for the block sentences including the preposition "avec" (with) in the complex NP ("la fille avec Charles", i.e. "the girl with Charles"). For all sentences, independent analyses were performed on each of 6 sentence segments, corresponding to: the beginning of the sentence, the complex NP, the beginning of the relative clause, the disambiguating adjective, the relative pronoun, the final region. We report here the results obtained at the disambiguating adjective region, as this is the region of theoretical interest. It is noteworthy, nonetheless, that analyses of the data for the non-reported regions did not reveal significant effects of any of the experimental factors. The measures used were: first fixation in a region, first pass gaze duration (i.e. all fixations in a region coming from the left of that region, from the first fixation until the eye left the region, to the left or right) and second pass reading times (i.e. all re-readings of a region, subsequent to the first reading of the region). These means are presented in Table 1.

Sentences with the preposition "de" (of) in the complex NP

First pass and total reading times at the disambiguating adjective for N1-*de*-N2 sentences were analysed as a function of RC attachment (N1 vs. N2) and Order of presentation (the "de" block first vs. following the "avec" block).

The analysis of first fixations revealed no significant effects: RC Attachment (264 vs 275 ms for N1 and N2 attachment, respectively; $F1(1,8) = 1.96$, NS; $F2 < 1$); Order ($F1 < 1$; $F2(1,28) = 3.06$, ns). This was to be expected, given that the disambiguating gender information was provided at the end of adjectives which were generally long. The effects of experimental factors were evidenced, however, in the analysis of first pass gaze durations, which revealed a significant effect of RC attachment ($F1(1,8) = 6.05$, $p<.05$; $F2(1,28) = 5.11$, $p<.03$). Gaze durations were longer when the adjective forced "low" N2 attachment than "high" N1 attachment (418 vs. 375 ms, respectively). The effect of RC attachment was not modified by Order of presentation ($F1(1,8) = 2.69$, ns, $F2(1,28) = 2.38$, ns), nor did Order affect performance in itself (F1 and F2 <1).

	"N1 de N2" sentences							
	Adjective region				Adjective + "que"			
	Block1		Block2		Block1		Block2	
	N1	N2	N1	N2	N1	N2	N1	N2
1st Fix.	270	292	257	258	*same as adjective region*			
Gaze	343	415	407	421	391	474	494	512
2ndPass	433	439	281	369	584	591	375	470

	"N1 avec N2" sentences							
	Adjective region				Adjective + "que"			
	Block1		Block2		Block1		Block2	
	N1	N2	N1	N2	N1	N2	N1	N2
1st Fix.	258	247	285	285	*same as adjective region*			
Gaze	398	380	441	371	473	432	505	461
2ndPass	366	399	365	373	408	454	398	417

Table 1. Reading Times: Mean first fixations, first pass gaze durations, and second pass reading times of the disambiguating adjective region and this region plus the word "que", according to Type of preposition in the complex NP ("de" versus "avec"), Order of presentation of sentences (first (block 1) or second block (block 2) of sixteen sentences with a given preposition, and Disambiguation (towards the first NP (N1) or towards the second NP (N2)).

Order of presentation tended to have a late effect, as demonstrated by the following results. First, when the disambiguating region was extended beyond the adjective to include the three letter word following the adjective (i.e."que"), the analysis of first pass gaze durations revealed both an effect of RC attachment ($F1(1,8) = 10.07$, $p<.01$; $F2(1,28) = 3.82$, $p<.06$) and a trend towards the interaction with Order of presentation in the subject analysis ($F1(1,8) = 4.09$, $p<.07$; $F2(1,28) = 1.89$, ns). French readers were faster to read this disambiguating region following N1 (442 ms) than N2 attachment (493 ms). However, this high attachment preference, obtained for sentences containing "of" in the complex NP, tended to be attenuated when subjects first read the block of sentences containing the preposition "with" in the complex NP, as compared to when the "of" sentences were given first. Specifically, gaze durations were faster for N1 than N2 attachment by 83 ms when subjects were given "of" sentences at the outset of the experiment (391 vs 474 ms, respectively; $F1(1,4) = 16.53$, $p<.01$; $F2(1,28) = 6.08$, $p<.02$), but by a mere 18 ms when subjects read the "of" sentences only after having read the block of "with" sentences (494 vs 512 ms, respectively; F1 and $F2<1$). Moreover, the factor Order affected RC attachment in second pass reading times. At the disambiguating adjective, the analysis of second pass reading times revealed a main effect of RC attachment ($F1(1,8) = 13.43$, $p<.01$; $F2(1,28) = 3.69$, $p<.06$), which was qualified by Order in the subject analysis ($F1(1,8) = 10.24$, $p<.01$; $F2(1,28) = 1.04$, ns). In contrast to first pass reading times, no difference in second pass reading times was apparent for N1 and N2 attachment when subjects received the "of" sentences at the outset of the experiment (433 vs. 439 ms, respectively; F1 and $F2<1$). However, second pass reading times revealed a difference, in favor of N1 over N2 attachment, when subjects received the "of" sentences in the second half of the experiment, i.e. only after having read the "with" block (281 vs. 369 ms, respectively; $F1(1,4) = 14.92$, $p<.02$; $F2(1,28) = 4.11$, $p<.05$). Apparently, when subjects received the "of" sentences at the outset of the experiment, they immediately resolved the RC attachment ambiguity in favor of N1, and no spill-over effects were found on second pass reading times. However, when subjects received the "of" sentences only after having read the "with" sentences, they were hesitant to resolve the ambiguity in favor of N1, and did so only upon an extended reading of the disambiguating zone.

The analysis of first pass regressions launched from the disambiguating region revealed that subjects made relatively few regressions, and no significant effects of the experimental factors as a function of this dependent variable.

Sentences with the preposition "avec" (with) in the complex NP

The reading times obtained at the disambiguating adjective for N1-*avec*-N2 sentences ("the girl with Charles") revealed the following.

The analysis of first fixations revealed no effects: RC attachment (271 vs 266 ms for N1 and N2 attachment, respectively; F1 and F2 <1); Order (F1<1; F2(1,28) $=4.65$, $p<.05$). This is line with the results for the "of" sentences, and is a reflection of the fact that disambiguating information was provided at the end of generally long adjectives. The effects of experimental factors showed up in the analysis of gaze durations. The latter revealed a main effect of RC attachment, by subjects, (F1(1,8) $= 5.79$, $p<.04$; F2(1,14) $= 2.53$, ns) which was not modified by the factor Order of presentation (F1(1,8) $= 2.10$, ns; F2<1). In contrast to the results reported above, subjects tended to take longer to resolve the ambiguity when it necessitated N1 attachment of the RC than when it necessitated N2 attachment (420 vs. 376 ms, respectively). This effect was not significantly influenced by whether the subjects read the "with" sentences at the outset of the experiment (398 vs 380 ms for N1 and N2 attachment, respectively) or only after having read a block of sentences containing the preposition "of" in the complex NP (441 vs 371 ms for N1 and N2 attachment, respectively).

The effect of ambiguity was apparently resolved at the adjective, as the analysis of the extended region, i.e. including the three-letter word immediately following the adjective, did not reveal any effects of the experimental factors: RC attachment (F1 and F2 <1); Order (F1 and F2 <1). Moreover, the analysis of second pass reading times at the adjective region failed to reveal effects of either RC attachment (F1 and F2 <1) or Order of presentation (F1 and F2 <1).

DISCUSSION

The results of our study show a definite effect of "syntax setting", introduced by varying the preposition included in the complex NP preceding a RC. For the sentences where the preposition was "de" ("of"), as in "Jacques saw the daughter of Charles who seemed happier (fem.) than usual", we found a strong N1 preference, as revealed by faster first pass reading times of the disambiguating adjective following N1 than N2 attachment, which is in line with previous work by Zagar et al. (1997)[3]. This was true, however, only when subjects read these sentences at the outset of the experiment. When subjects first read a block of sentences containing the preposition "avec" (i.e. "with"), as in "Jacques saw the girl with Charles who seemed happier (fem.) than usual", they showed an N2 preference for these sentences, and thereafter, showed virtually no difference in preference for N1 or N2 when reading the block of sentences containing the preposition "de" (i.e. "of"). In other words, the prior reading of sentences for which N1 attachment was difficult, nay ungrammatical, seriously undermined subjects' later decision to attach to N1 in sentences for which this was not only possible, but generally preferred. Quite interestingly, this "syntax setting" effect was not apparent for sentences containing the preposition "avec" (with). For these sentences, subjects showed an N2 preference, whether they read these sentences at the outset of the experiment, or only after having read the block of "de" sentences.

The above results provide important insight as concerns factors affecting attachment preferences for this particular structure. First, it can be noted that the preposition "with" apparently leads to an N2 preference which is rather systematic in that it has been found for Spanish, Italian, French and English. Secondly, the role of this factor may explain why previous studies have failed to find an N1 preference for this structure when the preposition was "of". Notably, DeVincenzi & Job (1993; 1995) and Baccino et al. (this volume) found, in self-paced reading studies, that Italian and French subjects demonstrated an on-line N2 attachment preference when the preposition was "del/della" or "de" (as in "the niece of the dancer"). Two facts must be highlighted, however. First, in all three studies, the N1-"of"-N2 sentences were presented along with others of the same structure but containing the preposition "con" or "avec" (as in "the man with the daughter"). While the effect of this factor would quite certainly have been smaller than the one we found here, in French, given that De Vincenzi and Job (1995) and Baccino et al. (this volume) presented their test sentences along with numerous fillers, it is nonetheless plausible that mixing the two prepositions had an effect on attachment preferences. Second, it is not in fact entirely clear that any of these studies has actually demaonstrated an immediate N2 preference for sentences containing the preposition "of." In all three studies, statistics are reported which show a global N2 preference for on-line reading times, that is, for N1-"of"-N2 and N1-"with"-N2 sentences considered together. No statistics are provided for the N1-"of"-N2 sentences considered independently, in either French (Baccino et al., this volume) or

Italian (De Vincenzi & Job, 1993, 1995). Given, as shown previously and in the present study, the strong and apparently universal preference to attach the RC low, to N2, when the preposition has lexical content, it is vital to show that the "N2 preference" reported by De Vincenzi and colleagues for their N1-"of"-N2 sentences holds on its own.

The main result to emerge from the present study is the non-obligatory nature of RC attachment. That is, whereas an immediate preference for high (N1) attachment of the RC for French sentences such as "He knows the councilors(masc) of the queen who seemed more anxious(fem/masc) than usual," has been found (Zagar et al., 1997), we showed herein that the N1 preference in French can be disrupted (see also, Pynte & Colonna, 1998). However, our results do show, indeed, that in the absence of other factors, French readers prefer high (N1) attachment of the RC for sentences such as the one illustrated above. Baccino et al. (this volume) have argued that this "N1 preference" is due to particularities of the linguistic construction that we employed. On the one hand, they suggest that low attachment should be relatively difficult given the properties of the complex NP, in which the second noun was systematically a proper noun (i.e. "the daughter of Charles"). As correctly stated by Baccino et al., for the relative clause to attach to N2 in this case, the RC would have to be considered as an appositive rather than as a restrictive clause. However, there is simply no data to back their claim that appositive clauses are introduced by a comma (cf. Hill & Murray, in press, for a discussion of the role of punctuation in parsing), nor, by virtue of this, any substance to their claim that readers should initially consider the RC as a restrictive clause. On the other hand, Baccino et al. claim the immediate N1 preference we found to be due to the "type" of RC we employed[4], which was headed by the verb "seem" (i.e. "who seemed more nervous(masc/fem) than usual"). Baccino et al.

argue, on the basis of ENGLISH grammar, that this construction is ambiguous. Most unfortunately for their argument, French grammar behaves quite differently from English, first, as concerns the relative pronoun, and secondly as concerns the verb "seem" In French, subject relative pronouns are introduced by "qui" (i.e. "who") not "que" (i.e. "that"). Moreover, the verb "sembler" ("seem") always has an overt, pronominal subject, "il" (i.e. "it"). Following the subject relative pronoun "qui" the verb "sembler" must attach to either N1 or N2 of the preceding complex NP. In order to attach the RC elsewhere, the relative pronoun would have to be "que" and the abstract pronominal subject of the verb "seem" would be stated, as in "qu'il semble."[5] In other words, a completely different structure from the one we used ("qui semble") would be necessary. Hence, the arguments forwarded by Baccino et al. (this volume) are invalid and do not account either for the N1 preference we observed or for the difference in results across the present study and theirs.

Over and above the implications the present results may have concerning modifier attachment in romance languages, they speak to another, more general issue related to the immediate effect of "syntax setting" that we observed. Ours is certainly not the first study to have demonstrated an effect of prior context on subjects' subsequent choice of syntactic structure. It is well established that subjects can be induced to produce a given structure amidst two or more alternatives by either reading (Pickering & Branigan, 1995; reported in Branigan et al., 1996) or repeating that structure (Bock, 1986). This type of structural priming has been demonstrated despite variations in semantic content, the animacy of arguments, and the underlying roles encoded in the prime sentences (cf. Bock & Loebel, 1990). The comparison of our results to those found in production is not immediately obvious, nonetheless. Notably, whereas production studies have systematically revealed a facilitatory effect of prior exposure to a given structure, we ourselves found evidence of inhibition. A more viable comparison is to be made with prior studies of comprehension which have shown effects of experimental manipulations on readers' choice of ambiguity resolution. One such study, cited in Cuetos et al. (1996), revealed that Spanish-speaking school children who were exposed to a particular ambiguity resolution during a two-week period later increased their already existing preference for that resolution.

Which of the models reviewed so far can best account for these "syntactic priming" effects? The class of model which lends itself most readily to this type of manipulation is unquestionably a frequency model, and, more precisely, the "tuning hypothesis" which by definition should be sensitive to changes in the distribution of structures. This is stated clearly in Cuetos et al. (1996, p. 175): "The model predicts that parsing preferences will change if, during some period prior to testing, the reader or listener has been exposed to an unusual preponderance of one ambiguity resolution rather than another." This prediction was indeed borne out in the study with Spanish-speaking children, at least for resolutions which were already favored prior to testing, and, more importantly for the model, more prevalent in the larger corpus of everyday Spanish.

At first blush, the tuning hypothesis would seem to be tailored to our results. Following a barrage of NP PP RC sentences which were preferentially resolved in favor of "N2",(i.e. N1-avec-N2-RC), our French readers momentarily dropped their normal "N1" strategy. This is exactly what would have been predicted by a frequency-based tuning model. However, there is a remaining glitch. As formulated, the model would predict symmetrical effects, that is, the processing of a preponderance of "N1-biased" resolutions should have affected subjects' subsequent processing of "N2-biased" sentences. This was not true of our data. The effect we observed was asymmetrical; whereas subjects were induced to abandon their "N1 strategy", they did not show an influence of prior processing of a set of "N1-biased" sentences on the subsequent processing of "N2-biased" sentences. It would appear that to fully explain our results, the tuning hypothesis would have to augment itself with some mechanism that took lexical content, not only frequencies of structures, into account. The need to "fine-tune" the model to account for observed parsing preferences has also been pointed out by Gibson and colleagues (Gibson, Schutze and Saloman, 1996).

The constraint-satisfaction model proposed by MacDonald and colleagues (1994) places lexical properties at the heart of syntactic ambiguity resolution. Although the strong lexical flavor of this proposal makes it difficult to ascertain whether the type of priming we report would be predicted, the model does make a case for the immediate intervention of "contextual" influences - provided that the frequency of lexical items in a given structure matches the contextual manipulation. If one considers the finding that all languages studied so far have systematically shown an "N2" preference for NP-PP-RC ambiguity when the preposition has lexical content (i.e. "with", "near, "on", or their equivalents), it is possible to predict that "N1-avec-N2" would provide a stronger priming context than "N1-de-N2". As such, the priming asymmetry that we found as a function of prepositional content could possibly be accommodated by this model.

In principle, a purely "structural account" should not predict the type of experimentally induced attachment preferences we found. However, in view of the construal hypothesis (Carrreiras & Clifton, 1993; Frazier & Clifton, 1996; Gilboy et al., 1995), this may be called into question for the type of ambiguity we examined, namely RC attachment. According to Frazier and

Clifton (1996, p. 73) "a relative clause will associate to the maximal projection of the last thematic role assigner. If N2 is an argument of N1 as (e.g.) in "the picture of the girl", then the NP headed by N1 will define the current processing domain and the relative clause will associate to the entire NP. Hence either N1 or N2 (or their projections) will be available as potential hosts for the relative. By contrast, when N2 is an argument of the preceding preposition (the man with the girl), then the PP will constitute the current processing domain. Hence, only N2 (and its projections) will be available to host the relative clause." On the basis of the above, one might expect that the processing of a set of "N2 biased" sentences, i.e. N1-avec-N2-RC, would influence subjects' later processing of a set of N1-de-N2-RC sentences, for which Construal does not predict an a priori preference for the host site. Our results show exactly that. "N1-de-N2" should not, by virtue of the predicted null preference, exert the same effect on the subsequent processing of "N1-avec-N2" sentences, which is also in agreement with our results. The fact that for "N1-de-N2" sentences N1 is preferred (in French) outside of any contextual manipulation can be explained by Frazier's "referentiality principle", one of the six unranked interpretative principles governing the association of non-primary relations.

In light of the above three models, one might well enquire about the exact locus of the priming effect we observed. The asymmetry between the "avec-de" manipulation (i.e. "N1-avec-N2" followed by "N1-de-N2") and the "de-avec" manipulation (i.e. "N1-de-N2" followed by "N1-avec-N2") lends credit to the hypothesis that the effect is an interpretive one rather than one of structural bias. This would explain why we were unable to force a highly unacceptable semantic interpretation despite a strong preceding structural bias, i.e. the impermeability of N2 attachment for "N1-avec-N2" sentences to a prior N1 context. It also fits with our finding that the influence of the N2 biasing context on later "N1-de-N2" sentences was rather late, occurring more or less one word downstream from the word which determined RC attachment.

If one accepts the hypothesis that the priming effect we found intervenes late, and is of an interpretive nature, this has implications for previous studies of modifier attachment. In particular, it suggests that claiming this type of attachment to be the product of immediate, structural preferences (cf. Baccino et al., this volume; DeVincenzi & Job, 1993, 1995) may be quite simply incorrect. Indeed, were the effect a purely structural one, based on universal principles of syntactic parsimony, we should not have been able to override on-line attachment preferences in the way we did. The fact that we could--at least when N2 was introduced by a non theta-assigning preposition--argues in favor of the position that "interpretive principles determine or at least influence judgements of preferred readings when several potential heads are available within the current thematic domain" (Frazier & Clifton, 1996, p. 92). The list of factors which could possibly influence sentence interpretation is infinite - list composition, segmentation, subjects' language background, the grammatical properties of a given language are just a few. It may thus reveal impossible to isolate any common set of interpretive principles across languages, even for closely related ones, viz. Italian, French and Spanish. Any attempt to do so would necessitate, however, careful control of known interpretive biases, such as, for example, the one we examined here.

NOTES

[1] Another structure which has been the subject of debate is PP attachment, where the PP in an English sentence such as "John identified the man in the store" can be attached to either the immediately preceding NP (the man) or to the preceding VP (identified). A structural account of parsing (cf. Clifton, Speer & Abney, 1991; Frazier, 1990; Frazier & Clifton, 1996) assumes that VP attachment should be preferred on the basis that NP attachment is structurally more costly, which has indeed been supported by various on-line studies. Furthermore, it has been shown in certain studies that VP attachment is preferred even when the arguments/semantic biais is toward NP attachment (Clifton et al., 1991; Rayner et al., 1982). This latter conclusion was somewhat brought to question, nonetheless, by subsequent studies showing that PP attachment can be influenced by information provided by the verb, such as its argument structure (Frenck-Mestre & Pynte, 1997), semantic category (Sedivy & Spivey-Knowlton, 1994) or thematic frame (Taraban & McClelland, 1988). In these latter studies, it has been argued that the apparently immediate use of this type of lexical information undermines the idea of a strictly structurally based parser. However, in defense of the structural account, Frazier and Clifton (1996; cf. also Frazier, 1990) have argued that the use of verb subcategorization information does not rule out a structural account, because while this information may come into play as soon as it is available, nothing proves that it must be present for the parser to begin acting upon the input. The PP structure is a good case in point, as the PP is treated one constituent downstream from the VP, i.e. following the NP, and subcategorization information provided by the verb may have come into play only after the parse based on structural principles had been initiated.

[2] An "N1" preference has also been reported for Dutch (Brysbaert & Mitchell, 1996) and German (Hemforth, Konieczny & Sheepers, 1994, cited in Brysbaert & Mitchell, 1996) while no clear preference has been reported for English (a nul preference has been found for American English (Carreiras & Clfiton, 1993) whereas an N2 preference is reported for British English (cf. Cuetos et al, 1996).

[3] Frenck-Mestre (1997) also showed, via the recording of eye-movements, that French readers prefer the relative clause to be attached to the first rather than to the second NP of a preceding complex NP. The structure of the relative clause and the disambiguation differed, however, from that used by Zagar et al. (1997) and in the present study. In Frenck-Mestre (1997),

disambiguation was provided by number agreement on the subordinate verb, as in "Jean téléphone aux filles de la gouvernante qui revient de Paris en train" vs. " Jean téléphone à la gouvernante des filles qui revient de Paris en train."

[4] Pynte and Colonna (1998) as well as Frenck-Mestre (1997) have shown a high (N1) attachment preference when the relative clause is immediately disambiguated by the subordinate verb, as in "Il connaît les filles du type qui entre/entrent dans le magasin." (He knowxs the girls of the guy who enters/enter the store).

[5] No confusion with "qui" is possible, as only "que" can contract with the pronoun "il," thereby forming "qu'il."

REFERENCES

Bock, J.K. (1986). Syntactic persistence in language production. *Cognitive Psychology*, 18, 355-387.

Bock, J.K. & Loebel, H. (1990). Framing sentences. *Cognition*, 35, 1-39.

Branigan, H. P., Pickering, M.J., Liversedge, S.P., Stewart, A.J. & Urbach, T.P. (1996). Syntactic priming: Investigating the mental representation of language. *Journal of Psycholinguistic Research*, 24, 489-506.

Brysbaert, M. & Mitchell, D.C. (1996) . Modifier attachment in sentence parsing: Evidence from Dutch. *The Quarterly Journal of Experimental Psychology,* 49A, 664-695.

Carreiras, M. & Clifton, C. (1993). Relative clause interpretation preferences in Spanish and English. *Language and Speech*, 36, 353-372.

Clifton, C., Speer, S. & Abney, (1991). Parsing arguments: Phrase structure and argument structure as determinants of initial parsing decisions. *Journal of Memory and Language,* 30, 251-271.

Corley, M. & Caldwell, C. (1996). Towards a simple statistical model of the HSPM. Poster presented at *Architectures and Mechanisms of Language Processing (AMLaP),* September 20-21st, Torino, Italy.

Cuetos, F. & Mitchell, D.C. (1988). Cross-linguistic differences in parsing: Restrictions on the late-closure strategy in Spanish. *Cognition*, 30, 73-105.

Cuetos, F., Mitchell, D.C. & Corley, M. (1996). Parsing in different languages. In M. Carreiras, J. Garcia-Albea and N. Sebastien-Galles (Eds.) *Language Processing in Spanish* Mahwah, NJ: LEA

De Vincenzi, M. and Job, R. (1995). An investigation of late closure: The role of syntax, thematic structure and pragmatics in initial and final interpretations. *Journal of Experimental Psychology: Learning Memory and Cognition,* 21, 1303-1321.

De Vincenzi, M. and Job, R. (1993). Some observations on the universality of the late closure strategy. *Journal of Psycholinguistic Research,,* 22, 189-206.

Frazier, L. (1987). Sentence processing: A tutorial review. In M. Coltheart (Ed). *Attention and performance XII.* Hillsdale, NJ: LEA

Frazier, L. (1989). Against lexical generation of syntax. In W. Marslen-Wilson (Ed.). Lexical representation and process. Cambridge, Mass: MIT Press

Frazier, L. (1990). Parsing modifiers: Special purpose routines in HSPM? In D.A. Balota, G.B. Flores d'Arcais & K. Rayner (Eds.), *Comprehension Processes in Reading.* Hillsdale, NJ: LEA

Frazier, L. & Clifton, C. (1996). *Construal.* Cambridge, MA.: MIT Press.

Frenck-Mestre, C. (1997). Examining second language reading: An on-line look. in A. Sorace, C. Heycock and R. Shillcock (Eds.) *Proceedings of the GALA '97 Conference on Language Acquisition.* Human Communication Research Centre: Edinburgh

Frenck-Mestre, C. & Pynte, J. (1995). Lexical influences on parsing strategies: Evidence from eye movements. In J.M. Findlay, R.W. Kentridge & R. Walker (Eds.) *Eye movement research: Mechanisms, Processes and Applications.* Amsterdam: Elsevier, North Holland.

Frenck-Mestre, C. & Pynte, J. (1997). Syntactic ambiguity resolution while reading in second and native languages. *The Quarterly Journal of Experimental Psychology,* 50A, 119-148.

Gibson, E., Pearlmutter, N., Canseco-Gonzales, E. & Hickok, G. (1996). Cross-linguistic attachment preferences: Evidence from English and Spanish. *Cognition,* 59, 23-59.

Gibson, E., Schutze, C. & Saloman, A. (1996). The relationship between the frequency and complextity of linguistic structure. *Journal of Psycholinguistic Research,* 25, 59-92.

Gilboy, E., Sopena, J.M., Clifton, C. & Frazier, L. (1995). Argument structure and association preferences in Spanish and English complex NPs. *Cognition,* 54, 131-167.

Gilboy, E., & Sopena, J.M. (1996) Segmentation effects in processing complex noun pronouns with relative clauses. In M. Carreiras, J. Garcia-Albea and N. Sebastien-Galles (Eds.) *Language Processing in Spanish* Mahwah, NJ: LEA

Hill, R. & Murray, W.S. (in press). The role of punctuation in parsing. In A. Kennedy and J. Pynte (Eds.)

MacDonald, M.C., Pearlmutter, N.J. & Seidenberg, M.S. (1994). Lexical nature of syntactic ambiguity resolution. Psychological Review, 101, 676-703.

Mitchell, D.C. (1994). Sentence parsing. In M.A. Gernsbacher (Ed.), *Handbook of Psycholinguistics*. New York: Academic Press.

Mitchell, D.C. & Brysbaert, M. (in press). Challenges to recent theories of cross-linguistic variation in parsing: Evidence from Dutch. In D. Hillert (Ed.) *Sentence processing: A cross-linguistic perspective*. Academic Press.

Mitchell, D.C., Brysbaert, M. & Grondelaers, S. (1997). An evaluation of exposure-based accounts of ambiguity resolution: Evidence from Dutch. Paper presented at *Architectures and Mechanisms of Language Processing (AMLaP)*, Sept. 11th-13th, Edinburgh.

Pynte, J. & Colonna, S. (1998). Relative Clause attachment revisited: French readers sometimes prefer to attach low. Poster presented at *Architectures and Mechanisms of Language Processing (AMLaP)*, Sept. Frieburg, Germany.

Sedivy, J. & Spivey-Knowlton, M. (1994). The use of structural, lexical and pragmatic information in parsing attachment ambiguities. In C. Clifton, L. Frazier and K. Rayner (Eds.), *Perspectives on sentence processing*. Hillsdale, NJ: Lawrence Erlbaum Associates.

Steedman, M.J. (1989). Grmmar, interpretation, and processing from the lexicon. In D.A. Balota, G.B. Flores d'Arcais & K. Rayner (Eds.), *Comprehension Processes in Reading*. Hillsdale, NJ: LEA

Tanenhaus, M.K. & Carlson, G.N. (1989). Lexical structure and language comprehension. In D.A. Balota, G.B. Flores d'Arcais & K. Rayner (Eds.), *Comprehension Processes in Reading*. Hillsdale, NJ: LEA

Zagar, D., Pynte, J. & Rativeau, S. (1997). Evidence for early closure attachment on first-pass reading times in French. *Quarterly Journal of Experimental Psychology*, 50A, 421-438.

APPENDIX

Thirty two sentences were presented in each of four possible versions, defined by the type of preposition (avec versus de) and gender marking on the adjective (masculine versus feminin).

1. Jean-Yves suit la gouvernante (avec/de) Joseph qui se montre plus pédant(e) que pendant sa jeunesse.
A. Jean Yves follows the governess (with/of) Joseph who is seemingly more pedantic(masc/fem) than in his/her youth.
2. Claire agace la petite fille (avec/de) Francis qui paraît plus taquin(e) que les autres fois.
B. Claire aggravates the little girl (with/of/) Francis who seems more of a tease(masc/fem) than on other occasions.
3. Jean-Marie questionne le boucher (avec/de) Nathalie qui semble plus méchant(e) que de raison.
C. Jean-Marie questions the butcher(masc) (with/of) Nathalie who seems meaner(masc/fem) than necessary.
4. Zoé accompagne la domestique (avec/de) Baptiste qui semble plus niais(e) que l'autre fois.
D. Zoé accompanies the servant(fem) (with/of) Baptiste who seems sillier(masc/fem) than the last time.
5. Xavier accueille la cuisinière (avec/de) Léon qui semble plus tatillon(ne) que l'été précédent.
E. Xavier greets the chef(fem) (with/of) Léon who seems more finicky(masc/fem) than last summer.
6. Danièle interroge la voisine (avec/de) Bernard qui a l'air plus fanfaron(ne) que de coutume.;
F. Danièle queries the neighbor (fem) (with/of) Bernard who seems to be more boastful(masc/fem) than usual.
7. Georges accuse le gérant (avec/de) Nicole qui semble moins famili(er/ère) que d'ordinaire.;
G. George accuses the manager(masc) (with/of) Nicole who seems more informal (masc/fem) than usual.
8. Paul conseille l'infirmière (avec/de) Daniel qui semble plus grossi(er/ère) que l'été passé.;
H. Paul advises the nurse(fem) (with/of) Daniel who seems coarser(mascfem) than last summer.

9. Marc critique le médecin (avec/de) Martine qui paraît plus discr(et/ète) que lors de son arrivée.;
I. Marc criticises the doctor(masc) (with/of) Martine who appears more disrete(masc/fem) than
10. Françoise console l'institutrice (avec/de) Bernard qui semble plus inqui(et/ète) que l'hiver passé.;
I. Françoise consoles the teacher(fem) (with/of) Bernard who seems more concerned(masc/fem) than last winter.
11. Damien observe le comptable (avec/de) Catherine qui a l'air plus pensi(f/ve) que la normale.
J. Damien observes the accountant(masc) (with/of) Cathrine who seems more thoughtful(masc/fem) than usual.
12. Cyril sert le client (avec/de) Marguerite qui paraît plus agressi(f/ve) que ce matin.
K. Cyril serves the client(masc) (with/of) Margaret who seems more aggressive (masc/fem) than this morning.
13. Olivier divertit la malade (avec/de) Gilbert qui semble plus attenti(f/ve) que la fois précédente.
L. Oliver amuses the patient(masc) (with/of) Gilbert who seems more attentive (masc/fem) than the last time.
14. Laurent distrait l'impresario (avec/de) Julie qui est plus naï(f/ve) que la moyenne.
M. Laurence distracts the impresario(masc) (with/of) Julie who is more naive(masc/fem) than most.
15. Léonard ennuie l'assistant (avec/de) Lucile qui a l'air plus crainti(f/ve) que jamais.
N. Leonard bothers the assistant(masc) (with/of) Lucile who looks more timid(masc/fem) than ever.
16. Claude salue le grand-père (avec/de) Sophie qui paraît plus moqueu(r/se) que la semaine dernière.
O. Claude greets the grandfather (with/of) Sophie who appears more mocking(masc/fem) than last week.

17. Sylvie frappe le gamin (avec/de) Cécile qui semble plus rouspéteu(r/se) que tout à l'heure.
P. Sylvia hits the kid(masc) (with/of) Cécile who seems grouchier(masc/fem) than a while ago.
18. Maxime amuse le chauffeur (avec/de) Marion qui est plus blagueu(r/se) que par le passé.
Q. Maxim amuses the driver (masc) (with/of) Marion who is more joking(masc/fem) than in the past.
19. Jean photographie la fille (avec/de) Charles qui semble plus dédaigneu(x/se) que d'habitude.
R. Jean photographs the girl/daughter (with/of) Charles who seems more disdainful(masc/fem) than usual.
20. Jacques écoute le locataire (avec/de) Paulette qui a l'air plus malheureu(x/se) que le mois dernier.
S. Jacques listens to the lodger(masc) (with/of) Paulette who looks unhappier(masc/fem) than last month.
21. Marie surveille la serveuse (avec/de) Thierry qui est plus grincheu(x/se) que les autres jours.
T. Marie watches the waitress (with/of) Thierry who is grumpier(masc/fem) than the other days.
22. Yves surprend la boulangère (avec/de) Marc qui paraît plus hargneu(x/se) que la nuit dernière.
U. Yves surprises the baker(fem) (with/of) Marc who seems more belligerent(masc/fem) than last night.
23. Mireille admire la femme (avec/de) Joël qui est plus rêveu(x/se) que d'habitude.
V. Mireille admires the woman/wife (with/of) Joël who is more distracted(masc/fem) than usual
24. Aline reçoit la belle-mère (avec/de) Denis qui est plus vaniteu(x/se) que la veille.
W. Aline receives the mother-in-law (with/of) Denis who is vainer(masc/fem) than on the prior eve.

25. Michèle réconforte la standardiste (avec/de) Gérald qui semble plus anxieu(x/se) que lundi matin.
X. Michèle comforts the receptionist(fem) (with/of) Gerald who seems more anxious(masc/fem) than on Monday morning.
26. Olga consulte l'avocat (avec/de) Béatrice qui a l'air plus querelleu(x/se) que pendant son stage.
Y. Olga consults the lawyer(masc) (with/of) Beatrice who looks more argumentative(masc/fem) than during training.
27. Igor emmène le professeur (avec/de) Patricia qui paraît plus amoureu(x/se) que la fois d'avant.
Z. Igor takes (somewhere) the professor (masc) (with/of) Patricia who appears more in love(masc/fem) than the last time.
28. Céline auditionne le scénariste (avec/de) Corinne qui est plus studieu(x/se) que l'année passée.
AA. Céline auditions the script-writer(masc) (with/of) Corinne who is more studious(masc/fem) than last year.
29. Pierre sollicite le patron (avec/de) Josiane qui paraît plus élogieu(x/se) que dans mon souvenir.
AB. Pierre solicits the boss(masc) (with/of) Josiane who seems more elogious(mascfem) than I recall.
30. Gérard attend l'employé (avec/de) Monique qui a l'air plus méticuleu(x/se) que l'instant d'avant.
AC. Gérard waits for the employee(masc) (with/of) Monique who looks more meticulous(mascfem) than a moment ago.
31. Régis cherche la gardienne (avec/de) Luc qui paraît plus soucieu(x/se) que dimanche dernier.
AD. Régis looks for the gardien (fem) (with/of) Luc who seems more worried(mascfem) than last Sunday.
32. Jeanne énerve la couturière (avec/de) Jules qui apparaît moins joyeu(x/se) que tantôt.
AE. Jeanne aggravates the seamstress (with/of) Jules who appears less joyful(mascfem) than earlier on.

Matthew J. Traxler, Martin J. Pickering, Charles Clifton Jr., and Roger van Gompel

ARCHITECTURES AND MECHANISMS FOR SENTENCE PROCESSING: IS SYNTACTIC PARSING A FORM OF LEXICAL AMBIGUITY RESOLUTION?

Some accounts of syntactic parsing propose that readers and listeners determine a sentence's syntactic structure in much the same way that they determine the meaning of a word (MacDonald, Pearlmutter, & Seidenberg, 1994). Namely, they recover information from a mental lexicon that describes what syntactic structures are permissible and preferred. MacDonald et al. note (p. 692), "...recent types of theorizing eliminate the strong distinction between accessing a meaning and constructing a syntactic representation, an idea which was central to previous accounts." Other accounts of syntactic parsing propose that readers and listeners consult grammatical principles and guide their syntactic structure-building decisions by determining (at least) the lexical categories of the words in the sentence (e.g., Frazier, 1979, 1987; Frazier & Clifton, 1996). In this chapter, we will contrast these different accounts by describing three dimensions on which they differ and by examining their compatibility with the empirical record.

THREE PARSERS

Because natural language is full of ambiguity, readers and listeners are constantly compelled either to delay analyzing some aspects of the input stream or entertain syntactic analyses that may turn out to be wrong. Empirical evidence suggests that

M. De Vincenzi and V. Lombardo (eds.), Cross-linguistic Perspectives on Language Processing, 149–174.

syntactic processing is rarely delayed (e.g., Altmann & Steedman, 1988; Frazier & Rayner, 1982; Trueswell, Tanenhaus, & Garnsey, 1994). Thus, two general classes of models are viable: those that propose that only a single analysis is ever considered at any given time and those that propose that multiple analyses are constructed and ranked. These two kinds of model differ as to how serial versus how parallel processing is presumed to be, as to whether the parser is limited to particular sources of information during an initial stage of processing, and as to the criteria the parser uses to rank analyses (or decide which single analysis to construct).

The *garden-path* model (Frazier, 1979, 1987) falls at the serial end of the serial-parallel dimension, as it presumes that readers and listeners construct only a single syntactic analysis at a time. Further, the garden-path parser ignores some potentially useful information during an initial stage of parsing. For example, referential context may influence the plausibility of alternative syntactic analyses (see, e.g., Altmann & Steedman, 1988), but according to the garden-path model, the parser does not use this information until after it has built an initial syntactic structure. The parser bases its preferences on *minimal attachment* and *late closure* strategies. Minimal attachment posits that readers and listeners minimize analysis time by building the phrase structure tree with the fewest nodes that is consistent with the input. Late closure posits that readers and listeners conserve processing resources by attaching incoming material to the most recently constructed phrase or clause rather than moving to a new or previously constructed phrase or clause.

The *construal* hypothesis (Frazier & Clifton, 1996) differs from the garden path model in that it resolves some (but not all) syntactic ambiguities in parallel. Construal proposes that text can be divided into *primary relations* and *non-primary* relations.

Frazier and Clifton (p. 41) propose, "Primary phrases and relations include a. the subject and predicate of any (+ or -_) finite clause; b. complements and obligatory constituents of primary phrases." For primary relations, the construal parser acts just like the garden path parser. Text that instantiates primary relations is attached deterministically in a phrase-structure tree and is subject to minimal attachment and late closure. Text that instantiates non-primary relations is associated to the currently active theta domain (the entire extended maximal projection of the most recent theta assigner), rather than attached to a specific node in the phrase-structure tree. Once the non-primary phrase has been associated to the active theta domain, all attachment sites within the domain are assessed as hosts for the non-primary phrase simultaneously. Non-structural factors like semantic plausibility and referential context can inform the assessment of alternative attachments. Thus, construal proposes that the parser is a partially parallel mechanism and is only sometimes prevented from using non-syntactic information to construct an initial syntactic analysis. Its preferences for text instantiating primary phrases are the same as for the garden-path parser (i.e., it still prefers to construct the simplest phrase-structure tree), but simplicity does not determine its preferences for text instantiating non-primary phrases.

Constraint-based parsers differ from garden-path and construal parsers in that they consider and rank multiple syntactic analyses for all ambiguous fragments (e.g., Boland, 1997; Boland, Tanenhaus, Garnsey, & Carlson, 1995; MacDonald et al., 1994; Spivey-Knowlton & Sedivy, 1995; Trueswell, Tanenhaus, & Kello, 1993). They draw no substantive distinctions between initial and later stages of processing (or between initial analysis and re-analysis), they do not ignore potentially useful sources of information (e.g., referential context), and they prefer likely analyses (as opposed to simple analyses). Finally, constraint-based theories propose that ambiguity resolution results from competition between alternative syntactic analyses. Spivey-Knowlton and Sedivy propose (p. 260), "Near equal activation of the two alternatives will result in lengthy competition, hence greatly slowed reading times at the point of ambiguity."

A constraint-based parser determines which analysis to foreground by accessing information about the syntactic structures that a particular lexical item permits and prefers. For example, the verb *realized* can take a simple noun-phrase object as its post-verbal argument (as in *The investor realized a profit.*), but it may also take a full sentence complement (as in *The investor realized that a profit would save the company.*), or a reduced complement (as in *The investor realized a profit would save the company*). Further, the verb *realized* most commonly takes a reduced complement as its post verbal argument (Pickering, Traxler, & Crocker, 1999), whereas a verb like *doubted* most commonly takes a noun-phrase object as its post-verbal argument. When parsing syntactically ambiguous sentence fragments like *The man realized a profit...* the parser may take into account the fact that the verb *realized* or some larger class of verbs including *realized* prefers to take a reduced complement and therefore assign more activation to the sentence-complement interpretation and less to the noun-phrase object interpretation. In contrast, when the parser encounters the fragment *The man doubted the explanation...*(*would satisfy the police.*) it may take into account the fact that the verb *doubted* prefers to take a noun-phrase object and assign more activation to the noun-phrase object interpretation and less to the sentence-complement interpretation (see, e.g., Ford, Bresnan, & Caplan, 1983). Further, the amount of activation assigned to the alternative syntactic analyses will depend on how strongly the individual verb prefers one structure over another. If a verb greatly prefers sentence complements, information available from the sentence fragment and preceding context supports this interpretation, and if the actual sentence requires this interpretation, then processing should proceed smoothly. If the verb has no strong preference, and context does not strongly bias one way or the other, then alternative analyses will receive similar amounts of activation and processing will be slowed or disrupted by competition between alternative syntactic analyses.

EXPERIMENTAL EVIDENCE FOR PARALLELISM, LIKELIHOOD PREFERENCES, AND COMPETITION

Evidence for parallel consideration of alternative interpretations in language processing is most prevalent in experiments on lexical ambiguity resolution. Swinney's (1979) classic study demonstrated that readers and listeners activate multiple meaning for ambiguous words before selecting a contextually appropriate meaning. Although some experimental work suggests that strongly biasing discourse context may cause readers and listeners to activate only the contextually appropriate meaning (e.g., Seidenberg, Tanenhaus, Leiman, & Bienkowski, 1982), consideration of alternative interpretations in parallel seems to occur commonly in lexical processing.

Lexical ambiguity resolution also offers some evidence for competitive resolution of ambiguity. In one eye-movement monitoring study (Rayner & Duffy, 1986), fixation times were collected for ambiguous words that had either one frequently occurring and one infrequently occurring meaning (biased words) or two equally frequent meanings (equibiased words). Equibiased words were defined as having no more than a 67% preference for the more frequent meaning, and biased words as having no less than 78% preference. Compared to unambiguous control words, readers spent more time fixating equibiased words. By contrast, biased words produced fixation times equal to unambiguous control words. Rayner and Duffy proposed that the two meanings of equibiased words became available at the same time, thereby forcing the reader to do additional processing to select one meaning for integration into the discourse representation. A competition between alternative meanings is one possible description of this additional processing (MacDonald, Pearlmutter, & Seidenberg, 1994).

A further study investigated context effects on the processing of equibiased and biased ambiguous words (Duffy, Morris, & Rayner, 1988). Equibiased words were preceded by context that made one of two meanings appropriate. Biased words were preceded by context that made the subordinate meaning appropriate. Fixation times on equibiased words preceded by biasing context did not differ from unambiguous control words. By contrast, readers spent more time fixating biased ambiguous words than unambiguous words when context supported the less-frequent meaning of the ambiguous word. Duffy et al. provide two possible explanations for these findings. The first proposes that word meanings are delivered for integration serially. On this view, frequency and context interact to determine when different meanings become available. The other explanation proposes that all of the meanings of an ambiguous word are activated simultaneously, but with different amounts of evidence favoring the different meanings. According to Duffy et al. (p. 441), "Selection (of a single meaning for integration) would be relatively fast when the evidence clearly supported one meaning; it would be slow when equal amounts of evidence accrued for both meanings." Where discourse context supports the dominant meaning of an ambiguous word, lexical preferences and contextual information are in accord and the dominant meaning quickly out-competes the non-dominant meaning. When discourse context supports the non-dominant meaning, lexical and contextual information conflict, and it takes longer for the contextually appropriate non-dominant meaning to out-compete the inappropriate dominant meaning. Thus, the data from this study may offer additional evidence that, in some circumstances, lexical ambiguity is resolved by a competitive process.

Evidence for parallel consideration of alternative syntactic structures comes from studies that manipulate the lexical preferences of individual verbs (Garnsey, Pearlmutter, Myers, & Lotocky, 1997; Spivey-Knowlton & Sedivy, 1995; Trueswell et al. 1993, 1994). Trueswell et al. (1993) monitored readers' eye-movements while they processed sentences like 1a - d:

(1a) The student forgot the solution was in the back of the book.
(1b) The student hoped the solution was in the back of the book.
(1c) The student forgot that the solution was in the back of the book.
(1d) The student hoped that the solution was in the back of the book.

The verb *forgot* prefers to take a noun-phrase object (as opposed to a reduced complement) as its post-verbal argument; whereas the verb *hoped* prefers to take a sentence-complement. In all of the test sentences, the correct interpretation was the sentence-complement analysis. Sometimes the post-verbal argument was a reduced complement (as in 1a & b), sometimes it was a full complement (as in 1c & d). Sentences with full complements provided baseline data, as the complementizer makes the direct-object interpretation impossible. If readers referred to detailed lexical information to rank alternative analyses, then they should have experienced greater disruption processing sentences like 1a, where the verb prefers the inappropriate noun-phrase object interpretation, than sentences like 1b, where the verb prefers the sentence-complement interpretation that actually appears. In the event, readers showed greater disruption while processing the syntactically disambiguating material was in the in sentence 1a than in 1b, as predicted. Trueswell et al. also noted that the magnitude of the difference between the ambiguous forms (1a & b) and the unambiguous forms (1c & d) correlated with the degree to which the verbs preferred to take a full (vs. reduced) sentence complement. Thus, they concluded that the verbs activated alternative syntactic structures to differing degrees, and that resolution time was a function of how much evidence was available for alternative syntactic analyses. Finally, since difficulty at disambiguation was a function of whether the disambiguating material confirmed or disconfirmed the verbs' preferences, these studies also provide some evidence that the parser initially foregrounds (or adopts) the analysis that is most likely in the circumstances. A further eye-movement monitoring study produced compatible results using a semantic plausibility manipulation (Garnsey, Pearlmutter, Myers, & Lotocky, 1997; but see also Ferreira & Henderson, 1990; Pickering, Traxler, & Crocker, 1999).

RESEARCH ON MODIFIER ATTACHMENT IN 6 1/2 LANGUAGES

Processing of modifiers has been studied in Dutch, (American & British) English, French, German, Italian, and Spanish, which makes a discussion of this work especially appropriate for this volume. In this section, we will describe some of the work on modifier attachment in languages other than English and some of the work that has been done in the Eye-Tracking Lab at the University of Glasgow (Traxler, Pickering, & Clifton, 1998; van Gompel, Pickering, & Traxler, 1999). We will focus particularly on the question of whether attachment ambiguity is resolved by competition between alternative analyses.

Consider processing of sentence 2 (an English translation of a Spanish sentence tested by Cuetos & Mitchell, 1988):

(2) Someone shot the (male) servant of the actress who was standing on the balcony with her husband.

In this sentence, the modifying expression *who was standing on the balcony with her husband* could modify either *servant* or *actress*. Gender marking on the noun-phrase *her husband* compels readers to attach the modifier to *actress*. Cuetos and Mitchell presented sentences like 3 to readers and found that they had greater difficulty processing disambiguating material (e.g., *her husband*) when the modifier attached to the second noun-phrase (*actress*) than when the attachment was left ambiguous. Cuetos and Mitchell also collected judgments that suggested that Spanish speakers prefer to attach modifiers to the first noun in the complex. Thus, their results provided evidence against the late closure principle (which would predict that attachment to the second noun phrase would be preferred) and in favor of a likelihood preference. Brysbaert and Mitchell (1996) tested Dutch translations of sentences like 3, and Zagar, Pynte, & Rativeau (1997) tested similar French sentences with compatible results, showing faster reading times when the relative clause modified the first noun-phrase than when it modified the second (note, however, that the off-line preference in Dutch seems to be for attachment to the second noun-phrase, and thus could be taken as evidence against a likelihood preference; cf. Pickering et al., 1999; Traxler et al., 1998).

Other studies on similar constructions in English (Carreiras & Clifton, 1993; Clifton, 1988), Italian (De Vincenzi & Job, 1993, 1995), and French (Baccino et al., this volume, Frenck-Mestre & Pynte, this volume) produced different results. Carreiras and

Clifton used self-paced reading to investigate sentences with relative clause modifiers and did not find a consistent attachment preference for English, although they found faster times for first than for second noun-phrase modifiers in Spanish. Similarly, Clifton used self-paced reading to investigate sentences with relative-clause modifiers in English and did not find a consistent attachment preference. De Vincenzi and Job tested prepositional phrase and relative-clause modifiers in Italian. In questionnaire studies, they found a consistent preference among Italian speakers to attach modifiers to the first noun phrase in noun-phrase complexes when the noun-phrase complex contained the preposition of, which is what Cuetos and Mitchell found for Spanish speakers. However, De Vincenzi and Job found that when they changed the preposition in the noun-phrase complex to with, Italian speakers preferred to attach the modifier to the second noun in the noun-phrase complex. Despite this difference in off-line preferences, self-paced reading experiments demonstrated that Italian speakers had less difficulty attaching both prepositional-phrase and relative-clause modifiers to the second noun-phrase than to the first noun-phrase in the complex. We return to the Baccino and colleagues' and Frenck-Mestre and Pynte's results below.

A further study compared Spanish and English speakers' preferences in experiments that manipulated the semantic relation between the first and second noun, the referentiality of the noun phrase, and the type of preposition in the noun-phrase complex (Gilboy, Sopena, Clifton, & Frazier, 1995). Gilboy et al. compared preference judgments for native Spanish and English speakers. In questionnaire studies, they found that the relationship between the nouns in the complex affected attachment preferences similarly for both Spanish and English speakers. Some relationships resulted in a strong preference for modification of the first noun phrase in both languages, and other relationships resulted in a strong preference for modification of the second noun phrase. Further, they demonstrated that Spanish speakers preferred to attach modifiers to the second noun in the complex for some kinds of sentences and that English speakers preferred to attach modifiers to the first noun in the complex for some sentences. These findings challenged the assumption that readers treat all sentences containing noun-phrase complexes followed by modifiers in the same fashion. Gilboy et al. proposed that Cuetos and Mitchell's (1988) results reflected the specific characteristics of their test sentences rather than a general difference in parsing between English and Spanish.

In the Eye-Tracking Lab at the University of Glasgow, we looked for competition between alternative syntactic analyses by examining different attachment resolution problems (Traxler et al., 1998; Van Gompel et al., 1999). The experiments tested additional predictions of garden-path, construal, and constraint based models. The first experiment tested construal's claim that readers process text that instantiates primary relations differently than text that instantiates non-primary relations. The second experiment used a different kind of disambiguation to confirm and extend novel findings from the first experiment. The third experiment tested construal's claim that attaching non-primary phrases outside the active theta domain is difficult. The final experiment tested sentences where modifying expressions could attach either to the matrix verb or to the matrix verb's direct object (so called high-low attachment ambiguities).

The first experiment tested sentences like 3a - f (Traxler, et al., 1998). Consider first sentences 3a - c:

(3a) The driver of the car with the moustache was pretty cool.

(3b) The car of the driver with the moustache was pretty cool.

(3c) The son of the driver with the moustache was pretty cool.

All of the sentences begin with a noun-phrase complex containing two noun-phrases. A modifier (here a prepositional phrase) that must be assigned to one of the other of the noun phrases in the complex followed. Semantic plausibility compels readers to attach the modifier to the first noun in the complex in 3a, because drivers can have moustaches but cars normally do not. In 3b, the modifier must attach to the second noun phrase; and in 3c the modifier can attach to either noun phrase (because both sons and drivers can have moustaches). However, prior to any semantic processing, either site could host the modifier. Previous eye-tracking studies have found that readers spend greater amounts of time fixating text that produces an implausible semantic interpretation (Clifton, 1993; Rayner, Carlson, & Frazier, 1983; Traxler & Pickering, 1996; Pickering & Traxler, 1998). Thus, we would expect to see elevated reading times if a syntactic analysis produces an attachment with an implausible interpretation (e.g., if the parser attached moustache to car).

Next, consider sentences 3d - f:

(3d) The driver of the car that had the moustache was pretty cool.

(3e) The car of the driver that had the moustache was pretty cool.

(3f) The son of the driver that had the moustache was pretty cool.

3d - f differ from 3a - c only in that the modifier is a relative clause as opposed to a prepositional phrase. According to construal, processing of the modifier depends on whether it is taken as a primary or non-primary phrase. While the construal hypothesis claims that a prepositional phrase is taken as a primary phrase in an environment in which it could serve as an argument (e.g., in the environment Verb-NP-PP), it is vague concerning exactly how the relevant environment must be specified. If the fact that a prepositional phrase can be an argument in some environments is enough for it to be treated as a potentially primary phrase in any environment, it should be subject to late closure. Thus, in sentences like 3a - c, the construal parser may prefer to attach the modifier to the second noun-phrase in the complex. Because relative clauses cannot instantiate primary relations, the modifier in sentences 3d - f will be associated to the current theta domain, which contains both noun-phrases in the complex, and both alternative syntactic analyses will be evaluated simultaneously. The garden-path parser does not recognize the distinction between primary and non-primary relations, and so processing of 3a - c and 3d - f should look exactly the same. More specifically, the garden-path parser will prefer to attach the modifiers to the second noun in the complex (as determined by the late closure principle).

Two possible patterns of results would be consistent with the operation of a constraint-based parser. The constraint-based parser will consider both attachment sites as host for the modifier simultaneously, because it constructs and ranks alternative analyses in parallel. On the one hand, attachment to the second noun-phrase may be easier than attachment to the first noun-phrase, because questionnaire studies demonstrate that (British) English speakers prefer to attach modifiers to the second noun in the complex in sentences like 3a - f. For sentences with prepositional-phrase modifiers (3a - c), raters preferred to attach the modifier to the second noun in the complex 74% of the time. For sentences with relative clause modifiers (3d-f), raters preferred to attach the modifier to the second noun in the complex 68% of the time. On the other hand, processing of the modifier in 3c and 3f may be more difficult than in 3a - b and 3d - e, because two syntactic analyses produce plausible interpretations in 3c and 3f, but only one of the syntactic analyses produces a plausible interpretation in 3a -b and 3d - e. If the available evidence supports more than one analysis, it should take some time for one alternative to out-compete the other, thus reading times should be elevated.

Total reading times on the modifier for sentences like 3a - c differed only weakly from one another, in the direction predicted by all of the accounts. Plausible attachment to the second noun-phrase produced shorter reading times than plausible attachment to the first noun phrase (but this difference was not statistically significant). Total reading times on the modifier in sentences like 3d - f, where the modifier was a relative clause, produced stronger differences. Total reading times on the modifier were less for sentences like 3f than for sentences like 3d and 3e (whose total reading times did not differ). Thus, the pattern of reading times for sentences with relative-clause modifiers differed from sentences with prepositional-phrase modifiers. This is consistent with the Gilboy et al. off-line findings and with the operation of a construal-type parser. The findings are inconsistent with the operation of a garden-path parser, as reading times for modifiers that attached to the second noun-phrase in the complex were sometimes elevated. The findings are also inconsistent with the operation of a constraint-based parser. On the one hand, reading times should have followed readers' off-line preferences, and they did not. On the other hand, reading times should increase as competition between alternative analyses increases, and they did not.

One final phenomenon requires comment. Reading times on the modifier for sentences like 3e were elevated in comparison with reading times for sentences like 3f. They were also elevated for sentences like 3d, but we emphasize 3e here because it is the form that is preferred in our off-line data and, following the logic of constraint-satisfaction models, should be read faster in an on-line study. In sentences like 3e, the modifier had to be attached to the second noun-phrase in the complex, as attachment to the first noun-phrase produced an implausible semantic interpretation. The only difference between sentences like 3e and sentences like 3f is that both attachments in 3f produced a plausible semantic interpretation. Thus it appears that readers sometimes attached the modifier to the first noun-phrase in sentences like 3e, even though that attachment was dispreferred and even though that attachment was implausible. We will return to this finding below.

The finding of slow reading times when relative clauses must modify the second noun phrase in a complex, compared to when it could modify either one, seems to have strong theoretical implications. Because of this, we attempted to reproduce the phenomenon using different materials. Thus, a further experiment examined processing of sentences like 4a - c (Traxler et al., 1997):

(4a) The daughter of the colonel who shot herself on the balcony had been very depressed.
(4b) The daughter of the colonel who shot himself on the balcony had been very depressed.
(4c) The brother of the colonel who shot himself on the balcony had been very depressed.

These sentences differ from sentences 4d - f in that the relative-clause modifier contains a reflexive pronoun that disambiguates attachment to the first noun-phrase in the complex in 4a or the second noun-phrase in the complex in 4b and in that the relative clause begins with the relativizer who instead of that. In 4c the relative-clause modifier could attach to either noun phrase in the complex. Thus, whereas sentences 3a -f used plausibility to disambiguate the attachment, these sentences used gender agreement. Sentences like 4a -c resemble sentences 3d -f in that they begin with a noun-phrase complex, the complex contains two noun-phrases, the noun-phrases are connected by the non-theta-assigning preposition of, and the modifier is a relative clause. Thus, the processing implications are the same for sentences 4a - c and 3d - f.

Reading times on sentences 4a - c confirmed the results from the previous experiment. Total reading times on the modifier were less for sentences like 4c than for sentences like 4a and 4b (whose total reading times did not differ). The data thus allow more confident conclusions about the processing of relative clause modifiers. Again, the total reading times did not conform to readers' off-line preferences; and again, the fully ambiguous sentences produced faster reading times than either of the disambiguated versions. In addition, lengthy reading times were observed on the modifier in sentences like 4b (as compared to 4c), which would occur only if readers attempted to attach the modifier to the first noun-phrase in the complex. Construal can accommodate this phenomenon, as it predicts that relative clauses will be attached to all available host sites and the resulting interpretations evaluated in parallel, if one implausible interpretation causes disruption.

Note however that this explanation would conflict with explanations of other experimental results. For example, Boland, Tanenhaus, Garnsey, & Carlson (1995) investigated unbounded dependency constructions containing verbs like persuaded that have two obligatory argument slots. Readers in this study did not experience disruption on the matrix verb when the direct object analysis produced an implausible interpretation, as in That's the movie that John persuaded...(some kids to watch.) Boland and her colleagues proposed that this implausible interpretation did not produce disruption in processing because readers had constructed an alternative analysis in parallel under which movie was part of an infinitival complement of persuaded (as in John persuaded some kids to watch the movie). On this account, the readers quickly foregrounded the alternative analysis and thus did not experience any disruption of processing. If this same logic were applied to relative-clause attachment, then no disruption of processing should have occurred in sentences like 3e and 4b. If readers attached the relative clauses in parallel, then one plausible attachment was always available, and readers should have been able to change from foregrounding one analysis to foregrounding the other at little or no cost. Thus, the current results suggest that modifier attachment ambiguities may be resolved differently than ambiguities involving the assignment of a noun-phrase to one of two obligatory post-verbal argument slots.

A third experiment tested sentences like 5a - c (Traxler et al., 1998):

(5a) The steak with the sauce that was tough didn't win a prize.

(5b) The steak with the sauce that was runny didn't win a prize.

(5c) The steak with the sauce that was tasty didn't win a prize.

These contain relative-clause modifiers (as did sentences like 3d - f and 4a - c). The main difference between these sentences and the previous ones is that the noun-phrase complex in these sentences contains the theta-assigning preposition with; whereas the noun-phrase complexes in the previous sentences contained the non-theta-assigning preposition of. According to construal, relative-clauses are attached in parallel to all potential host sites in the currently active theta domain. With the theta-assigning preposition present, only the second noun-phrase in the complex is available in the active theta domain when readers encounter the relative-clause modifier. Thus, according to construal, it should be easier to process the relative clause in 5b and 5c, where it attaches to the second noun-phrase in the complex, than in 5a, where it attaches to the first. The garden-path model makes the same prediction, for different reasons. It proposes a preference for attachment to the second noun-phrase due to the late closure principle. The constraint-based model predicts the same pattern for these sentences as for 3a - f and 4a - c, because readers also prefer to attach modifiers to the second noun-phrase in the complex 81% of the time (according to a questionnaire study). In fact, total reading times on the modifier were greater for sentences like 5a than for sentences like 5b and 5c (whose total reading times did not differ). Thus, the results of this experiment were consistent with the operation of garden-path, construal, and constraint-based parsers; but the construal parser makes the additional prediction that relative clauses in sentences like 5a - c will be treated differently than relative clauses in sentences like 3d - f and 4a - c, which is the case.

One final experiment tested processing of sentences like 6a - c (Van Gompel, Pickering, & Traxler, 1999; see also Altmann & Steedman, 1988; Clifton, Speer, & Abney, 1991; Rayner et al., 1983; Spivey-Knowlton & Sedivy, 1995; Taraban & McClelland, 1988).

(6a) The hunter killed only the leopard with the rifle not long after sunset.

(6b) The hunter killed only the leopard with the scars not long after sunset.

(6c) The hunter killed only the poacher with the rifle not long after sunset.

Here, the prepositional-phrase modifier with the rifle/scars can attach either to the verb shot or to the verb's direct object the leopard/poacher. Off-line studies demonstrated that attachment to the verb and the direct object was equally preferred when the word only was inserted after the matrix verb. If alternative syntactic analyses compete, then processing of the modifier should take longer in the fully ambiguous version (e.g., sentences like 6c) than in either of the disambiguated versions (e.g., sentences like 6a and 6b). First pass reading times did not show any significant differences. However, first-pass regressions out of the spill-over region (e.g., not long after) demonstrated that the ambiguous sentences were easier to process than their unambiguous counterparts. There were fewer first-pass regressions out of the spill-over region for sentences like 6c than for sentences like 6a and 6b, which did not differ. This result is clearly incompatible with competitive resolution of the attachment ambiguity.

ONE PARSER

An account of human sentence processing must include an explanation of how modifier attachment is accomplished. It must explain why readers sometimes experience less disruption in processing when two modifier attachments produce plausible semantic interpretations than when only one attachment produces a plausible semantic interpretation. It must explain what causes readers to change their behavior when presented with prepositional-phrase modifiers and relative-clause modifiers. It must explain why changing the type of preposition in noun-phrase complexes changes the processing of a subsequent relative-clause modifier. Finally, it must explain why readers sometimes process modifiers slowly when the preferred attachment produces a semantically plausible interpretation.

The standard garden-path model fails some of these tests. The late closure principle suggests that readers will always attempt initially to attach modifiers to the last noun in a noun-phrase complex. Reading times should be fast when this attachment produces a plausible interpretation and slow when it does not. Lengthy reading times for relative-clause modifiers for sentences like 4e and 5b disconfirm this prediction. The garden-path parser also does not explain why changing the preposition in the noun-phrase complex changes readers behavior.

Constraint-based models also fail some of these tests. According to constraint-based accounts, readers should experience difficulty when the available evidence supports more than one syntactic analysis, because competition between analyses will proceed for a greater amount of time. Processing should be more difficult in the fully ambiguous sentences, especially where structural preferences are closely matched (as in, e.g., Van Gompel et al., 1999), but it is not. Further, reading times should conform to readers' off-line preferences, and they do not always do so. Finally, processing should proceed smoothly when a single preferred structural analysis produces a plausible semantic interpretation. However, readers' preferred structural analyses sometimes produced slow or disrupted reading.

The construal parser passes the bulk of the tests. It provides a ready explanation for why prepositional-phrase modifiers and relative-clause modifiers are processed differently and for why the type of preposition in the noun-phrase complex matters. Thus, none of the phenomena described above directly contradicts the construal account. The construal account is silent, however, on the question of why fully ambiguous sentences produce rapid processing of the modifiers. The construal account does propose that relative-clause attachment is processed in parallel, and that may provide a place to start developing an explanation.

Assume for the moment that relative clause attachment is done in parallel (i.e., that relative clauses are attached to all potential host sites within some attentional window and the resulting interpretations evaluated simultaneously). Assume further that the reader ceases processing the attachment as soon as one interpretation produces a plausible semantic interpretation. It is unlikely that all attachments would be completed and evaluated at precisely the same instant in time. On some occasions, attachment to the first host site would be completed a little before attachment to the second site. On other occasions, attachment to the second host site would be completed first. On this model, disambiguated sentences would produce disruption some of the time, because the first analysis would produce an implausible semantic interpretation. By contrast, fully ambiguous sentences would never produce disruption, because the first analysis would always produce a plausible semantic interpretation. Thus, parallel evaluation where there is some variability in how quickly the attachments are prepared could produce fast processing in fully ambiguous materials and slower average processing time in sentences where one analysis produces an implausible interpretation. Note that this account does not propose direct competition between alternative analyses, and thus there is no basis for lengthy reading times for fully ambiguous sentences. Rather, disruption occurs for the same reason it occurs in other garden-path sentences: Readers sometimes commit to a structural analysis that conflicts with other aspects of the input.

Before we conclude, we are compelled to address apparent conflicts between our results and those reported elsewhere in this volume (Baccino et al.; Frenck-Mestre & Pynte) and in previous studies (e.g., Cuetos & Mitchell, 1988). Let us address the French studies before turning to Spanish. Contrasting our results with the French results is not a straightforward task for several reasons. First, the two French studies produced different patterns. Baccino et al. found that attaching relative-clause modifiers to the second of two noun-phrases was easier than attaching relative-clause modifiers to the first of two noun-phrases. Frenck-Mestre and Pynte found the opposite pattern, except, apparently, when attachment to the second noun-phrase is primed by the prior presentation of sentences where the noun-phrase complex contains the preposition with. It is our view that further research is required to reconcile these two sets of results. We would note, however, that our findings with English relative-clause modifiers would be compatible with the aggregate of the French results, as we find no evidence of a preference either way for sentences that have only one plausible attachment. Second, neither the French nor Spanish studies included fully ambiguous sentences. Our central claim is that a race mechanism explains the pattern of processing we observed better than a competition between alternative syntactic analyses. Because none of the other studies included ambiguous sentences, they cannot be taken as evidence for competition and against a race. Finally, to address the issue of the Spanish results, we would point out that they, too, demonstrated that readers had less difficulty processing sentences where more than one attachment was possible than when attachment was forced to the second noun-phrase in a complex. Further, the English sentences that we tested were structured differently than the Spanish studies in ways that may be critical in terms of the ambiguity resolution problems that they present (see Gilboy et al., for a full discussion). Thus, any contradiction between the Spanish results and the English results we described above may be more apparent than real.

CONCLUSIONS

If competition resolves ambiguity at the level of word meanings, but does not resolve modifier attachment, then it may not be accurate or useful to describe processing at one level as being a version of processing at the other level. It may be that different processes are required at the word and syntax level, because different processing demands are involved and because the consequences of making a mistake are different. It may be that activating and comparing two word meanings is easier than activating and comparing two modifier attachments. Thus, the parser may choose to settle on the first available structural analysis, rather than exhaustively seek alternative analyses. Further, if a word's lexical identity is not disambiguated, this will have repercussions at the level of word-meaning and possibly also at the level of syntactic structure (if, for example, a noun were mis-identified as an adjective or a verb). However, there would be no further structural implications if a modifier attached to the first versus second noun-phrase in a complex. In other words, the reader could continue to construct appropriate syntactic representations for the rest of the sentence, even after attaching the modifier to the wrong noun phrase.

NOTES

Order of authorship is arbitrary. We acknowledge the assistance of Keith Edwards, Stephen Frisson, & Roger van Gompel. This research was supported by ESRC Grant No. R000234542 and a British Academy Post-Doctoral Fellowship (both awarded to Pickering). Clifton's participation in this research was supported by grant HD-18708 to the University of Massachusetts.

REFERENCES

Altmann, G.T.M., & Steedman, M.J. (1988). Interaction with context during human sentence processing. Cognition, 30, 191-238.

Boland, J.E. (1997). Resolving syntactic category ambiguities in discourse context: Probabilistic and discourse constraints. Journal of Memory and Language, 36, 588-615.

Boland, J.E., Tanenhaus, M.K., Garnsey, S.M., & Carlson, G.N. (1995). Verb argument structure in parsing and interpretation: Evidence from wh-questions. Journal of Memory and Language, 34, 774-806

Frazier, L. (1979). On comprehending sentences: Syntactic parsing strategies. Ph.D. Thesis, University of Connecticut. West Bend, IN: Indiana University Linguistics Club.

Brysbaert, M., & Mitchell, D.C. (1996). Modifier attachment in sentence parsing: evidence from Dutch. Quarterly Journal of Experimental Psychology, 49A, 664-695.

Carreiras, M., & Clifton Jr., C. (1993). Relative clause interpretation preferences in Spanish and English. Language and Speech, 36, 353-372.

Clifton Jr., C. (1988). Restrictions on late closure: Appearance and reality. Paper presented to the sixth Australian Language and Speech Conference, University of New South Wales, Australia.

Clifton Jr., C. (1993). Thematic roles in sentence parsing. Canadian Journal of Experimental Psychology, 47, 222-246.

Clifton Jr., C, Speer, S., & Abney, S. (1991). Parsing arguments: Phrase structure and argument structure as determinants of initial parsing decisions. Journal of Memory and Language, 30, 251-271.

Cuetos, F., & Mitchell, D.C. (1988). Cross-linguistic differences in parsing: Restrictions on the use of the Late Closure strategy in Spanish. Cognition, 30, 73-105.

De Vincenzi, M., & Job, R. (1993). Some observations on the universality of the late closure strategy: Evidences from Italian. Journal of Psycholinguistic Research, 22, 189-206.

De Vincenzi, M., & Job, R. (1995). An investigation of late closure: The role of syntax, thematic structure, and pragmatics in initial and final interpretation. Journal of Experimental Psychology: Learning, Memory, & Cognition, 21, 1-19.

Duffy, S.A., Morris, R.K., & Rayner, K. (1988). Lexical ambiguity and fixation times in reading. Journal of Memory and Language, 27, 429-446.

Ferreira, F., & Henderson, J. (1990). Use of verb information in syntactic parsing: Evidence from eye movements and word-by-word self-paced reading. Journal of Experimental Psychology: Learning, Memory, and Cognition, 16, 555-568.

Frazier, L. (1987). Sentence Processing: A Tutorial Review. In M. Coltheart (Ed.), Attention and Performance XII. Hillsdale, NJ: Erlbaum.

Frazier, L., & Clifton Jr., C. (1996). Construal. Cambridge, MA: MIT Press.

Frazier, L., & Rayner, K. (1982). Making and correcting errors during sentence comprehension: Eye movements in the analysis of structurally ambiguous sentences. Cognitive Psychology, 14, 178-210.

Garnsey, S.M., Pearlmutter, N.J., Myers, E., & Lotocky, M.A. (1997). The contributions of verb bias and plausibility to the comprehension of temporarily ambiguous sentences. Journal of Memory and Language, 37, 58-93.

Gilboy, E., Sopena, J.M., Clifton Jr., C., & Frazier, L. (1995). Argument structure and association preferences in Spanish and English compound NPs. Cognition, 54, 131-167.

MacDonald, M.C., Pearlmutter, N.J., & Seidenberg, MS. (1994). The lexical nature of syntactic ambiguity resolution. Psychological Review, 101, 676-703.

Pickering, M.J., & Traxler, M.J. (1998). Plausibility and recover from garden-paths: An eye-tracking study. Journal of Experimental Psychology: Learning, Memory, & Cognition, 24, 940-961.

Pickering, M.J., Traxler, M.J., & Crocker, M.W. (1999). Ambiguity Resolution in Sentence Processing: Evidence Against Likelihood. Unpublished manuscript.

Rayner, K., Carlson, M., & Frazier, L. (1983). The interaction of syntax and semantics during sentence processing: Eye movements in the analysis of semantically biased sentences. Journal of Verbal Learning and Verbal Behavior, 22, 358-374.

Rayner, K. & Duffy, S.A. (1986). Lexical complexity and fixation times in reading: Effects of word frequency, verb complexity, and lexical ambiguity. Memory & Cognition, 14, 191-201.

Spivey-Knowlton, M., & Sedivy, J.C. (1995). Resolving attachment ambiguities with multiple constraints. Cognition, 55, 227-267.

Swinney, D. A. (1979). Lexical access during sentence comprehension: (Re)consideration of context effects. Journal of Verbal Learning and Verbal Behavior, 18, 645-659.

Tanenhaus, M.K., Leiman, J.M., & Seidenberg, M.S. (1979). Evidence for multiple stages in the processing of ambiguous words in syntactic contexts. Journal of Verbal Learning and Verbal Behavior, 18, 427-440.

Taraban, R., & McClelland, J.R. (1988). Constituent attachment and thematic role assignment in sentence processing: Influence of content-based expectations. Journal of Memory and Language, 27, 597-632.

Traxler, M.J., & Pickering, M.J. (1996). Plausibility and the processing of unbounded dependencies: An eye-tracking study. Journal of Memory and Language, 35, 454-475.

Traxler, M.J., Pickering, M.J., & Clifton Jr., C. (1998). Modifier Attachment is not a Form of Lexical Ambiguity Resolution. Journal of Memory and Language, 39, 558-592.

Trueswell, J., Tanenhaus, M., & Garnsey, S. (1994). Semantic influences on parsing: Use of thematic role information in syntactic disambiguation. Journal of Memory and Language, 33, 285-318.

Trueswell, J., Tanenhaus, M.K., & Kello, C. (1993). Verb-specific constraints in sentence processing: Separating effects of lexical preference from garden-paths. Journal of Experimental Psychology: Learning, Memory, and Cognition, 19, 528-553.

Van Gompel, R., Pickering, M.J., & Traxler, M.J. (1999). Prepositional-Phrase Attachment Ambiguities are not Resolved via Competition. Unpublished manuscript.

Zagar, D., Pynte, J., Rativeau, S. (1997). Evidence for early-closure attachment on first-pass reading times in French. Quarterly Journal of Experimental Psychology A, 50, 421-438.

Michael Meng and Markus Bader

THE ROLE OF CASE AND NUMBER FEATURES IN SYNTACTIC AMBIGUITY RESOLUTION[1]

INTRODUCTION

Syntactic representations contain two kinds of information: information about phrase-structural relations and information about the distribution of syntactic features within the phrase-structure tree. Parsing theory has concentrated on the computation of phrase-structural relations during processing. Although syntactic features like case and number often play an important role in experimental investigations, for example for creating unambiguous control conditions, the representation and processing of these features has rarely been an issue.

Recently, interest in the representation and processing of syntactic features has been aroused by research on subject-verb agreement errors in production and comprehension (see Bock & Miller, 1991; Bock & Cutting, 1992, and Nicol, Forster, & Veres, 1997, among others). For example, if subjects are given a NP like *the visit of my sisters* and are asked to repeat this NP and continue to form a complete sentence, they occasionally produce continuations like (1) in which the finite verb does not agree with the head of the higher NP (*visit*) as required, but with the head of the embedded NP (*sisters*).

(1) *The visit of my sisters were great fun.

Agreement errors as in (1) have been observed in a number of experiments and also in natural speech. These experiments have

M. De Vincenzi and V. Lombardo (eds.), Cross-linguistic Perspectives on Language Processing, 175–204.

also shown an asymmetry between singular and plural NPs. While singular NPs with embedded plural NP like *the visit of my sisters* elicit a certain amount of agreement errors, agreement errors for plural NPs with embedded singular NP (*the visits of my sister)* are comparatively rare.

Agreement errors have been explained with recourse to the notion of feature attraction. As proposed by Eberhard (1997), the head noun (*visit*) can attract the number feature of the embedded noun (*sisters*). The attraction process is argued to be sensitive to the relative markedness of singular and plural in English. Only plural can trigger the attraction process. If this interpretation is correct, agreement errors demonstrate that the construction of syntactic representations involves processes which directly refer to syntactic features independently of any syntactic mechanism in which these features participate. The results on agreement errors furthermore imply that the processes responsible for number attraction interact with markedness properties of features.

In this paper, we will discuss a range of related processing phenomena in German which essentially lead to the same conclusion. Drawing on experimental results on the processing of object-object and subject-object ambiguities in German, we will explore the role that case and agreement features play in processes of syntactic ambiguity resolution and garden-path recovery. Our conclusion will be that a variety of processing phenomena in this domain cannot be explained solely in terms of mechanisms responsible for the computation of phrase-structure relations. Instead, we will propose that at least some parsing decisions are directly driven by properties of case and agreement features, in particular their relative markedness.

The paper is organized as follows. We begin with a brief exposition of our assumptions concerning the sentence structure of German, followed by a discussion of the German Case system which will focus on markedness distinctions therein. We will then discuss a range of processing phenomena involving the resolution of syntactic function ambiguities, case attraction, strength of garden-path effects and asymmetries in processing ungrammatical sentences. In all of these phenomena, markedness distinctions within the German Case system are relevant. We conclude with some remarks on how our assumptions generalize to related processing phenomena involving number features in subject-verb agreement.

SYNTACTIC BACKGROUND

Sentence structure of German

German is a SOV-language which exhibits the verb-second property (see Vikner, 1995). The SOV-nature of German is directly visible in embedded clauses where all verbs - whether finite or not - are located in clause-final position (see the underlined verbs in (2a)). In main clauses, the finite verb is raised to the second position, that is, to the position directly following the first constituent of the clause whereas non-finite verbs remain in clause-final position (see (2b)). If main clauses only contain a finite verb as in (2c), it also occupies the second position. In the following, we will discuss the processing of both embedded and main clauses. The syntactic structures of (2a) and (2c) are shown in (3a) and (3b), respectively.

(2) a. (Ich glaube), daß Fritz das Buch gelesen hat.
I believe that Fritz the book read has
"I belive that Fritz has read the book."

b. Fritz hat das Buch gelesen.
Fritz has the book read
"Fritz has read the book."

c. Fritz las das Buch.
Fritz read the book
"Fritz read the book."

(3)
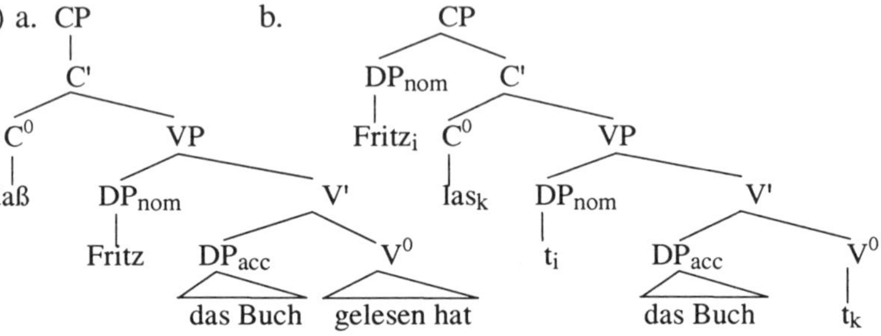

With these structures, we follow the assumption that German has no Inflectional Phrase (IP) but that instead all arguments are contained within the Verb Phrase (VP) (see Haider, 1993, 1997; Reuland & Kosmeijer, 1993). Therefore, a clause simply consists of a Complementizer Phrase (CP) dominating a VP. The embedded clause in (3a) transparently reflects the SOV-nature of German. The main clause in (3b) has been derived from an underlying verb-final structure by moving the finite verb to the position of C^0 and moving one further constituent, which in this case is the subject, to the specifier position of CP.

One reason for assuming that German is lacking an IP derives from the fact that there is no compelling evidence for an IP-VP-distinction in German. Furthermore, depending on the particular verb, the subject can be base-generated in a position preceding the object (see (2)) or following the object (see the passive sentences discussed in the next section). Therefore, syntactic functions like subject or object cannot be defined configurationally. Instead, in order to recover syntactic functions in German, the case marking on NPs has to be taken into account.

The Case system of German

German has four cases: nominative, accusative, dative and, genitive case. Genitive case is almost exclusively used for modifiers and complements of nouns and will therefore not be considered any further. Nominative and accusative case are structural cases which are assigned by default in certain syntactic contexts. Dative case, in contrast, is a lexical case which is directly tied to particular verbs. The distinction between structural and lexical cases is illustrated in (4) and (5). (4a) shows a simple two-place predicate with a nominative-marked subject and an accusative object. If such a predicate is passivized, the former accusative object is promoted to subject and the former subject can be expressed by an optional *von* (by) adjunct (4b). Sentence (5a) contains a two-place predicate with a dative object. This object is not affected by passivization, as shown in (5b). It receives dative case independent of the particular syntactic context, i.e. independent of whether the verb is in the active or the passive voice.

(4) a. Sie_{nom} unterstützt ihn_{acc}.
She supports him

b. Er_{nom} wird von ihr unterstützt.
He is by her supported
"He is supported by her."

(5) a. Sie_{nom} hilft ihm_{dat}
She helps him

b. Ihm_{dat} wird von ihr geholfen.
Him is by her helped.
"He is helped by her."

Since the assignment of dative case is dependent on specific lexical licensers, dative case can be considered a marked option in comparison to nominative and accusative case, which are assigned by default.

The markedness of dative case compared to nominative and accusative case is not only reflected syntactically but also by morphological and semantic properties: First, dative case is almost always distinctively marked morphologically whereas the morphological forms for nominative and accusative marked NPs often coincide. The only systematic exceptions to this latter claim are NPs without a determiner, for example proper names and bare NPs (see below). Secondly, dative case is tightly connected with a certain semantic interpretation. Simplifying somewhat, dative case is associated with the thematic roles of goal or beneficiary (see Wegener, 1985, for discussion). Nominative and accusative case, in contrast, are semantically almost empty. Although one can sometimes predict nominative and accusative case from thematic-conceptual information (e.g., if an NP-argument is an agent, it will be assigned nominative case), the reverse is not true. From knowing that an NP bears nominative case nothing can be concluded about the thematic role that this NP is associated with.

In sum, syntactic, morphological, and semantic facts indicate that dative case, as opposed to nominative and accusative case, has a marked status within the German case system. As we will now show, this marked status of dative case is reflected in a range of processing phenomena.

PARSING PREFERENCES IN PURE CASE AMBIGUITIES

Object-object ambiguities

The first phenomenon to be discussed concerns parsing preferences in a special type of syntactic function ambiguity, namely syntactic function ambiguities that can be classified as a pure case ambiguity (Bader, Bayer, Hopf, & Meng, 1996). A first example of a pure case ambiguity is given by the object-object ambiguity in (6). In (6a), the sentence-initial NP starting with *Personen* (*persons*) is the accusative object of the verb *unterstützen* (to support); in (6b), this NP is the dative object of *helfen* (to help). The distinction between accusative and dative object is not visible in (6b) at the object itself because the bare NP *Personen* is not marked with respect to its case. Only at the clause final verb, where the verb's subcategorization features become available, can it be determined that (6a) starts with an accusative object but (6b) with a dative object. Note that the ambiguity would be lost if the initial NP included an article. Then, (6a) would begin with *die Personen* but (6b) with *den Personen.*

(6) a. Personen, die in Not sind, sollte man *unterstützen.*
persons who in distress are should one support
"One should support persons who are in distress."

b. Personen, die in Not sind, sollte man *helfen.*
persons who in distress are should one help
"One should help persons who are in distress."

Sentence pair (6) is an instance of a pure case ambiguity because the single object of a two-place verb always occupies the same phrase-structural position, independently of whether it is an accusative or a dative object. The position of the object is within the VP. From this position, the object has been topicalized in (6a) and (6b), leaving a trace behind. The resulting syntactic structures are shown in (7).

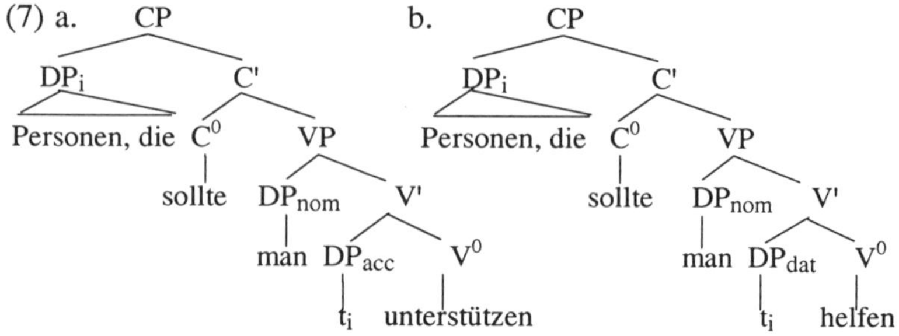

When processing a sentence from left to right, it becomes clear at the position of the auxiliary that the sentence-initial NP must be an object. This is so because the initial NP is marked for plural whereas the auxiliary is marked for singular. Therefore, the phrase-structural position of the trace associated with the sentence-initial object is uniquely determined from the auxiliary on. What remains open until the sentence-final main-verb is processed is only what case feature the object is bearing. In this sense, the object-object ambiguity in (6) is a pure case ambiguity.

Bader et al. (1996) (see also Hopf, Bayer, Bader, & Meng, 1998) have shown that sentences like (6b) elicit a garden-path effect at the main verb, where it turns out that the clause-initial NP must bear dative case. Such an effect was not found in sentences ending in an accusative verb and in dative sentences with an unambiguous dative NP. This indicates that the parser assigns accusative case to the case-ambiguous NP on first-pass parsing. In (6b), this initial case assignment has to be replaced by the assignment of dative case, with the result that a garden-path effect emerges. Due to the lack of a phrase-structural difference between (6a) and (6b), the preference of assigning accusative case to an ambiguous object cannot be explained by a parsing principle cast in phrase-structural terms. Bader et al.

(1996) have therefore proposed the *Case Preference Principles* in (8).

(8) *Case Preference Principles (CPP)*

a. Prefer structural Case to lexical Case.

b. Prefer nominative Case to accusative Case.

For the processing of the sentences in (6), the first clause of the CPP is relevant. After the lack of agreement between the clause-initial NP and the finite auxiliary has signalled that the initial NP cannot be the subject of the clause, two possibilities remain: this NP might either be an accusative or a dative object. According to the first clause of (8), accusative case will be preferred to dative case because the former is a structural case whereas the latter is a lexical case.

The finding of garden-path effects in object-object ambiguities like (6) is remarkable in two respects. First, this finding strongly indicates that the parser's first-pass decisions are sensitive to case-information. Otherwise, no processing difference would be expected between sentences like (6a) and (6b). In particular, the parser does not seem to wait until it encounters the disambiguating verb when making decisions about case assignment. Instead, decisions about case assignment seem to be made immediately when encountering NPs in need of case. Thus, decisions concerning case are on a par with attachment decisions as far as the incrementality of processing is concerned. Furthermore, the fact that accusative case is preferred to dative case shows that markedness relations within the case system govern initial parsing decisions. As outlined in the preceding section, accusative case as a structural case is the default case for an object whereas dative case is a lexical case which is dependent on a lexical licenser, i.e. a verb that subcategorizes for a dative object. Given this difference between accusative and dative case, it comes at no surprise that accusative case is preferred to dative case in a situation where the main verb has not yet been processed. The preferred case in such a situation is simply the default case, namely accusative.

Subject-object ambiguities

Pure case ambiguities are not confined to object-object ambiguities. Certain subject-object ambiguities are also pure case ambiguities. The existence of such ambiguities, namely subject-object ambiguities not involving phrase-structural differences between the SO- and OS-structure, is the reason for the second clause of the CPP. An example for an ambiguity which is both a subject-object ambiguity and a pure case ambiguity is given in (9). The embedded clause of (9a) is an active clause with *Maria* as subject and *das Buch* as accusative object. (9b), in contrast, contains an embedded passive clause with *Maria* as dative object and *das Buch* as subject. Since both *Maria* and *das Buch* are case-ambiguous NPs, the parser can determine the syntactic functions that these two NPs occupy in (9a) and (9b) only when it encounters the auxiliary in clause-final position.

(9) a. Ich glaube, daß Maria das Buch geliefert *hat.*
I believe that M. the book delivered has
"I believe that M. has delivered the book."

b. Ich glaube, daß Maria das Buch geliefert *wurde.*
I believe that M. the book delivered was
"I believe that the book was delivered to M."

Above we made the assumption that German clauses do not have an IP but simply consist of a VP dominated by a CP. For pairs of active-passive sentences like those in (9), this assumption has the consequence that an active sentence like (9a) does not differ phrase-structurally from a passive clause like

(9b). The shared phrase-structural representation is shown in (10).

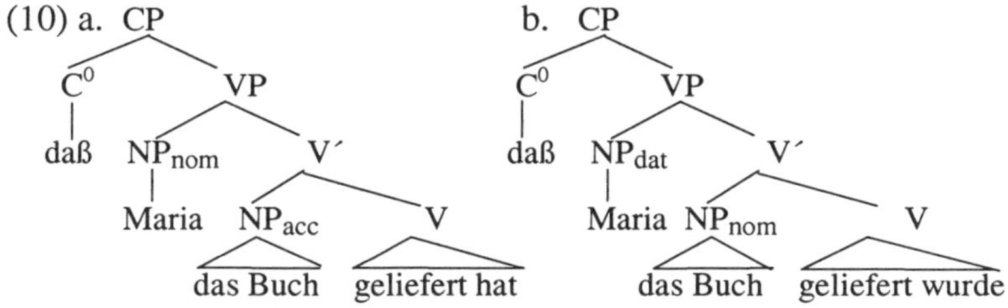

If the processing of such sentences is controlled by the Case Preference Principles in (8), the predictions are as follows: On first-pass parsing, the parser will assign nominative case to the first NP, *Maria*, and accusative case to the second NP, *das Buch*. If the sentence ends with the perfect auxiliary *hat*, nothing has to be changed and there should be no difference between ambiguous and unambiguous active clauses. If, in contrast, the sentence ends with the passive auxiliary *wurde*, the initial case assignment turns out to be false. The initial assignment of nominative case followed by accusative case has to be replaced by dative case followed by nominative case. Ambiguous passive clauses should therefore be at a disadvantage when compared to unambiguous passive clauses. These predictions have been confirmed in several experiments: Whereas ambiguous and unambiguous active clauses do not differ from each other, passive sentences elicit a garden-path effect in that ambiguous passive clauses are more difficult to comprehend than unambiguous passive clauses (see Bader, 1994, 1997).

To conclude this section, we have seen that garden-path effects can arise in the absence of phrase-structural differences between the alternative syntactic structures. This holds for the object-object ambiguity in (6) and the subject-object ambiguity in (9). In order to account for garden-path effects in pure case-ambiguities, we have invoked the Case Preference Principles which state that the parser prefers certain case assigments to others. The particular form of the CPP can be seen as a direct reflection of regularities inherent in the case system of German. Structural case is preferred to dative case, reflecting the distinction between marked and unmarked case assignment, and nominative case is preferred to accusative case, reflecting the dependence of an accusative object on the presence of a subject.

CASE ATTRACTION

The subject-object preference (SO-preference) found for the active-passive ambiguity was argued to follow from preferences on part of the parser with respect to case assignment. In particular, structural case is preferred to lexical case. In this section we will see that the SO-preference can turn into an OS-preference under highly specific circumstances, namely when an ambiguous noun attracts the case of a nearby case-marked element. The phenomenon of case attraction strengthens the point that the parser has access to syntactic features independently of the phrase-structural configurations of which these features are a part.

To introduce the phenomenon of case attraction, consider the sentences in (11) and (12). These sentences are identical to the sentences in (9), except that they contain a relative clause which modifies the case-ambiguous proper name. The relative clause in (11) is headed by the relative pronoun *die*. This relative pronoun is compatible with both structural cases, accusative and nominative case. In the particular example (11), *die* bears accusative case. The relative pronoun *der,* which heads the relative clause in (12), is unambiguously marked for dative case in (12).

(11) *Relative pronoun: structural case*

a. *Active*
Ich glaube, daß Maria, <u>die</u> ich vorhin getroffen
I believe that M. who I just met

habe, das Buch geliefert hat.
have the book delivered has

"I believe that Maria, who I have just met, has delivered the book."

b. *Passive*
Ich glaube, daß Maria, <u>die</u> ich vorhin getroffen
I believe that M. who I just met

habe, das Buch geliefert wurde.
have the book delivered was

"I believe that the book was delivered to Maria, who I have just met."

(12) *Relative pronoun: dative case*

a. *Active*
Ich glaube, daß Maria, <u>der</u> ich vorhin begegnet
I believe that M. who I just met

bin, das Buch geliefert hat.
am the book delivered has

"I believe that Maria, who I have just met, has delivered the book."

b. *Passive*
Ich glaube, daß Maria, der ich vorhin begegnet
I believe that M. who I just met

bin, das Buch geliefert wurde.
am the book delivered was

"I believe that the book was delivered to Maria, who I have just met."

Sentences like those in (11) and (12) have been investigated in a speeded grammaticality judgement experiment. The results can be summarized as follows (see Bader, 1997, for full discussion): For passive sentences, the presence of a relative clause has only minor consequences. When compared to passive sentences containing no relative clause, passive sentences containing a structural relative are slightly more difficult to process whereas sentences containing a dative relative pronoun are slightly easier. Active sentences containing a structural relative clause (11a) do not differ from active sentences without a relative clause (9a). A dative relative clause, however, strongly interferes with the processing of active sentences. Sentences like (12a) elicit a strong garden-path effect as reflected by a sharp decrease in the percentages of sentences judged as grammatical.

As several follow-up experiments have shown, the finding that the presence of a dative relative clause turns the usual SO-preference found in simple sentences into an OS-preference (which furthermore elicits a much stronger garden-path effect than the garden-path effect found in passive clauses containing a structural relative clause) is very robust (see Bader & Meng, 1998b). Given this finding, two things are in need of an explanation. How does the reversal of the SO-preference come about, and why is the garden-path effect found in active sentences like those in (12a) much stronger than the one in

(11b)? Our hypothesis is that the key to both questions can be found in the by now familiar distinction between structural and lexical case.

In the reminder of this section, we will concentrate on the first question and discuss the reversal of the SO-preference to an OS-preference under the influence of a dative relative clause. The basic idea is that this reversal reflects the attraction of the dative feature of the relative pronoun *der* by the ambiguous head noun *Maria*, similar to the attraction process that has been made responsible for number agreement errors in English, as outlined in the introduction. If the head noun *Maria* attracts the dative case of the relative pronoun, the whole NP turns into a dative marked NP. Consequently, the clause will receive an OS-structure. The first NP will be marked for dative by case attraction and the second NP marked for nominative, in accordance with the CPP. If the sentence ends with the auxiliary *hat* which requires an active structure with SO-order, a mismatch arises between the case features on the NPs and the subcategorization requirements of the verbal complex *geliefert hat*. The first NP is marked for dative case instead of nominative case, and the second NP is marked for nominative case instead of accusative case. This case mismatch will lead to the garden-path effect found in active sentences containing a relative clause.

Important in the context of the present discussion is the observation that the processes underlying case attraction are also sensitive to the relative markedness of features, on a par with what has been found for number attraction in English. In contrast to dative relative pronouns, structural relative pronouns do not seem to trigger case attraction. A first piece of evidence for this claim derives from the observation that there are no strong processing differences between simple passive clauses like (9b) and passive clauses like (11b) which contain a structural relative clause, a result which is in sharp contrast to the strong processing difference observed for the respective active sentences. The lack of a comparable processing effect for passive sentences can be explained under the hypothesis that case attraction is only induced by marked case features such as dative, but not by case features which are unmarked, such as nominative and accusative. In the absence of case attraction in (11b), there will be no syntactic difference between a simple proper name (as in (9b)) and a proper name modified by a structural relative clause besides the mere presence of the relative clause. The remaining slight differences between (9b) and (11b) can be traced back to the length difference between these two types of sentences, in accordance with other findings that lengthening an ambiguous region can increase the strength of a garden-path effect (see Frazier & Rayner, 1982; Ferreira & Henderson, 1991).

Furthermore, Bader & Meng (1998b) found that for sentences like (13) in which the proper name *Peter* precedes the relative pronoun *den* which is unambiguously marked for accusative case, the preference does not reverse. For sentences as in (13), no garden-path effect was observed, showing that the usual SO-preference persists in the presence of the accusative relative pronoun *den*.

(13) Ich glaube, daß Peter, <u>den</u> ich vorhin getroffen
I believe that P. who I just met

habe, das Buch geschickt hat.
have the book sent has

"I believe that Peter, who I have just met, has sent the book."

This finding clearly shows that case attraction does not apply across-the-board but is sensitive to markedness distinctions within the German case system. The results also suggest that markedness in this domain cannot be reduced to some superficial morphological factor, e.g. whether the relative pronoun is unambiguously case marked or not. Rather, markedness must be defined at a more abstract level by also taking into account syntactic and semantic differences between dative case on the one hand and nominative and accusative case on the other hand, as outlined above.

Summarizing this section, we have seen that the SO-preference found in simple active-passive pairs like (9) reverses to an OS-preference under the influence of a dative relative pronoun, resulting in a strong garden-path effect. This finding can be explained by the assumption that a dative case feature on a relative pronoun can be attracted by the head-noun of the relative clause. Case-attraction, which overrides the SO-preference found in simple sentences, shows quite clearly that case features must have a representation of their own within the phrase-structural representation computed by the parser. Furthermore, case attraction only occurs with dative relative pronouns but not with structural relative pronouns. This suggests that case attraction can only be induced by marked case features. In this respect, case attraction seems to be entirely parallel to number attraction in English which - as pointed out in the introduction - is confined to plural as the marked number feature in English. Therefore, the phenomenon of case attraction not only shows that case features play an essential role for human parsing processes but it also provides evidence for the more specific claim that markedness distinctions within the German case system are at work both within the competence grammar and within the parsing system.

GARDEN-PATH STRENGTH AND THE PROCESSING OF UNGRAMMATICAL SENTENCES

Up to this point, we have demonstrated how the assumptions adopted here with respect to the interplay of phrase-structural and case information can be used to account for a range of findings concerning first pass parsing, namely parsing preferences in pure-case ambiguities and the OS-preference which shows up under the influence of a dative relative clause. As we will now show, the same assumptions also provide a basis for deriving second-pass parsing effects, in particular the difference in garden-path strength between active sentences containing a dative relative clause and passive sentences. As pointed out when discussing the examples in (11) and (12), passive sentences only lead to slight garden-path effects, whether they contain a relative clause or not. In contrast, active sentences containing a dative relative clause do elicit a rather strong garden-path effect. How can this striking difference in garden-path strength be accounted for? For reasons of space, the following discussion will only consider (some variants of) serial models of the human parser (see Frazier, 1978). A discussion of alternative models, like the minimal commitment model of Weinberg (1993) or the parallel model of Gibson (1991) can be found in Bader & Meng (1998a).

In a serial parsing model, the general explanation for garden-path effects runs as follows: At the point of ambiguity, the parser selects a single preferred structure. At the point of disambiguation, a mismatch, that is, a temporary ungrammaticality, arises if the sentence is disambiguated in favor of the unpreferred continuation. This mismatch triggers a process of re-analysis during which the parser tries to replace the initial, incorrect structure by a correct structure. It is the need for the additional process of re-analysis which is responsible for the emergence of garden-path effects. Furthermore, differences in garden-path strength have been interpreted as reflecting the ease with which a given re-analysis can be carried out.

As argued in detail in Bader & Meng (1998a), the difference in garden-path strength between active sentences containing a dative relative clause and passive sentences is difficult to explain within current serial models of syntactic ambiguity resolution. Given our syntactic assumption that active and passive sentences do not differ phrase structurally, the main problem that our examples raise for current serial models is that neither in the active garden-path sentence nor in the passive garden-path sentence does re-analysis require any change to the phrase structural representation computed up to the point of disambiguation, leaving these models with no basis for deriving why re-analysis should be of different ease.

Our proposal is that it is possible for serial models to account for why active sentences like (12a) lead to stronger garden-path effects than passive-sentences like (11b) if the way garden-path effects are explained within serial models is extended. The basic idea is that the strength of a given garden-path effect is determined not only by the processes that follow the detection of a temporary mismatch but also by processes associated with the detection of the mismatch itself. In principle, after having detected a mismatch, the parser has two options: either it tries to re-analyse the initial syntactic representation or it simply assumes that the current input sentence is defective, that is, ungrammatical. If, for a particular syntactic ambiguity, the latter option is taken, a strong garden-path effect will emerge, as reflected, for example, in a sharp decrease in accuracy in a speeded-grammaticality judgement experiment. Put in a different way, we assume that within serial parsing models, strong garden-path may not only arise in cases where re-analysis is effortful and therefore difficult to achieve, however difficulty in this sense is defined. Under our hypothesis a strong garden-path effect may so result in cases where re-analysis would be quite easy to achieve, but where the parser does not even attempt re-analysis or stops re-analysis at a very early point and therefore erroneously abandons the structure as ungrammatical.

According to Bader & Meng (1998a), one factor determining the choice between trying to complete re-analysis or abandoning the sentence as ungrammatical before re-analysis has been completed pertains to the salience of the temporary syntactic mismatch that signals the garden-path. Operationally, we consider a syntactic mismatch as salient if sentences that exhibit this mismatch in a permanent way are judged as ungrammatical with high accuracy. The sentences in (14a) and (14b) contain the same kind of syntactic mismatch as the active garden-path sentence (12a) and the passive garden path sentence (11b), respectively. In both (14a) and (12a), the initial NP is marked for dative case instead of nominative case, the difference being that *der Frau* in (14a) is morphologically unambiguous whereas *Maria* in (12a) is marked for dative case only by case attraction. In (14b) as well as in (11b), the first NP is marked for nominative case instead of dative case. Here, the difference is that *die Frau* in (14b) is morphologically incompatible with dative case whereas *Maria* in (11b) is morphologically ambiguous and has acquired its nominative feature only by the CPP.

(14) a.* daß der Frau das Buch rechtzeitig geliefert hat.
that the woman the book on time delivered has

b.* daß die Frau das Buch rechtzeitig geliefert wurde.
that the woman the book on time delivered was

Experiments using the method of speeded-grammaticality judgements have shown that ungrammaticalities of the kind exhibited by (14a) are judged as ungrammatical with high accuracy whereas ungrammaticalities of the sort in (14b) are often erroneously classified as grammatical. In short, (14a) is an instance of a salient ungrammaticality, whereas (14b) is not salient. Given that the permanent ungrammaticalities in (14a) and (14b) correspond to the temporary ones in (12a) and (11b), we can observe what we will call the *Mismatch Effect*: A strong garden-path effect is associated with a salient syntactic mismatch at the point of disambiguation, whereas a weak garden-path effect is associated with a non-salient syntactic mismatch. Combined with the above extension of the serial model of syntactic ambiguity resolution, our claim is that salient ungrammaticalities may cause the parser to abandon an ambiguous sentences as ungrammatical without attempts to complete re-analysis. If this is correct, we can hypothesize that active sentences containing a dative relative clause elicit a strong garden-path effect because - due to the salient syntactic mismatch - the parser will often assume that the sentence is defective. Passive sentences, in contrast, contain only a non-salient ungrammaticality, one which does not lead the parser to stop re-analysis at an early point and to abandon the structure. Consequently, re-analysis - which turns out to be easy - will be completed successfully.

To conclude the argument, we have to ask why the ungrammaticality in (14a) is a salient one, whereas the one in (14b) is not. This brings us back to the main theme of this paper, namely the role of syntactic features for processes of syntactic ambiguity resolution and the impact of the markedness of features. Note that the ungrammaticality in (14a) involves the assignment of a structural case to a dative-marked NP. In (14b), the reverse situation is found. Dative case is assigned to an NP which is only compatible with structural case. Thus we again seem to have a situation where a marked syntactic feature can erroneously override an unmarked one, but not vice versa, similar to what we found for case attraction in German and what has been reported for number attraction in English. Dative as the marked feature can override the unmarked feature for structural case, but unmarked structural case features cannot override the marked feature for dative. The parser tends to overlook the ungrammaticality of (14a), whereas for sentences like (14b), the ungrammaticality is detected more reliably since the parser receives a clear error signal. However, for the garden path sentence (12a) which corresponds to (14b) as far as the type of syntactic mismatch is concerned, the clear error signal that the parser receives at the point of disambiguation has the effect that re-analysis is not pursued any further. The sentence is erroneously judged as ungrammatical because the parser does not consider the option that structural case overrides dative case a legitimate move. Consequently, re-analysis is not pursued any further although it would be possible. No such problems arise in garden-path sentences like (11b) which corresponds to (14a). There is nothing that would block re-analysis which therefore can be completed successfully, leading to a correct, albeit slowed, response in the speeded grammaticality judgement task.

NUMBER FEATURES AND THE PROCESSING OF FILLER-GAP AMBIGUITIES

In this section, we will turn to processing effects that can be related to different properties of structural case features on the one hand and number features on the other hand. The discussion will center around subject-object ambiguities in German that involve ambiguous filler-gap relationships. A typical example is given in (15). In (15a), the ambiguous wh-phrase *welche Tante* is the subject because the second NP is unambiguously marked for accusative case and therefore can only be the object. In (15b), in contrast, the second NP is the subject because it is unambiguously marked for nominative case. The initial wh-phrase therefore is the object.

(15) a. Welche Tante hat *t* den Neffen besucht?
which aunt has the-ACC nephew visited
„Which aunt visited the nephew?"

b. Welche Tante hat der Neffe *t* besucht?
which aunt has the-NOM nephew visited?
„Which aunt did the nephew visit?"

Filler-gap ambiguities have already received quite a lot of attention in the psycholinguistic literature, mainly with respect to the question of which word-order is preferred on first-pass parsing. Research on filler-gap ambiguities in German has converged on the conclusion that the SO-order is preferred. This SO-preference manifests itself in a garden-path effect in sentences like (15b) where the second NP disambiguates in favor of the unpreferred OS-structure. Such an SO-preference has not only been found in main clause questions, but also in embedded questions, in main-clause as well as embedded declaratives, and in relative clauses (e.g., Hemforth, 1993; Bader & Meng, in press; Schriefers, Friederici & Kühn, 1995).

SO- and OS-sentences like those in (15a) and (15b) differ with respect to their phrase-structural representation. It is therefore possible to explain the SO-preference found in filler-gap ambiguities with recourse to purely phrase-structural principles. For example, the Minimal Chain Principle of DeVincenzi (1991), which is given in (16), correctly predicts an SO-preference across all kinds of filler-gap ambiguities (see Gorrell, 1996, and Schlesewsky, Fanselow, Kliegl, & Krems, 1996, for alternative phrase-structural accounts).

(16) *Minimal Chain Principle (MCP)*
Avoid postulating unnecessary chain members at S-structure, but do not delay required chain members.

An alternative to a phrase-structure based principle like the MCP is provided by the CPP. According to the second clause of the CPP, nominative case is preferred to accusative case. This also predicts a general SO-preference in filler-gap ambiguities of the kind exemplified by (15).

In what follows, we will concentrate on some recent findings concerning garden-path strength in filler-gap ambiguities. It has been shown in a series of both self-paced reading and speeded grammaticality judgement experiments that garden-path strength in filler-gap ambiguities is dependent on how sentences are disambiguated (see Meng, 1997; Meng & Bader, 1998; Schlesewsky et al., 1996). One kind of disambiguation has already been shown in (15). In (15), disambiguation is achieved by the case-marking on the second NP. We will call this kind of disambiguation disambiguation by case. A second kind of disambiguation is exhibited by (17). As in (15), the first NP in (17) is ambiguous between nominative and accusative case. However, in contrast to (15), the second NP in (17) is a plural NP. Therefore in (17), the SO-order is ruled out already at the finite verb (the auxiliary) due to the fact that obligatory number agreement between subject and verb fails. We will call the disambiguation in (17) disambiguation by agreement.

(17) a. Welche Tante hat *t* die Neffen besucht?
which aunt-SG has-SG the nephews visited
„Which aunt visited the nephews?"

b. Welche Tante haben die Neffen *t* besucht?
which aunt-SG have-PL the nephews visited?
„Which aunt did the nephew visit?"

OS-sentences lead to garden-path effects independent of whether they are disambiguated by case or by agreement. However, disambiguation by agreement consistently leads to stronger garden-path effects than disambiguation by case. As the studies referred to above have shown, this contrast does not only hold for matrix Wh-questions as in (15) and (17) but also for embedded wh-questions and long extraction from complement clauses.

How can this difference in garden-path strength be accounted for? First of all note that the contrast between (15) and (17) is quite unexpected given that disambiguation in the easy garden-path sentence occurs at a later point than in the strong garden-path sentence. This contrast is therefore not amenable to parsing principles like the Late Revisions Principle of Frazier (1990) which has been proposed to hold for certain other kinds of syntactic ambiguity.

(18) *Late Revisions Principle*
Confirmed processing decisions take longer to revise than unconfirmed ones.

However, if we approach the problem of garden-path strength from the same perspective as we did in the preceding section, a solution will emerge that again underlines the importance of syntactic features for garden-path phenomena. Consider first the ungrammatical sentences in (19). (19a) contains the same kind of ungrammaticality as (15b) albeit in a permanent way. In both (19a) and (15b) the mismatch consists of the fact that the sentence contains two nominative marked NPs. Due to the morphological ambiguity of *welche Frau,* the mismatch in (15b) can be cured. The NP *welcher Onkel* in (19a), in contrast, is unambiguously marked for nominative and therefore the sentence contains a permanent ungrammaticality. (19b) and (17b) both contain an agreement mismatch because the first NP is nominative marked but does not agree with the finite verb. As before, the agreement violation in (19b) is permanent due to unambiguous nominative marking on the wh-phrase whereas the violation in (17b) can be cured.

(19) a.* Welcher Onkel hat der Neffe *t* besucht?
which uncle-NOM has the-NOM nephew visited?

b.* Welcher Onkel haben die Neffen *t* besucht?
which uncle-SG have-PL the nephews visited?

In several speeded grammaticality judgement experiments, Meng (1997) has shown that ungrammatical sentences like (19b) are judged as ungrammatical with higher accuracy than ungrammatical sentences like (19a) which elicit a high percentage of incorrect responses (see also Bader & Meng, 1998a). (19b) is a salient ungrammaticality whereas (19a) is not. Thus, we again find the pattern described by the Mismatch-Effect: A salient ungrammaticality is associated with a strong garden-path effect whereas a non-salient ungrammaticality is associated with a weaker garden-path effect. As before, we assume that this correlation follows from the assumption that the type of syntactic mismatch underlying a salient ungrammaticality can cause the parser to abandon processing and to classify the ambiguous sentence as ungrammatical.

We want to propose that the difference between (19a) and (19b) with respect to the salience of the respective ungrammaticality again finds an explanation in terms of the syntactic features that are involved in these ungrammaticalities. Note that nominative case is assigned by default to the first NP of a clause if there is no contradictory morphological information. If the parser then receives a second NP morphologically marked for nominative, as in (19a), the first NP cannot be nominative as well. The parser must decide whether to replace the case feature on the first NP or whether to judge that the sentence is truly ungrammatical. As shown by the poor performance on sentences like (19a), the parser often replaces the nominative feature without making sure that this is morphologically licit. Evidence for the claim that the case feature on the first NP is changed comes from a speeded-grammaticality judgments experiment in which subjects had to repeat each sentence after having judged its grammaticality. If sentences like (19a) are incorrectly judged as grammatical, subjects predominantly change the first NP to an accusative NP. For example, *welcher Onkel* (nominative) in (19a) would be replaced by *welchen Onkel* (accusative) in the repetition that subjects are forced to produce.

Let us now briefly turn to (19b). When the parser receives the finite auxiliary and checks for subject-verb agreement, it will notice that the first NP is singular but the auxiliary is plural. In this case, the parser cannot simply change the singular feature on the first NP because number features in German are not assigned by default. Number features are an integral part of the lexical representation of a word. Therefore, they are supplied by the lexical system. Note finally that number features share certain properties with features marking dative case: As dative case, agreement features must have a morphological spell-out and are tied to a specific semantic interpretation. It is therefore not surprising that - as far as processing consequences in the domains considered here are concerned - agreement features pattern with dative case rather than with nominative and accusative case.

CONCLUSION

In this paper we have reviewed some recent experimental findings which show that syntactic features play an essential role for the processing of subject-object and object-object ambiguities in German. Evidence for the parser's sensitivity to case and agreement features comes from three domains: preferences in first-pass parsing, case-attraction phenomena, and variation in garden-path strength. In all three domains, parsing decisions seem to be governed by the distinction between marked and unmarked features. Several factors (syntactic, morphological, and semantic) were pointed out which may contribute to this distinction. The relative weight of these factors remains to be specified by future research.

NOTES

[1] We would like to thank Josef Bayer, Janet D. Fodor, Paul Gorrell and the audience at AMLaP-96 for discussion and helpful comments.

REFERENCES

Bader, M. (1994). *Sprachverstehen: Syntax und Prosodie beim Lesen.* Doctoral dissertation, University of Stuttgart.

Bader, M. (1997). Syntactic and morphological contributions to processing subject-object ambiguities. Manuscript submitted for publication.

Bader, M., Bayer, J., Hopf, J.-M., & Meng, M. (1996). Case-Assignment in processing German verb-final clauses. In *Proceeding of the NELS 26 Workshop on Sentence Processing*, MIT Occasional Papers in Linguistics, Vol. 9, pp. 1-25.

Bader, M., & Meng, M. (in press). Subject-object ambiguities in German embedded clauses: An across-the-board comparison. *Journal of Psycholinguistic Research.*

Bader, M., & Meng, M. (1998a) Ungrammaticality detection and garden-path strength. Manuscript in preparation, University of Jena.

Bader, M., & Meng, M. (1998b) Case-attraction phenomena in German. Manuscript in preparation, University of Jena.

Bock, K., & Cutting J. C. (1992). Regulating mental energy: Performance units in language production. *Journal of Memory and Language, 31*, 99-127.

Bock, K., & Miller, C. A. (1991). Broken agreement. *Cognitive Psychology, 23*, 45-93.

DeVincenzi, M. (1991). *Syntactic parsing strategies in Italian*. Dordrecht: Kluwer.

Eberhard, K.M. (1997). The marked effect of number on subject-verb agreement. *Journal of Memory and Language, 36*, 147-164.

Ferreira, F., & Henderson, J.M. (1991). Recovery from misanalysis of garden-path sentences. *Journal of Memory and Language, 30*, 725-745.

Fodor, J.D., & A. Inoue (1994). The diagnosis and cure of garden-paths. *Journal of Psycholinguistic Research, 23*, 407-434.

Frazier, L. (1978). *On comprehending sentences: Syntactic parsing strategies.* Unpublished doctoral dissertation, University of Connecticut, Storrs.

Frazier, L. (1990). Exploring the architecture of the language-processing system. In G. Altmann (Ed.), *Cognitive models of speech processing. Psycholinguistic and computational perspectives*, pp. 409-433. Cambridge, MA: MIT Press.

Frazier, L., & Rayner, K. (1982). Making and correcting errors during sentence comprehension: Eye movements in the analysis of structurally ambiguous sentences. *Cognitive Psychology, 14*, 178-210.

Gibson, E. (1991). *A computational theory of human linguistic processing.* Unpublished doctoral dissertation, Carnegie Mellon University, Pittsburgh, Pennsylvania.

Gorrell, Paul (1996). Parsing theory and phrase-order variation in German V2 clauses. *Journal of Psycholinguistic Research, 25*, 135-156.

Haider, H. (1993). *Deutsche Syntax - generativ. Vorstudien zu einer projektiven Theorie der Grammatik.* Tübingen: Narr.

Haider, H. (1997). Projective economy. In F.-J. d'Avis & U. Lutz (Eds.), *Zur Satzstruktur im Deutschen*, pp. 31-54. Working Papers of the SFB 340, No. 90, University of Stuttgart.

Hemforth, B. (1993). *Kognitives Parsing: Repräsentation und Verarbeitung grammatischen Wissens.* Sankt Augustin: Infix Verlag.

Hopf J.-M., Bayer J., Bader, M., & Meng, M. (1998) Event-related brain potentials and case information in syntactic ambiguities. *Journal of Cognitive Neuroscience, 10*, 264-280.

Meng, M. (1997). *Grammatik und Sprachverarbeitung: Psycholinguistische Untersuchungen zur Berechnung syntaktischer Strukturen.* Doctoral dissertation, University of Jena.

Meng, M., & Bader, M. (1998). Mode of disambiguation and garden-path strength: An investigation of subject-object ambiguities in German. Manuscript submitted for publication.

Nicol, J.L., Forster, K.I., & Veres, C. (1997). Subject-verb agreement processes in comprehension. *Journal of Memory and Language, 36*, 569-587.

Reuland, E., & Kosmeijer, W. (1993). Projecting inflected verbs. In Fanselow, G. (Ed.), *The parameterization of Universal Grammar*, pp. 37-71. Amsterdam: John Benjamins.

Schlesewsky, M., Fanselow, G., Kliegl, R., & Krems, J. (1996). Preferences for grammatical functions in the processing of locally ambiguous wh-questions in German. To appear in B. Hemforth, & L. Konieczny (Eds), *Cognitive parsing in German.*

Schriefers, H., Friederici, A.D., & Kühn, K. (1995). The processing of locally ambiguous relative clauses in German. *Journal of Memory and Language, 34*, 499-520.

Vikner, S. (1995). *Verb movement and expletive subjects in the Germanic Languages*. Oxford: Oxford University Press.

Wegener, Heide (1985). *Der Dativ im heutigen Deutsch*. Tübingen: Narr Verlag.

Weinberg, A. (1993). Parameters in the theory of sentence processing: Minimal commitment theory goes east. *Journal of Psycholinguistic Research, 22*, 338-364.

Holly P. Branigan and Mercè Prat-Sala

A CROSS-LINGUISTIC PERSPECTIVE ON DISCOURSE CONTEXT AND SYNTACTIC PROCESSING IN LANGUAGE PRODUCTION

INTRODUCTION

Communication is a co-operative process. The speaker's purpose is to convey some information to the listener. The listener's task is to extract this information and integrate it with existing knowledge. Although considerable progress has been made in studying the listener and the mechanisms responsible for information extraction and integration, much less is known about the mechanisms which underlie the speaker's production of language. In particular, much of the existing evidence is limited to the production of isolated sentences. This chapter is, like Heydel and Murray's chapter (this volume), concerned with the way in which previous context can affect syntactic processing during cross-linguistic language production. Our particular focus is on the relationship between features of the discourse context and the syntactic structure that a speaker assigns to a sentence. We will be especially concerned with the relationship between pragmatic theories and processing theories, and whether processing mechanisms which have been proposed for the production of isolated sentences can also account for context effects in production.

Linguistic theories of pragmatics have long argued that different discourse contexts are associated with systematic variations in syntactic structure. These variations have been

M. De Vincenzi and V. Lombardo (eds.), Cross-linguistic Perspectives on Language Processing, 205–226.

linked to two factors: *referential status* and *information structure*. Referential status relates to an entity's status within a participant's *discourse model*, or mental representation of the entities involved in the current discourse, together with the attributes and links of these entities (Kintsch & van Dijk, 1978; Sanford & Garrod, 1981; Heim, 1983; Webber, 1983). Thus entities differ in referential status depending on whether, for example, they have been previously introduced in the discourse, they are new to the discourse, they are inferable, and so on (e.g., Prince, 1981,1992). Differences in referential status have been associated with the syntactic structure of referring expressions (Ariel, 1990). *Information structure* concerns the way in which information is articulated within a sentence. Thus some of the information conveyed in a sentence will be more informative for the listener than other information (Halliday, 1967; Dahl, 1974; Li & Thompson, 1976; Chafe, 1976; Sgall *et al.*, 1986). The exact terminology used to refer to this information structure varies between theories (e.g., *theme-rheme*, *topic-comment*, *given-new*, *topic-focus*). Variations in information structure have been claimed to impact upon the syntactic structure of a sentence, more specifically the relative ordering of constituents (e.g., Halliday, 1967; Sgall *et al.*, 1986). For example, Sgall *et al.* (1986) proposed the notion of communicative dynamism (CD), under which the elements of the sentence can be ranked in a continuum which is determined by their relative communicative values. The left-to-right linear order of words in a sentence reflects communicative value: the less communicative elements tend to appear at the beginning of the sentence and the more communicative elements at the end of the sentence. Such an ordering has been claimed to be language-universal (Clark & Clark, 1978).[1]

Pragmatic theories are essentially concerned with declarative characterisations of patterns of data. However, the data which they aim to characterise are the sentences which people produce and comprehend. Hence we would expect that the distinctions which they make and the regularities which they discover can be associated with psychological processes. Many experimental studies of language comprehension have demonstrated that the distinctions outlined above are indeed important (e.g. Haviland and Clark, 1974; Clark & Haviland, 1977; Sanford & Garrod, 1981). For example, Sanford and Garrod (1981) found evidence that reference resolution is faster for some entities in the discourse model than for others. They suggested that in a discourse model, some entities are more foregrounded or salient than others, and that at any given point only a certain number of entities are foregrounded and hence available for reference. This is in keeping with the idea that entities have different referential statuses. Processing models of comprehension have also suggested a functional explanation for the relative ordering of less informative elements before more informative elements: the less informative elements usually specify an address to which the more informative elements should be attached. Thus the less informative elements appear first, to allow the listener to access the appropriate address in memory for subsequent update (Clark & Clark, 1978).

There has been much less study of the relationship between discourse context and language production. Discourse context should nevertheless be equally likely to affect production as comprehension. Listeners can exploit cues such as word order and syntactic structure during the task of information extraction and integration only if speakers co-operatively provide them in the sentences which they produce. Perhaps more importantly, the processes by which the speaker retrieves and assembles information during production may themselves be affected by previous discourse. In the remainder of this paper, we examine how prior discourse context affects language production. In particular, we examine the relationship between the referential status of entities and the syntactic structure of a subsequently produced sentence. We begin by reviewing cross-linguistic evidence that non-linguistic factors may affect syntactic processing in isolated sentences. We also review the limited evidence from English that some aspects of discourse context may affect syntactic processing of sentences embedded within a discourse. We then discuss new cross-linguistic evidence from three languages that one particular contextual factor, discourse salience, can affect the realisation of different syntactic structures during production. We suggest that these effects can be explained in the same way as other non-linguistic influences on syntactic structure. Finally, we discuss how cross-linguistic differences in the realisation of discourse effects can be captured within a single processing architecture.

NON-LINGUISTIC AND CONTEXTUAL INFLUENCES ON SYNTACTIC PROCESSING

The syntax of a language can be regarded as the system that allows the conversion of a multidimensional thought into a linearly ordered sequence of words. Current models of language production distinguish between three levels of processing: message generation, linguistic encoding (which includes the assignment of grammatical functions, the determination of word order and phonological encoding), and articulation (e.g., Garrett, 1975; Bock, 1987; Bock & Levelt, 1994). These three levels account for the translation of a message in the speaker's mind into a syntactically and semantically well-formed sentence which is articulated with an appropriate prosodic contour.

There is substantial experimental evidence that non-linguistic factors can affect the processes of linguistic encoding, and specifically syntactic processing. A number of studies have shown that differences in the predicability, animacy, imageability, concreteness or prototypicality of different entities are systematically associated with variations in syntactic structure (Clark, 1965; Clark & Begun, 1971; Osgood & Bock, 1977; Harris, 1978; Bock & Warren, 1985; Kelly *et al.*, 1986; Mcdonald *et al.*, 1993). Words that are animate or more predicable, imageable, concrete or prototypical typically appear in more prominent syntactic positions. Bock (1987) suggested that these apparently disparate influences can be brought together under a common heading of conceptual accessibility. Conceptually more accessible words are those whose referents are more easily activated in, or retrieved from, memory. Bock suggested that the lemmas (semantic/syntactic content of lexical entries) (Kempen & Huijbers, 1983) associated with conceptually more accessible words are retrieved more quickly from the mental lexicon. Under the assumption that language production is incremental, as a means of promoting fluency (Kempen & Hoenkamp, 1987), this means that they will have priority during syntactic structure generation, and hence will tend to appear in prominent syntactic positions. We will return in the final section to the syntactic mechanisms which underlie these effects.

The precise syntactic manifestation of this prominence differs from language to language. For example, sentence recall and picture description experiments have shown that conceptual accessibility (indexed by concreteness and animacy) is associated with the production of active and passive sentences in English and German (Bock & Warren, 1985; Mcdonald *et al.*, 1993; Teufel *et al.*, 1996); canonical actives, passives and dislocated actives in Catalan and Spanish (Prat-Sala, 1997) (although there may also be an effect of lexical accessibility); and canonical actives and topicalised actives in Greek (Feleki & Branigan, 1997).

Thus there is substantial cross-linguistic evidence that at least some non-linguistic factors can affect syntactic processing in the production of isolated sentences. Entities which are conceptually more accessible, as indexed by one or a combination of these factors, tend to appear in syntactically more prominent positions. We now turn to discourse context, and the evidence that it too can influence syntactic processing in production. Until recently, this evidence has been limited to written language production in English. Using a written recall task, Bock (1977) examined the relationship between Given and New information in the production of different syntactic structures in English. The sentences to be recalled were prompted by a question. For example the question in (1) was used to prompt recall of the active sentence in (2a) or the passive sentence in (2b) (Bock (1977) used ten different syntactic structures). In this particular example, the NP *a psychologist* is mentioned in both answer sentences. However the Given-New structure is only preserved in (2a); in (2b), New information precedes Given information. Thus (2a) is an appropriate answer to (1) but (2b) is an inappropriate answer.

(1) A psychologist acquired fame and fortune after his appearance on the Tonight Show with Johnny Carson. What happened?

(2a) A psychologist cured a neurotic poodle.

(2b) A neurotic poodle was cured by a psychologist.

Participants tended to recall answer sentences in the form that preserved the Given-New ordering which pragmatic theories identify as the favoured ordering, even when this necessitated altering the syntactic structure of the sentence (e.g. from an active to a passive or vice versa). Bock concluded that speakers use alternative syntactic structures in order to place Given information earlier in sentences than New information. She suggested that this Given-New ordering might reflect lexical priming, with a lexical expression in the question priming a lexical expression in the answer.

In subsequent experiments, Bock and Irwin (1980) used the same recall task to distinguish between effects resulting from referential availability, where preceding context provides a referent, and those resulting from lexical availability, where preceding context provides a lexical expression. They presented participants with questions containing a word that was either both lexically and referentially related, or only referentially related, to a word appearing in the answer. For example in (2a-b) above, the words might be *poodle* (lexically and referentially related) and *dog* (referentially related). The answer could be either an appropriate answer to the question (preserving the Given-New structure) or an inappropriate answer to the question (not preserving the Given-New structure).

The results showed that both lexical and referential availability affected the production of syntactic structure. Again, participants tended to recall a sentence in whichever form preserved the Given-New structure. These effects were stronger when a word mentioned in the question was lexically identical to a word in the answer than when it was coreferential but not identical. Bock and Irwin's results suggest that both lexical and referential availability contribute to the preference for Given-New ordering.

These experiments suggest that discourse context can influence syntactic processing in written language production. Speakers prefer to place an entity which has been made referentially or lexically available in a preceding linguistic context (here, question) before an entity which has not been previously introduced. Bock suggested that this tendency results from two aspects of information retrieval: the conceptual content of Given information is more easily retrieved than that of New information; and the lexical content associated with Given information may have been primed by the previous context and hence be more easily retrieved. Because production is incremental, such that information which is retrieved first is also output first (all other things being equal), both factors favour Given information to be produced preceding New information.

Many questions about the possible influence of discourse on language production remain, however. One important issue is whether the same influences operate on other languages. Pragmatic theories have observed Given-New ordering for many languages, and suggest that it may be a language universal. If we ascribe this ordering at least in part to processing constraints upon the speaker, we would expect to find evidence for the same or related effects in other languages. A second question is whether the only discourse influences on production are those that can be captured using a binary Given/New distinction. Recent pragmatic theories argue against a binary articulation of referential status (Prince, 1981; Sgall *et al.*, 1986), with empirical support from studies of language comprehension (Sanford & Garrod, 1981). A third question concerns how discourse influences are realised cross-linguistically. As we saw above, other non-linguistic factors have been shown to have different syntactic manifestations in different languages.

DISCOURSE SALIENCE AND SYNTACTIC PROCESSING

These issues were explored in a series of experiments by Prat-Sala and Branigan (1998) (see also Prat-Sala, 1997). They examined how the relative salience of entities in a discourse affects syntactic processing in production. Following Sanford and Garrod's (1981) proposals for comprehension, they suggested that not all entities encoded in the discourse model (i.e. Given) are equally accessible: entities which are salient (or foregrounded) are more accessible than less salient entities. They hypothesised that this difference would be reflected in the syntactic structure which a speaker assigned to a subsequent sentence. Specifically, an entity which had been made salient by previous discourse would have priority in syntactic encoding over an entity which had also been previously introduced, but which had not been made salient. They predicted that these effects would not be restricted to English, but would also be found for other languages.

These predictions were tested experimentally in three languages (English, Catalan and Spanish). Participants listened to short stories and then immediately afterwards orally described a picture. In the first three experiments, the picture depicted a transitive action involving an inanimate agent and an animate patient. The short stories were constructed in such a way that they mentioned both entities, but made one of the entities in the picture more salient or foregrounded. Each story ended with the open question *What happened?* For example, if the picture depicted the action of a swing hitting a man, the story could make salient either the inanimate agent (here, the swing), as in (3), or the animate patient (here, the man), as in (4). However, the target picture was the same for both stories.

(3) There was this old rusty swing standing in a playground near a man, swaying and creaking in the wind. What happened? (Inanimate-agent salient)

(4) There was this little old man standing in a playground near a swing, going for a walk after a very tiring day at work. What happened? (Animate-patient salient)

The results showed a relationship between salience and the syntactic structure of the picture description in all three languages. Participants tended to produce a syntactic structure that allowed them to produce the salient entity earlier in the sentence than the less salient entity. They produced active descriptions (e.g. *The swing hit the man*) more often when the agent was made salient than when the patient was made salient. Conversely, they produced more passive descriptions (e.g. *The man was hit by the swing*) when the patient was made salient than when the agent was made salient. Additionally, Catalan and Spanish participants produced dislocated active description (e.g. *A un home l'ha colpejat un gronxador*, 'A man, a swing has hit him') more frequently following patient-salient stories than following an agent-salient stories. In this latter case, the salient entity appeared as a sentence-initial direct object and the non-salient entity as a post-verbal subject. This latter finding shows clearly that discourse salience affected the production of word order, and not simply which entity became the subject of the sentence. Table 1 shows the percentages of each type of sentence produced in each condition.

	Inanimate Agent Salient			Animate Patient Salient		
	Act	Pass	Disloc	Act	Pass	Disloc
English	87.0%	13.0%	N/A	48.0%	52.0%	N/A
Catalan	96.5%	2.0%	1.5%	60.5%	23.0%	16.5%
Spanish	96.0%	2.5%	1.5%	51.5%	26.0%	22.5%

Table 1: Percentage of responses by scoring category (Inanimate agent/animate patient)

Note that the influence of discourse salience in these experiments overrode another potential influence on syntactic structure, that of animacy. In previous experiments studying the production of isolated sentences, Prat-Sala (1997) found that pictures involving inanimate agents and animate patients tended to induce passive descriptions in the same three languages. Here, when the inanimate agent was salient, participants overwhelmingly produced active descriptions. Hence discourse salience appears to impose a strong influence on syntactic processing.

In subsequent experiments, Prat-Sala and Branigan examined whether discourse salience alone could induce variations in word order. We noted above that animacy independently influences syntactic processing in production, in particular the production of passive clauses (McDonald *et al.*, 1993; Prat-Sala, 1997). The experiments discussed above found that participants tended to produce more passive clauses when an animate patient was made salient than when an inanimate agent was made salient. Hence, two features were confounded: animacy and salience. Thus while the results show that discourse salience influences syntactic processing, they do not show that discourse salience alone can induce variations in syntactic structure.

The subsequent experiments therefore employed the same experimental method, but with pictures which depicted two inanimate entities. Again, the preceding short story made either the (inanimate) agent or the (inanimate) patient more salient. For example, if the picture depicted a swing hitting a scooter, the agent-salient story would be (5) and the patient-salient story would be (6).

(5) There was this old rusty swing standing in a playground near a scooter, swaying and creaking in the wind. What happened?

(6) There was this old red scooter standing in a playground near a swing, with rusty wheels and scratched paint. What happened?

Again, the results showed a relationship between salience and syntactic structure. In all three languages, participants tended to produce a syntactic structure that allowed them to produce the salient entity earlier than the less salient entity. Active descriptions were more frequent following agent-salient stories, whilst passive descriptions were more frequent following patient-salient stories. Additionally, Catalan and Spanish participants produced more dislocated active descriptions when the patient was made salient than when the agent was made salient. Table 2 shows the percentages of each type of syntactic structure produced in each condition.

	Inanimate Agent Salient			Animate Patient Salient		
	Act	Pass	Disloc	Act	Pass	Disloc
English	90.0%	10.0%	N/A	72.5%	27.5%	N/A
Catalan	100.0%	0.0%	0.0%	75.5%	20.0%	4.5%
Spanish	99.5%	0.5%	0.0%	83.5%	12.0%	4.5%

Table 2: Percentage of responses by scoring category (Inanimate agent/patient)

These results suggest that variations in the discourse salience of different entities can alone induce variations in syntactic structure, independent of other non-linguistic factors.

The results of these experiments clearly demonstrate a cross-linguistic influence of salience upon syntactic processing in spoken language production. In all three languages, the type of syntactic structure which participants produced to describe a picture varied systematically according to variations in the salience of one of the entities depicted in the picture. More specifically, participants produced syntactic structures that allowed them to produce a more salient entity earlier in the sentence than a less salient entity.

Prat-Sala and Branigan therefore concluded that discourse context affects language production not only in English, but also in other languages. They further concluded that the influence of discourse does not reduce to a simple distinction between entities which are Given within a discourse and those which are

New. Instead, the relative salience of entities within a discourse (with Given and New as areas on a continuum) affects syntactic processing. They also concluded that discourse context does not only affect the production of actives and passives; in languages which have more flexible word order possibilities, discourse salience may also be associated with variations in word order.

Thus we can conclude that discourse context exerts a cross-linguistic influence on syntactic processing in spoken language production. The resulting tendency for more salient information to precede less salient information reflects the ordering preferences observed by pragmatic theories. However, languages differ in how this tendency is manifested: in English, it is in the alternation of active and passive structures, whilst in Catalan and Spanish a third alternative (dislocated actives) is also found. In the next section we will consider the mechanisms which are responsible for these effects.

THE MECHANISMS UNDERLYING DISCOURSE INFLUENCES UPON PRODUCTION

We suggest the influence of discourse salience on the production of sentences within a discourse context can be explained in the same way as other non-linguistic influences on the production of isolated sentences: discourse salience is linked to variations in conceptual accessibility (Bock & Warren, 1985). That is, just as animate entities are conceptually more accessible than inanimate entities, we suggest that entities that are more salient in a discourse are conceptually more accessible than entities that are less salient. Because of the architecture of the processing system, in particular the incremental nature of processing, such variations in conceptual accessibility inevitably affect the course of syntactic processing, with corresponding impacts on the syntactic structure of the eventual utterance.

We will now consider in more detail how this takes place, and how it can account for cross-linguistic discourse influences on production. Our discussion will be presented in terms of Bock's (1987) model of language production, in keeping with Bock's original proposals about conceptual accessibility. However, our account is also compatible with other models (e.g., Levelt, 1989). Under Bock's model, production is parallel and incremental: more than one alternative may be considered at a time, and processing at one stage may begin as soon as minimal input has been received from the previous stage. Syntactic processing comprises two discrete stages. During *functional processing*, appropriate lemmas to convey the message are retrieved from the mental lexicon and linked with the grammatical functions associated with the retrieved verb, by a process of *functional integration*. Bock proposed that lemmas which are retrieved more easily (i.e. are conceptually more accessible) will be retrieved earlier and hence assigned grammatical functions earlier than less easily retrieved lemmas. She also proposed that grammatical functions are assigned following the NP-Accessibility Hierarchy proposed by Keenan and Comrie (1977), such that subject assignment has priority over direct object assignment, and so on. Thus because conceptually more accessible words are retrieved first, they are more likely to claim the subject function.

However, grammatical function assignment is also influenced by competition between alternative structures: different verb forms (e.g. the forms associated with active and passive structures) and the grammatical functions associated with them compete for activation. Functional integration is thus affected not only by the accessibility of the lemmas, but also by the strength of the verb form. Overall, active forms tend to be more highly activated than passive forms, though the precise degree of activation varies (in part between languages; passive forms are relatively stronger in English than in Catalan and Spanish, for example). If the agent of a transitive event is accessed first, it is most likely to become the subject of an active verb form. If the patient of a transitive event is accessed first, it is likely to become the subject of a passive verb form. However, in this latter case there will also be competition from the active verb form. This means that sometimes the patient will end up as the subject of a passive and sometimes it will end up as the object of an active. Overall, actives tend to be preferred over passives.

The second stage of syntactic processing is *positional processing*. Here, the lexemes, or phonological content associated with the lemmas, are retrieved and assigned a position in the syntactic framework which has been constructed on the basis of the syntactic information contained in the lemmas. This constitutes *constituent integration*. Bock proposed that the relative accessibility of lexemes play a role here, with more accessible (e.g. more frequent) lexical forms claiming an early position (Bock, 1987). In addition, however, we might expect that the order in which lemmas are retrieved will also influence the order in which lexemes are retrieved, since processing is incremental. All other things being equal (e.g. assuming that all of the lexemes are equally accessible), the first lemma to be assigned a grammatical function will also undergo lexical retrieval first, and the lexeme associated with it will be retrieved first. In other cases, there may be a competition for first serial position between a lexeme which has low inherent accessibility but which was activated first (because its associated lemma was retrieved first) and a lexeme which has high inherent accessibility but which was activated later (because its associated lemma was retrieved later). Thus positional processing is influenced by both the relative accessibility of the lexemes themselves and the order in which they are activated.

Bock proposed this model to account for the non-linguistic influences on the production of isolated sentences which we discussed above. However, we have claimed that both these influences and discourse influences are linked to variations in conceptual accessibility. Hence we suggest that this model can also explain how discourse context influences syntactic processing. Our discussion will be couched in terms of discourse salience, but this should be taken to include the distinction between entities which have been introduced in previous discourse and those which have not.

When an agent is made more salient by preceding discourse, it becomes conceptually more accessible. This increase in conceptual accessibility means that the lemma associated with the agent is retrieved first and seeks to be bound to the grammatical function of subject. The verb form associated with an active structure is also highly activated, hence it is very likely that the salient entity will become the subject of an active clause. Because this lemma is first to be retrieved, retrieval of its associated lexeme will also be initiated first. This, and any additional lexical priming effect (from previous mention of the word in the preceding discourse) (cf. Bock and Irwin's (1980) results), means that the lexeme associated with the salient entity should be retrieved first. (Though note that in Prat-Sala and Branigan's experiments, both entities were lexically introduced in the preceding short story, suggesting that the effects found by Prat-Sala and Branigan did not involve lexical priming). Hence the word associated with the conceptually accessible concept will tend to appear sentence-initially, as the subject.

This model can also account for the tendency in Prat-Sala and Branigan's experiments for participants to produce passives, and also dislocated actives in Catalan and Spanish, following stories which made the patient salient. When a patient is made salient, its conceptual accessibility increases and hence the lemma associated with it is retrieved faster than those of less accessible entities. This increases its likelihood of claiming a subject function. Hence it will try to be linked to the subject of a passive structure. However, there will be a competition between the active and the passive verb forms; sometimes one will win and sometimes the other. If the passive verb form wins, the lemma will claim the subject function and initiate retrieval of the corresponding lexeme, resulting in the salient entity appearing as the sentence-initial subject. If the active verb form wins, then the conceptually more accessible patient will fulfill the object function. In English, where grammatical function largely determines word order, this means that the conceptually more accessible word will appear post-verbally. Thus even though the conceptually more accessible word has an advantage during syntactic processing, the syntactic options available in the language prevent it from ultimately appearing in an early word order position.

In other languages, however, where word order is more flexible, grammatical function assignment does not determine word order. In these languages, potential variations in word order will be exploited to allow the first lexeme which is successfully retrieved to appear first. This explains why Prat-Sala and Branigan's experiments found higher proportions of dislocated active structures following patient-salient stories in Catalan and Spanish: when the lexeme associated with the more salient entity was retrieved first, as a (partial) consequence of its priority in lemma retrieval, a dislocated active structure allowed it to appear first, even though it fulfilled the object function. In the experiments involving animate patients, this tendency may have been increased by the higher lexical accessibility (as indexed by frequency) of the words associated with the animate entities. However, the same tendency was found in the second set of experiments where the words associated with the agent and patient were of equivalent frequency and hence accessibility.

Note that the dislocated active structure will be in competition with the canonical active structure, which will also be activated. Which structure is ultimately chosen will depend upon the order in which the relevant lexemes are retrieved, which we have suggested depends upon an interaction between the order in which retrieval is initiated and the relative accessibility of the lexemes themselves. In some cases, an inherently highly accessible lexeme associated with a conceptually less accessible entity may be retrieved before the lexeme associated with a conceptually more accessible entity, resulting in production of a canonical active structure.

CONCLUSIONS

We have shown how discourse context can influence syntactic processing in language production. We propose that its primary influence is to make the conceptual representations associated with entities that are highly salient within the discourse more accessible than those associated with entities that are less salient or have not been previously introduced in the discourse model. More specifically, we suggest that a common factor, conceptual accessibility, underlies the effects of discourse salience on the production of sentences within a discourse context and of other influences on the production of sentences in isolation.

We suggest that its effects are a consequence of the architecture of the processor. The overriding aim of the speaker is to produce language fluently under real time constraints. The processor achieves this through incremental processing, in which information is processed in the order in which it is retrieved. Because discourse context makes some entities more accessible, those entities will have priority during syntactic processing, resulting in their eventual appearance in syntactically prominent positions. Discourse context can also increase lexical accessibility (through lexical priming), which may also influence syntactic processing at the positional level. Hence we follow Bock (1977) in suggesting that at least some of the systematic variations in syntactic structure that pragmatic theories identify can be explained by the way in which discourse context affects how a speaker retrieves and processes information during language production.

We further propose that discourse context influences language production in the same way across languages. That is, we suggest that in all languages it affects conceptual accessibility. We also suggest that cross-linguistic language production involves a common architecture and common processing mechanisms. We have shown that cross-linguistic variations in the syntactic structures associated with different discourse contexts need not be explained by invoking different mechanisms for different languages, but instead can be explained by variations in the syntactic options available in each language.

NOTES

The order of authors is arbitrary. HB was supported by a British Academy postdoctoral fellowship. MP-S was supported by an ESRC Research Studentship No. R00429434261. Correspondence should be addressed to Holly Branigan, Human Communication Research Centre, Department of Psychology, 53 Hillhead Street, Glasgow G12 8QF.

[1] As in much early work on these issues, Clark and Clark did not distinguish between referential status and information structure, but conflated both under a Given/New distinction.

REFERENCES

Ariel, M. (1990). Accessing noun phrase antecedents. London: Routledge.

Bock, J. K. (1977). The effect of a pragmatic presupposition on syntactic structure in question answering. *Journal of Verbal Learning and Verbal Behavior*, 16, 723-734.

Bock, J. K. (1987). Co-ordinating words and syntax in speech plans. In A. W. Ellis (Ed.), *Progress in the Psychology of Language* (Vol. 3, pp. 337-389). London: Lawrence Erlbaum.

Bock, J. K. & Irwin, D. E. (1980). Syntactic effects of information availability in sentence production. *Journal of Verbal Learning and Verbal Behavior*, 19, 467-484.

Bock, J. K. & Levelt, W. J. M. (1994). Language production: grammatical encoding. In M. A. Gernsbacher (Ed.), *Handbook of Psycholinguistics.* (pp. 945-984). San Diego: Academic Press.

Bock, J. K. & Warren, R. K. (1985). Conceptual accessibility and syntactic structure in sentence formulation. *Cognition*, 21, 47-67.

Chafe, W.L. (1976). Givenness, contrastiveness, definiteness, subject, topics, and point of view. In C.N. Li (Ed.), *Subject and Topic*, pp.25-55. San Diego: Academic Press.

Clark, E. & Clark, H. (1978). Universals, relativity and language processing. In J. Greenberg (Ed.), *Universals of Human Language, Volume 1: Method and Theory* (pp. 225-277). Stanford: Stanford University Press.

Clark, H. H. (1965). Some structural properties of simple active and passive sentences. *Journal of Verbal Learning and Verbal Behavior*, **4**, 375-390.

Clark, H. H. & Begun, J.S. (1971). The semantics of sentence subjects. *Language and Speech*, **14**, 34-46.

Clark, H. H. & Haviland, S. E. (1977). Comprehension and the Given-New Contract. In R. O. Freedle (Ed.), *Discourse Production and Comprehension* (pp. 1-40). Ablex Publishing Corporation, Norwood, New Jersey.

Dahl, O. (1974). Topic-comment revisited. In O. Dahl (Ed.), *Topic and comment, contextual boundedness and focus,* pp.1-24. Hamburg: Buske.

Feleki, E. & Branigan, H.P. (1997). Animacy effects in Greek sentence production: Evidence for single-stage syntactic processing?. Poster presented at The Third Architectures & Mechanisms of Language Processing Conference. Edinburgh, September 1997.

Garrett, M. F. (1975). The analysis of sentence production. In G.H. Bower (Ed.), *The Psychology of Learning and Motivation*, Volume 9, pp.133-177, San Diego: Academic Press.

Halliday, M. (1967). Notes on transitivity and theme in English, Part II. Journal of *Linguistics*, 3, 199-244.

Harris, M. (1978). Noun animacy and the passive voice: A developmental approach. *Quarterly Journal of Experimental Psychology*, **30**, 199-244.

Haviland, S. E. & Clark, H. H. (1974). What's new? Acquiring new information as a process in comprehension. *Journal of Verbal Learning and Verbal Behavior*, 13, 512-521.

Heim, I. (1983). File change semantics and the familiarity theory of definiteness. In R. Bäuerle, C. Schwarze, & A. von Stechow (Eds.), *Meaning, Use and Interpretation of Language,* pp.164-189. Berlin: de Gruyter.

Keenan, E.L. & Comrie, B. (1977). Noun phrase accessibility and universal grammar. *Linguistic Inquiry*, **8**, 22-99.

Kelly, M. H., Bock, J. K. & Keil, F. C. (1986). Prototypicality in a linguistic context: Effects on sentence structure. *Journal of Language and Memory*, 25, 59-74.

Kempen, G. & Hoenkamp, E. (1987). An incremental procedural grammar for sentence formulation. *Cognitive Science*, 11, 201-258.

Kempen, G. & Huijbers, P. (1983). The lexicalization process in sentence production and naming: Indirect election of words. *Cognition*, **14**, 185-209.

Kintsch, W. & van Dijk, T.A. (1978). Toward a model of text comprehension and production. *Psychological Review,* **85**, 363-394.

Levelt, W. J. M. (1989). *Speaking: From Intention to Articulation.* Cambridge, Ma: MIT Press.

Li, C. N. & Thompson, S. A. (1976). Subject and topic: A new typology of language. In C. N. Li (Ed.), *Subject and Topic*, pp.458-489. San Diego: Academic Press.

McDonald, J. L., Bock, J. K., & Kelly, M. H. (1993). Word and world order: Semantic, phonological, and metrical determinants of serial position. *Cognitive Psychology*, **25**, 188-230.

Osgood, C. E. & Bock, J. K. (1977). Salience and sentencing: Some production principles. In S. Rosenberg (Eds.), *Sentence Production: Developments in Research and Theory*, pp. 89-140. London: Lawrence Erlbaum.

Prat-Sala, M. (1997). *The Production of Different Word Orders: A Psycholinguistic and Developmental Approach.* Ph.D. thesis, Centre for Cognitive Science, The University of Edinburgh.

Prat-Sala, M. & Branigan, H.P. (1998). Discourse constraints on syntactic processing in language production: A cross-linguistic study in English & Spanish. Ms.

Prince, E. F. (1981). Toward a taxonomy of given-new information. In P. Cole (Ed.), *Radical Pragmatics*, pages 223-255. New York: Academic Press.

Prince, E. F. (1992). The ZPG letter: Subjects, definiteness, and information-status. In W. C. Mann & S. A. Thompson (Eds.), *Discourse Description: Diverse Linguistic Analyses of a Fund-Raising Text* (pp. 295-325). John Benjamins Publishing Company.

Sanford, A. J. & Garrod, S. C. (1981). *Understanding Written Language*. New York: Wiley.

Sgall, A. J., Hajicova, E., & Panevova, J. (1986). *The Meaning of the Sentence in its Semantic and Pragmatic Aspects*. Dordrecht: D. Reidel.

Teufel, S, Branigan, H.P. & Feleki, E. (1996). Conceptual accessibility and subjecthood in German sentence production. Poster presented at The Second Architectures & Mechanisms of Language Processing Conference. Turin, September 1996.

Webber, B.L. (1983). So what can we talk about now? In M. Brady & R.C. Berwick (Eds.), *Computational Models of Discourse*, pp. 331-371. Cambridge, Ma: MIT Press.

Maren Heydel and Wayne S. Murray

CONCEPTUAL EFFECTS IN SENTENCE PRIMING: A CROSS-LINGUISTIC PERSPECTIVE

It is now well established that the production (or perception) of one sentence is capable of increasing the probability that the speaker will subsequently produce another utterance of the same or a related type. This phenomenon, which we shall refer to as 'sentence level priming', has generally been taken to reflect a facilitation of syntactic processes and/or representations as a result of their repeated occurrence. Whilst it is clear that various conceptual features of the utterance also play a role in the production process, it has generally been concluded (e.g. Bock 1986; Bock, Loebell, & Morey 1992) that these do not underlie the priming phenomenon and that they exert independent additive effects on the likelihood of production of a particular sentence type.

In this chapter we argue that there are substantial reasons for reconsidering this conclusion. We suggest that the evidence derived from monolingual (English) priming studies does not unequivocally support such a conclusion, but that, in any case, the close link within any one language between conceptual features and syntactic form makes it extremely difficult to tease apart the two types of effect. Since, within any given language, particular conceptual structures will normally be realised by certain syntactic structures, the repeated production of the same syntactic structure does not necessarily imply that it is the syntactic form, or syntactic processes, which are primed. We suggest that a more profitable approach to this question is

M. De Vincenzi and V. Lombardo (eds.), Cross-linguistic Perspectives on Language Processing, 227–254.

provided by a cross-linguistic methodology using structures which have differing syntactic and conceptual counterparts in the two languages. The results from two studies, using this methodology, show that sentence priming effects extend cross-linguistically, from German to English, and further suggest that sentence priming may be more closely linked to conceptual rather than to syntactic form.

REPRESENTATION AND PROCESS

Linguistics and psychology bring different perspectives to bear on the study of language, but they share an underlying foundation. They both assume a psychological reality to the representations they postulate and that there is some necessary level of correspondence between the linguistic and the psychological. This correspondence is, arguably, most apparent at the level of 'representation' and it is, perhaps, for what it can tell us about representation that the phenomenon of sentence level priming is most valuable.

While it may be argued that the business of linguistics is simply to provide an adequate description of the competence grammar, and this doesn't necessarily involve questions of psychological plausibility or adequacy, it is clear that the vast majority of linguists wish to have their theories at least informed by what is known about psychological process. Similarly, even though it became clear in the 1960s that a fairly straightforward translation of linguistic theory into concomitant psychological processes wasn't going to work, theories of psychological processes have, on the whole, shown a considerable debt to the form of linguistic theory. But, of course, this correspondence is not surprising, since linguistic and psychological theories are built from the same stuff - the performance of human beings dealing with language. While most linguistic theory is predicated on the linguist's intuitions concerning allowable structures and processes, these must be derived from (or at least be informed by) the apparent consequence of attempting to process such a structure.

Traditionally, linguists have considered language at a number of different levels of representation. These can be described in terms of the rules that instantiate the structures at any particular level of description. For example, it has been proposed that the categorial component of a syntactic subsystem determines the lexical insertion rules for the generation of a deep structure (D). A rule, move-α, maps D to an abstract surface structure (S), leaving traces coindexed with their antecedents. S is represented as a phonetic form (π) and as a logical form (λ) (Chomsky, 1981). These derivations are not directional; they correspond to levels of linguistic representation. 'Movement' in this context refers to various instantiations of the rule, move-α, at different levels, and does not refer, and is not implied to refer to actual mechanisms involved in perception or production.

Within a minimalist framework (Chomsky, 1995) the syntactic variation of languages arises from morphological properties which restrict the allowable derivations. Similarly, both phonetic form and logical form are determined by the morphologically allowable derivations and it is not necessary to postulate the existence of D structure. A derivation is legitimate if it yields a legitimate structural description at the levels of phonetic form and logical form and if internal principles allow π and λ to be paired.

In contrast, while a certain amount of psycholinguistic work has attempted to find performance correlates of these types of operations and representations, the emphasis in psychology in recent years has been very much on the derivation of a set of principles or heuristics which are concerned principally with only the surface structure parsing of an incoming string, to allow for rapid incremental interpretation of the utterance. What is common to both approaches is the belief (or assumption) that there is an underlying representation - the structure of our knowledge about language - which is fundamental and forms the basis for any use of language[1]. The assumption is that even if, for example, deep structure relations are not directly computed during the process of sentence comprehension, they may still capture a level of representation of the *linguistic knowledge*, present in the hearer, which can give rise to measurable psychological consequences, such as 'gap filling' (e.g. Stowe, 1986; Frazier & Clifton, 1989), 'reactivation' (e.g. Nicol & Pickering, 1993; Love & Swinney, 1996), etc.

Similarly, from a linguistic perspective, if it were the case that there were two alternative competence grammars, which were equally acceptable on formal grounds, a principle of 'transparency' suggests that a measure of the most appropriate could be determined by the extent to which the structures it proposes map onto psychologically plausible representations of that knowledge. As suggested by J.D. Fodor (1993, p.351), "... any experiment that reveals how a sentence is mentally represented by language users could in principle show something about its derivation that linguistics would like to know." Such a mental representation must be based on the set of knowledge, the units and structures, which provides the speaker with the ability to turn messages into utterances and which underlies the hearer's ability to perform the translation in the opposite direction. While it seems unlikely that these opposing processes will be successfully characterised simply in terms of a single mechanism which can be run forward or backward, it must be the case that the knowledge - the functional representation upon which they are both based - is the same (in so far as the message derived by the hearer corresponds to the message intended by the speaker).

For the most part, psycholinguists have addressed the question of the nature of this representation rather indirectly - for example by processes such as determining whether there are psychological consequences of different types of linguistically defined gaps (e.g. Bever & McElree, 1988; Clifton & Frazier, 1986; Love & Swinney, 1996; McElree & Bever, 1989) or whether violation of particular linguistic principles results in a measurable processing cost (e.g. Freedman & Forster, 1985). However, the tying together of linguistic theory with processing consequences frequently involves a rather extended level of inference, and even where the inference is straightforward, the evidence is not always unequivocal.

MONOLINGUAL SENTENCE PRIMING

While the link between linguistic theory and sentential processing may be difficult to trace, it appears that the examination of sentence production processes might provide a more direct window onto the nature of linguistic knowledge and representation. As Bock, Loebell and Morey (1992) point out, the link between the elements of messages and the units and structures of language is one of the more remote components in the language system. But the nature of this link may provide a fairly direct window onto the nature of linguistic representation. Studies of speech errors (e.g. Garrett, 1980; Harley, 1984) and agreement phenomena (e.g. Bock & Miller, 1991; Vigliocco, Butterworth & Semenza, 1996) have provided valuable insights into the levels of linguistic representation and the way that the mapping from message to utterance may be performed. However, it seems that recent work on sentence level priming (e.g. Bock, 1986: Bock & Loebell, 1990; Bock et al., 1992; Branigan, Pickering, Liversedge, Stewart & Urback, 1995; Pickering & Branigan, in press) may provide an even more direct means for empirical investigation of at least some aspects of the mapping process and the nature of the representations which underlie it. Indeed, Branigan et al argue that this type of priming provides a means for tapping into underlying communalities of representation that are basic across language processes, underlying both perception and production.

We use here the term "sentence priming" rather than the more commonly used "syntactic priming" both to be theoretically neutral and also, as will become apparent later, because we feel that the possible influences on the phenomenon of other levels of representation and process have not yet been adequately assessed. Since the early work of Chomsky (e.g. 1965) it has been assumed that syntactic structure is central to linguistic knowledge and representation. This is not to say that other approaches which place more emphasis on detailed lexical knowledge and semantic roles, such as Fillmore's (1968) generative grammar and Kaplan and Bresnan's (1982) lexical functional grammar, have not attracted attention, but it has been fairly widely agreed (or assumed) that syntactic processes represent the core of what must be explained or understood. Within such a framework it becomes easy to assume that sentence level priming is likely to have its basis in syntactic processes and/or representations.

This sort of priming was first described in terms of syntactic parallelism effects found in natural discourse: under certain conditions, a similar syntactic structure, such as a passive, occurs repeatedly across utterances. Such parallelism effects have been described by Schenkein (1980), Weiner and Labov (1983), Estival (1985), and they have been examined by Levelt & Kelter (1982) under both laboratory and non-laboratory conditions. However, from these studies it is not clear what the basis of such parallelism effects might be. Sociolinguistic factors have been implicated (Giles & Powesland, 1975). Discourse effects also seem likely to be involved. Particular speech acts are associated with particular syntactic structures and particular registers and/or functional styles. Persistence of a discourse topic may also lead to persistence of a syntactic structure, either for rhetorical purposes (Tannen 1989), or because similar communicative intentions are realised by similar syntactic structures. Persistence of discourse topic can also lead to lexical overlap, with the consequence that similar lexical items facilitate similar syntactic structures. For example, given a preference for a particular serial order of constituents, use of members of a set of transitive verbs with the same argument structure would tend to lead to replication of the same active or passive sentence form across subsequent utterances. Prosodic effects, too, might be implicated, particularly in question and answer sessions where the form of the question favours the production of successive sentences with the same prosodic contours, and this in turn facilitates sentences with the same syntactic structure (Levelt & Kelter, 1982).

It appears, therefore, that syntactic repetition effects which occur in natural discourse might be explained in terms of a number of factors, other than the activation or facilitation of mapping processes from messages to utterances. The sentence priming task first used by Bock (1986), however, allows the possibility of experimentally differentiating between these sorts of discourse and/or semantic factors and facilitation effects derived from underlying sentence production processes. Her procedure, which masked the task as a memory test in which participants were required to repeat priming sentences and then provide descriptions of line drawings, provides a situation in which sentences are produced, but there is little possibility of confounding discourse or semantic effects.

Bock found clear priming effects for both transitive and dative structures. Following prepositional dative primes, the production of prepositional dative picture descriptions increased in frequency by 23% compared to its rate following double-object primes. Double object datives similarly increased in relative frequency by 22% following double object primes. Active primes increased the frequency of active responses by 8% relative to their frequency following passives, and the same 8% increase was observed for passive responses following passive primes.

Since grammatical sentences do not constitute a discrete set, and consequently the activation of syntactic structures cannot be along the same lines as activation of elements of lexical knowledge, Bock suggested that there are two factors which could be responsible for syntactic repetition effects:

1) The representation of a previously encountered sentence may directly influence the formation of a subsequent utterance. That is, the syntactic structure of a previously encountered sentence may be used by speakers as a blueprint for a subsequent utterance.

2) There may be a direct influence on the syntactic processes responsible for understanding and producing an utterance, involving some form of activation, strengthening or threshold reduction that persists over time and increases the probability that the activated or strengthened information will be used in a subsequent syntactic process.

Bock favoured the latter of these possibilities and argued that such syntactic processes can be differentiated from processes associated with meaning, involving conceptual features such as animacy, human vs. non-human agency, etc. However, it is clearly not the case that conceptual features play no role in the priming procedure. The results from this first study showed that passive primes did not produce a significant effect if the associated target pictures contained human agents. The ideal conditions for a passive to be produced were with a picture showing a non-human or inanimate agent and a human or animate patient. This suggests that conceptual features, such as animacy, have some relation to syntactic processes, since they appear to be able to inhibit the application of syntactic procedures such as passivisation. It is not the case that passive sentences with an animate agent and an inanimate patient are ungrammatical in English, but they do occur less frequently than passive sentences with animate patients. This may reflect the application of a conceptual feature precondition or bias associated with the use of a particular syntactic structure. However, this would not necessarily imply that conceptual features interact *directly* with syntactic processes.

In her second and third experiments, Bock systematically manipulated human agency in both the priming sentences and pictures, but found no significant variation in the magnitude of the syntactic priming effect in response to variation in animacy in the primes. She concluded that either syntactic processes may not have access to certain conceptual features, or that it is sufficient for the application of certain syntactic processes (such as passivisation) if there is at least a partial match between the conceptual features of a message and the syntactic structure normally associated with these features. The optimum condition for a passive may be a non-human agent and a human patient, with the patient being the theme of the sentence (what the message is about; its starting point), but these conditions may not be necessary for passivisation to occur. Thus, the results suggest that certain syntactic processes may be informationally encapsulated and can be manipulated irrespective of the conceptual features of the utterance.

An alternative explanation is that the results could arise from the priming of specific lexical items. For example, in the case of passives, priming of the preposition "by", which introduces the agent of the action, could result in an increase in subsequent passive responses. If, as suggested by Garrett (1980), closed-class elements are already in place when the phonological forms of open-class words are integrated into a phrasal planning frame, then the priming of "by" might increase the probability of use of a sentence frame which contains this word. However, results by Bock (1989) suggest that such specific lexical priming is unlikely. She found an equal priming effect on prepositional 'to-datives' from both to- and for-datives, suggesting that the presence of a specific lexical item is not critical. The fact that prepositional datives prime prepositional datives (irrespective of the particular preposition) and double-object datives prime double-object datives is taken as evidence for *syntactic* priming.

Double-object / to-dative alternations, in fact, produce a very robust sentence priming effect. However, it would be a mistake to conclude that to-datives and double-object datives differ only syntactically. They also differ conceptually. Following Pinker's theory of extended conceptual structure (Pinker, 1989), there are differences between the double-object and the to-dative form. In the prepositional form, the transferred object is the patient; in the double-object form, the recipient is the patient. This causes differences in the entailments of these utterances. The statement in (1a) does not entail the suggestion that the action was completed successfully. The statement in (1b) does.

(1a) (PP) John taught English to the students (unsuccessfully)

(1b) (DO) John taught the students English (successfully)

Also in the double object form, the change of possession is expressed not as an analogue of motion (as in the PP) but as a causation-state whereby the possessor has the object. This is apparent in the way that the double-object form is not available with some verbs, while with other verbs the prepositional object form is not available (see examples 2a-2d). If these forms were conceptually identical then every verb which allows for a double-object should have a prepositional object form and vice versa.

(2a) (PP) She carried the letter to the mailbox.

(2b) (DO) *She carried the mailbox the letter.

(2c) (PP) *They spared the punishment to the policeman.

(2d) (DO) They spared the policeman the punishment.

Bock and Loebell (1990), however, provide evidence against the suggestion that priming may be based on a more abstract, intermediate level of linguistic encoding involving conceptual features of utterances. They found that passive target sentences were primed equally well by passives, such as (3), and locatives, like (4).

(3) The construction worker was hit by the bulldozer.

(4) The construction worker was digging by the bulldozer.

They interpreted this as evidence for a direct meaning-to-form mapping that does not involve an intermediate level of conceptual representation. That is, one without intervention of a level of representation involving, for example, thematic roles. Thematic roles are a kind of shorthand for frequently occurring conceptual structures. Following Fillmore (1968) and Jackendoff (1972, 1983), thematic roles relate the arguments of a verb to the meaning of that verb. So, 'agent' is the instigator of an action - the subject of verbs like 'kill', 'eat', 'kick' etc. 'Patient' is someone or something affected by an action - the object of these verbs. In the preceding examples, on the most plausible interpretation, "the bulldozer" fills the agent role of the verb 'hit' in (3), while in (4), "the bulldozer" is simply part of a prepositional phrase adjunct which fills no thematic role associated with the verb "digging". Thus, the two sentences are conceptually quite distinct, and the evidence of equivalent priming counts against any claim for a conceptual level involvement in the effect.

There may, however, be another reason for this apparent lack of effect. The experiment tested whether both of these structures would prime a passive. The target pictures were all consistent with active or passive descriptions, but not with locatives. If, indeed, locatives are better able to prime locative rather than passive structures, there would have been no potential for producing one in this situation, and under such circumstances, it wouldn't be surprising if a structure similar at a superficial phrase structure level - the passive - received some benefit.

Bock, Loebell and Morey (1992) carried out an experiment which provided a more direct test of whether syntactic processes can be manipulated irrespective of conceptual information. They noted that the conceptual feature 'animacy' is frequently connected with subjecthood and used this property as a 'tracer' in the mapping process in order to determine whether there is direct mapping between functional-level and surface syntactic categories, or whether this is mediated by the equivalents of subjects/objects at D-structure. They reasoned that it should be possible to trace this mapping process by systematically varying the animacy of the subject and object arguments (the lexical items which fill these syntactic roles) in the priming sentences. Their assumption was that the production of a particular sentence form would be facilitated when preceded by a prime which contains subject and object arguments having the same animacy as the subject and object in the target. Since their target pictures all depicted events with an inanimate agent and an animate patient, this means that for the production of active sentences, such as (5a), primes such as (6a), which maintain the same animacy relations, should be more effective than (6b), where the animacy relations are reversed. The same should be true of the passive primes, (6c) and (6d), if the direct mapping hypothesis is correct. However, if mediated mapping is involved, then it is the animacy of the underlying D-structure subject and object relations which is important, and the pattern should reverse with passive primes.

(5a) The alarm clock awakened the boy.

(5b) The boy was awakened by the alarm clock.

(6a) The boat carried five people.

(6b) Five people carried the boat.

(6c) Five people were carried by the boat.

(6d) The boat was carried by five people.

Their results showed priming of actives, like (5a), by actives, and passives, like (5b), by passives. In addition, they report an additive effect of a match in the animacy of the surface subject and object arguments on the proportion of actives produced. That is, where the animacy of the prime and target matched (6a & 6d), proportionally more actives were produced regardless of the structural form of the prime. These results appear to support the direct mapping hypothesis and also suggest that conceptual and syntactic factors have additive effects. However, if we instead consider the number of passives produced in the study, these conclusions are not so robustly supported. More passives were produced following passive primes, and more so following primes with the same animacy relations. However, the animacy effect was not repeated following active primes. More passives were produced following active primes with inanimate subject arguments (6a) than following actives with animate subjects

(6b). That is, the converse animacy relations applied when the prime was active and the response a passive[2].

It is an open question as to which is the most appropriate measure of the strength of the priming effect in this study. The proportions used in the figures in the paper seem a reasonable way of assessing it, but there must be at least some question concerning the appropriate interpretation of the results when one measure (the number of passives produced) shows a converse pattern. This would be especially true if it were the case that priming applied principally to the more marked structure (the passive). It is unfortunate that subjects describing pictures of events with animate agents and inanimate patients use passives so infrequently or it would be possible to fully-cross this design and perhaps gain a better understanding of the relationship between conceptual and syntactic factors that way. When participants are very unlikely to produce passive utterances containing human agents, there may be little margin for these types of conceptual features to influence the syntactic processes which are engaged. The nature of the task may therefore mitigate against finding such effects.

CONCEPTUAL FORM AND SENTENCE PRODUCTION

The role played by conceptual form in sentence production has been the subject of a number of recent studies. It is beyond the scope of this chapter to discuss these in detail, but the emerging consensus appears to be that the role played by conceptual features is perhaps larger than was previously envisaged. While this does not *necessarily* suggest that conceptual form may be closely implicated in the sentence priming phenomenon, it is at least consistent with that proposal.

Sentence production studies involving languages other than English have provided evidence of conceptual effects that appear to be unrelated to syntactic form. Prat-Sala and Branigan (this volume), for example, examined the influence of discourse saliency on the production of actives and passives in English and on the production of actives, passives and 'dislocated' actives in Catalan and Spanish (that is, actives where the direct object appears before the subject). They found increased production of passives following a patient-salient context in English. For Spanish and Catalan, this effect, however, does not appear to be related to a preference for filling the *surface subject* role with the patient. The same pattern was found for *both* passives and 'dislocated' actives in Catalan and Spanish. While the subject precedes the verb in the passive, in the 'dislocated' active, it does not. The effect therefore appears to be conceptual and related to the fact that in both passives and 'dislocated' actives the focus is on the patient rather than on the agent of the action.

The results derived from another paradigm - the production of subject-verb agreement errors - lead to a similar conclusion. Early findings (e.g. Bock & Miller, 1991) suggested a purely syntactic basis to the effect of mismatching number of a local noun on verb agreement errors. However, in a series of experiments, Vigliocco and colleagues (e.g. Vigliocco, Butterworth & Semenza, 1996; Vigliocco, Hartsuiker, Jarema & Kolk, 1996) have shown that complex noun phrases with multi-token head nouns (e.g. "the label on the bottles") are more likely to result in agreement errors (e.g. "*the label on the bottles are...") than single token head nouns (e.g. "the road to the mountains"). Thus, again, it appears that conceptual factors play a larger role in production processes than was initially believed.

CROSSLINGUISTIC SENTENCE PRIMING

Even if we restrict consideration to the domain of sentence priming, it is apparent that the basic effect of actives priming actives and passives priming passives is not necessarily driven purely by syntactic factors. We have seen that it can be overlaid with effects of animacy and conceptual factors related to agency. Actives and passives also differ in focus: with passives, focus is on the patient; with actives, it is on the agent of an action. Within any given language, different conceptual forms[3] will normally be realised by different syntactic structures, and it is therefore not surprising that it becomes very difficult to draw clear distinctions between syntactic and conceptual effects. It also does not seem plausible to assume that different syntactic structures are likely to be conceptually identical. In English there is a direct link between structure and word order. There is also a direct link between word order and focus. It follows that there must, therefore, be a link between syntax and focus.

The central question, therefore, is not *whether* conceptual factors are involved in sentence level priming, but the precise nature of the involvement. It may be, as Bock argues, that syntactic and conceptual features of the prime have independent additive effects. Alternatively, conceptual features may play a more critical role. It is, for example, the particular combination of an animate agent and an inanimate patient which so potently inhibits the production of passives. It also seems plausible to suggest that priming could result from the activation of a particular cluster of conceptual features, if these features are closely associated with a particular surface form. For example, in English, focus on the patient rather than on the agent of an action is normally expressed by a passive. Thus, if participants reproduce the conceptual form of the prime, they will be biased towards producing the same surface structure. It is therefore not surprising that it is so difficult, within a monolinguistic framework, and particularly in English, to tease apart the effects produced by conceptual features on the one hand and by syntactic structure on the other.

One way of attempting to separate these effects is to adopt a cross-linguistic methodology. There is evidence of cross-linguistic lexical priming in both word recognition (Ketley, Spinks & de Gelder, 1994) and word fragment completion tasks (Basden, Bonilla-Meeks & Basden, 1994). The results from both of these studies suggest that cross-linguistic priming takes place if and only if subjects are encouraged to access the underlying conceptual form of an expression. Ketley et al suggest that the representations of words expressed in different languages may be interconnected by one-to-one links between translation equivalents as well as by meaning-integration processes, and that cross-linguistic priming takes place when these meaning-integration processes are activated. Basden et al explain the same phenomenon in terms of study-activated processing components which include the conceptual features of the word. When these features are accessed, cross-linguistic priming takes place. If this conclusion is correct, and if priming occurs at a sentence level across languages, this would suggest that it is the conceptual form rather than syntactic structure of the sentences involved which is responsible for the priming effect. This hypothesis can be further tested if the same type of conceptual form can be expressed by two different syntactic structures in the first language, but by only one syntactic structure in the second. If the two different syntactic structures in the first language are equally good primes for the corresponding structure in the second we can assume that the locus of the priming effect must be at the level of conceptual rather than syntactic form.

German has a choice of two syntactically different structures which allow focus to be established on the patient of an action and which are conceptually similar: a passive and a topicalization[4]. 'Focus' used in this sense refers to a range of expressive linguistic devices which allow us to identify the most salient element in a message. Normally this would be the starting point of the message. In active sentences the starting point is the agent. One reason for using a passive in English is to allow speakers to establish the patient of an action as the most salient element. In German, too, this can be achieved with use of the passive, but a topicalization can also serve the same purpose.

Unlike English, German has kept the availability of V2-movement as an unmarked option. It is possible to front syntactic components before the finite verb which is the second element of a main clause. A sentence containing a topicalized constituent differs from its untopicalized version at the level of phonetic form, but not at a more abstract functional level: all syntactic components stay in the slots assigned to them during functional level processing. That is, a surface subject argument remains a surface subject argument and a surface object argument remains a surface object argument. Thus they are identical in ‘voice’. However, in a topicalization, the surface object can appear before the finite verb and become the starting point of the message.

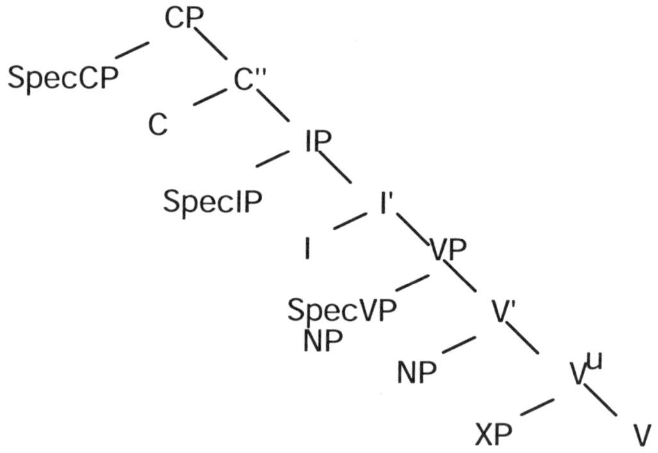

Figure 1.

The structural similarity of topicalized and untopicalized phonetic representations is obvious when we look at the basic structure of German sentences as illustrated in Figure 1 (c.f. Grewendorf, 1992). The structure rests on the two basic functional categories C (complement) and I (inflection) and reflects a weak configurational analysis of German (that is, word order is restricted by the verb phrase). SpecCP (complement specifier) is the basic position for the subject, if we assume that there is always a CP (and there seems to be no compelling reason not to). SpecCP is also the landing place for topicalizations. Indeed it can be argued that SpecCP is not reserved for any particular constituent (such as the subject, as is the case in English), but represents a cluster of syntactic features. IP is the landing place for VP-external local adjuncts, V' for VP-adjuncts (e.g. object arguments), and V^u is for certain V-adjuncts (such as some directional adverbials which bind closely to the verb) (Maienborn, 1994). Because the subject is base-generated in VP, subjects and objects are not separated by a boundary that blocks governments (I) and therefore an object can change its case while remaining in the same serial position. This is the main difference to English where the subject is not in VP. In a strongly configurational language, such as English, word order is constrained by VP in such a way that it blocks government from outside. Thus, there is no way to assign nominative case to an NP inside VP, because nominative case is assigned by I, which is not part of VP. Therefore the subject must precede VP. Figure 2 shows this structure.

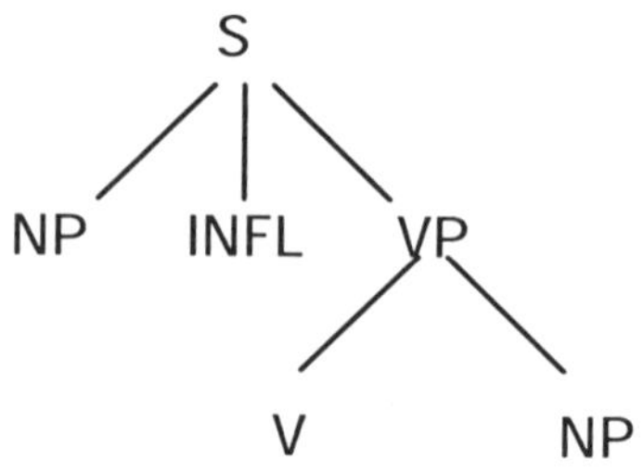

Figure 2.

Within a non-configurational analysis of German (c.f. Haider, 1995) differences between topicalized and untopicalized clauses are explained instead by the argument structure of the verb, which favours a particular serial order. This, however, does not make a difference to the present argument, since both accounts show *syntactic similarity* between topicalized and untopicalized actives but *different conceptual behaviour*. Cross-linguistically, English actives and German (untopicalized) actives are similar both syntactically and conceptually. The same applies to English passives and German passives. Both exhibit focus on the patient of the action, which is the surface subject. In both languages, passivisation involves an auxiliary and the agent is contained in a prepositional noun phrase.

This syntactic similarity, however, is at the level of underlying syntactic form rather than superficial word order or phrase structure. As shown in examples 7 and 8, German word order does not usually match the word ordering of an English translation of the primes. Specifically, since German is underlying verb final, the relative positions of verbs and complements are different. If structures such as actives and passives can be primed crosslinguistically from German to English, it therefore seems likely that the priming effect must be based on a level of representation at least as abstract as underlying syntactic form.

(7a) Die Feuerwehr konnte den Brand nicht löschen.
(literally: The firebrigade could the blaze not extinguish.)

(7b) The firebrigade could not extinguish the blaze.

(8a) Der Igel wird von einem Auto überfahren.
(literally: The hedgehog is by a car run over.)

(8b) The hedgehog is run over by a car.

The presence and strength of crosslinguistic priming of actives and passives therefore comments on the question of the degree of abstraction of the representation(s) involved in the priming effect. Further, the inclusion of German topicalizations allows us to tease apart the influences of syntactic and conceptual factors on sentence priming. The effect of German topicalizations on the production of either English actives or English passives provides a measure of the extent to which the effect is syntactic, on the one hand, or conceptual, on the other. Specifically, if sentence priming is solely related to syntactic structure, we would expect German actives and topicalizations to both prime English actives, and to a simiiar extent. (And German passives should of course prime English passives.) If, however, conceptual structure is critically involved in the priming effect, we would expect German topicalizations to prime English passives.

Heydel and Murray (1997, 1998a) carried out experiments which tested these possibilities. Participants were presented with picture pairs and German sentence primes. For each pair of pictures they had to decide whether the German sentence related to the events shown in the picture (this was never the case for experimental items) and to describe each picture in one complete sentence. Examples of the three prime types are shown below:

Prime Types:

(Active) Ein PR-Mann berät den Manager.
(Passive) Der Manager wird von einem PR-Mann beraten.
(Topicalization) Den Manager berät ein PR-Mann.

(A PR-man advises the manager / The manager is advised by a PR-man)

The results showed clear cross-linguistic priming, with the frequency of production of actives increasing by 7% following an active rather than a passive prime and passive responses increasing by 8% following their corresponding primes. These results are very similar in magnitude to the effect found with monolingual priming of English actives and passives. This is true both with respect to the original Bock studies and also in a more recent study by Heydel and Murray (1998b) using identical methodology to the cross-linguistic experiment. In all cases, the magnitude of the priming effect was around 8%. The effect, however, does not appear to be a syntactic one. The conceptual form of the prime was crucial, since topicalizations behaved like passives in that they, too, facilitated passive responses. The production of passives increased by 11% following topicalization primes and there was no evidence of a difference in the form of the priming effect resulting from passive and topicalization primes[5].

Although the close similarity in magnitude of the priming effects found with monolingual and cross-linguistic procedures suggests that they engage similar processes, it might nonetheless be argued that there is something 'odd' about the cross-linguistic procedure which inhibits syntactic effects. It could, for instance, be suggested that it involves an element of translation not found in 'normal' discourse. It's unlikely, however, that 'translation' could account for the nature of these findings. To do so, it would need to be suggested that translation somehow promotes conceptual effects at the expense of syntactic ones. The opposite, however, appears to be the case. Rather than diminishing syntactic effects in translation, syntax plays a role which can best be described as 'excessive'. Inexperienced translators, in particular, tend to reproduce the syntactic surface structure of the original utterance, at times regardless of conceptual or grammatical constraints (Krings, 1986; Bosshardt & Hagen, 1988). The reason for this inappropriate echoing of syntactic form is unclear, but one possibility, of course, is syntactic priming.

In order to assess directly the role played by translation in the cross-linguistic procedure, we conducted a second experiment specifically involving translation. It employed the same materials as the first experiment, except that the associated 'priming' sentences always described the events shown in the right hand picture. Participants were asked to provide a description of the left hand picture and to translate a German sentence, such as those below, into English.

(A) Ein Auto überfährt den Igel.

(P) Der Igel wird von einem Auto überfahren.

(T) Den Igel überfährt ein Auto.

Possible responses could be:

(A) A car runs over the hedgehog.

(P) The hedgehog is run over by a car.

(A*) *The hedgehog runs over a car.

As expected, there was a massive effect of syntactic form; active responses increased by 59% and passive responses by 54% following their corresponding primes. From the magnitude of this effect it might be suggested that the translation task involves only 'syntactic echoing' and does not engage any of the same processes as the priming procedure. However, while there are clearly differences between the tasks, this does not appear to be the case. There were a substantial number of 'other' responses (20%), which did not follow either of the possible syntactic forms, and participants never produced semantically anomalous sentences such as (A*). In fact the results show topicalizations pulled in both directions, with evidence for both syntactic and conceptual effects. Conceptual effects were also shown overall insofar as conceptual features such as the animacy of the agent influenced the overall production rate of actives vs. passives for all prime types. This effect however, was largest with topicalizations. For topicalizations with animate agents (15 items) there were 56% actives, but for those with inanimate agents (9 items) the percentage of active responses dropped to only 14%. We concluded therefore that 'translation' shows influences of both conceptual and syntactic form. It seems clear, however, that it is not 'translation' in the first experiment which gives rise to the results.

The fact that a cross-linguistic form of the priming task does not seriously impinge on the magnitude of the effect lends support to Bock's contention that it arises as a consequence of the priming of abstract forms, rather than anything which may be specific to particular lexical items, metrical form or even the ordering of particular lexical types. It also seems clear that the priming effect does not critically depend on precise details of the priming procedure. While Bock required participants to repeat the prime and produce spoken target responses, we used, in both the cross-linguistic and monolingual studies, a read prime and a written response. It appears therefore that priming is not dependent upon engaging the same set of output processes twice in succession. Again, this adds weight to the argument that the basis of the effect lies in underlying abstract representations.

If, however, we wish to argue that these representations are syntactic in form, we rapidly run into difficulty when looking at the crosslinguistic data. German topicalizations and English actives have a similar syntactic form, and topicalizations and English passives do not. Yet we find topicalizations priming English passives. Furthermore, the magnitude of this effect is equivalent to the strength of the priming from passives to passives.

It appears therefore that, in some way, underlying conceptual form must be critically involved in the priming effect, since this is the only thing shared by passives and topicalizations which is not also shared by actives. If, as we have suggested, crosslinguistic priming engages the same set of mechanisms which are responsible for monolinguistic priming, then it appears that this too cannot be critically based on surface syntactic form per se. Rather, it seems likely that it is the close relationship between the nature of the conceptual representation and the choice of surface form which leads to repetition of the same structure.

NOTES

[1] In using the term "representation" here, we don't mean to imply that this necessarily takes the form of an isolatable mental process or state. It could, from a connectionist viewpoint, be realised diffusely and in conjunction with other processes. We simply refer to something which can, at some *functional* level of description, be referred to as a representation.

[2] The reason for this, of course, is that there was some variation in the number of 'other' responses produced across the experimental conditions.

[3] We use the term 'conceptual form' to refer to a complete description of the relationships between the conceptual features of an utterance, including factors such as agenthood, focus, etc.

[4] The topicalization is equivalent to what Prat-Sala and Branigan (this volume) refer to as a 'dislocated active' in Spanish and Catalan.

[5] In fact there was a trend numerically, but not statistically, towards a slightly larger amount of passive response priming by topicalizations.

REFERENCES

Basden, B.H., Bonilla-Meeks, J.L., & Basden, D.R. (1994). Cross-language priming in word-fragment completion. *Journal of Memory and Language, 33,* 69-82.

Bever, T.G., & McElree, B. (1988). Empty categories access their antecedents during comprehension. *Linguistic Inquiry, 19,* 35-43.

Bock, K.J. (1986). Syntactic persistence in language production. *Cognitive Psychology, 18,* 355-387.

Bock, J.K. (1989). Closed class immanence in sentence production. *Cognition, 31,* 163-186.

Bock, J.K., & Loebell, H. (1990). Framing sentences. *Cognition, 35,* 1-39.

Bock, J.K., Loebell, H., & Morey, R. (1992). From Conceptual roles to structural relations: Bridging the syntactic cleft. *Psychological Review, 99,* 15-171.

Bock, J.K., & Miller, C.A. (1991). Broken agreement. *Cognitive Psychology, 23,* 45-93.

Bosshardt, H., & Hagen, B. (1988). Einfluß der englischsprachigen Textoberfläche auf ihre deutsche Übersetzung. *Archiv der Psychologie, 140,* 127-135.

Branigan, H.P., Pickering, M.J., Liversedge, S.P., Stewart, A.J., & Urbach, T.P. (1995). Syntactic priming: Investing the mental representation of language. *Journal of Psycholinguistic Research.*

Branigan, H.P., & Prat-Sala, M.(1998). A cross-linguistic perspective on discourse context and syntactic processing in language production. In this volume.

Chomsky, N. (1965). *Aspects of the theory of syntactic structure.* Cambridge Mass.: MIT Press.

Chomsky, N. (1981). *Lectures on Government and Binding.* Dordrecht: Foris.

Chomsky, N. (1995). *The Minimalist Program.* Current Studies in Linguistics, 28. Cambridge, Mass.: MIT Press, 1995.

Clifton, C., & Frazier, L. (1986). The use of syntactic information in filling gaps. *Journal of Psycholinguistic Research, 15,* 209-224.

Estival, D. (1985). Syntactic priming of the passive in English. *Text, 5,* 7-21.

Fillmore, C (1968). The case for case. In E. Bach & R. T. Harms (Eds.), *Universals of linguistic theory*. New York: Holt, Rhinehardt, & Winston.

Fodor, J.D. (1993). Processing empty categories: A question of visibility. In G.T.M. Altmann & R. Shillcock (Eds.), *Cognitive models of speech processing: The second Sperlonga meeting*. Hillsdale, N.J.: Erlbaum.

Frazier, L., & Clifton, C. (1989). Successive cyclicity in the grammar and parser. *Language and Cognitive Processes, 4*, 93-126.

Freedman, S.E., & Forster, K.I. (1985). The psychological status of overgenerated sentences. *Cognition, 19*, 101-131.

Garrett, M. (1980). Levels of processing in sentence production. In B. Butterworth (Ed.), *Language Production, 1*. London: Academic Press.

Grewendorf, G. (1992). Parametrisierung der Syntax. Zur "kognitiven Revolution" in der Linguistik. In L Hoffmann (Ed.). *Deutsche Syntax, Ansichten und Aussichten*. Berlin/N. York: de Gruyter.

Haider, H. (1995). *Studies in comparative Germanic syntax*. Dordrecht: Kluwer.

Harley, T.A. (1984). A critique of top-down independent levels models of speech production: Evidence from non-plan-internal production. *Cognitive Science, 8*, 191-219.

Heydel, M., & Murray, W.S. (1997). Conceptual form and the basis of sentence priming: Cross-linguistic evidence. *10th CUNY Sentence Processing Conference*, Santa Monica, March.

Heydel, M., & Murray, W.S. (1998a). Conceptual structure in sentence production: Evidence from cross-linguistic priming. Submitted for publication.

Heydel, M., & Murray, W.S. (1998b). Syntactic priming? Maybe not! *11th CUNY Sentence Processing Conference*, New Brunswick, March.

Jackendoff, R. (1972). *Semantic interpretation in generative grammar*. Cambridge Mass.: MIT Press.

Jackendoff, R. (1983). *Semantics and Cognition*. Cambridge Mass.: MIT Press.

Kaplan, R., & Bresnan, J. (1982). Lexical-functional grammar: a formal system for grammatical representation. In J. Bresnan (Ed.), *The mental representation of grammatical relations*. Cambridge Mass.: MIT Press.

Ketley, C. W., Spinks, J. A., & de Gelder, B. (1994). Asymmetrical cross-language priming effects. *Memory and Cognition, 22*, 70-84

Krings, H. P. (1986). *Was in den Köpfen von Übersetzern vorgeht: Eine empirische Untersuchung zur Struktur des Übersetzungsprozesses an fortgeschrittenen Französischlernern.* Tübingen: Narr.

Levelt, W., & Kelter, S. (1982). Surface form and memory in question answering. *Cognitive Psychology, 14*, 78-106.

Love, T., & Swinney, D. (1996). Coreference processing and levels of analysis in object-relative constructions; Demonstration of antecedent reactivation with the cross-modal priming paradigm. *Journal of Psycholinguistic Research, 25*, 5-24.

Maienborn, C. (1994).Überlegungen zum Fokusverhalten von Adjunkten am Beispiel der Lokaladverbiale. *Hamburger Arbeitspapiere zur Sprachproduktion, 15*, 29-66.

McElree, B., & Bever, T.G. (1989). The psychological reality of linguistically defined gaps. *Journal of Psycholinguistic Research (Special Issue), 18*, 21-35.

Nicol, J.L. & Pickering, M.J. (1993). Processing syntactically ambiguous sentences: Evidence from semantic priming. *Journal of Psycholinguistic Research, 22*, 207-237.

Pickering, M.J., & Branigan, H.P. (in press). The representation of verbs: Evidence from syntactic priming in language production. *Journal of Memory and Language.*

Pinker, S. (1989). *Learnability and Cognition: The acquisition of argument structure.* MIT Press. Cambridge, Mass.

Schenkein, J. (1980). A taxonomy for repeating action sequences in natural conversation. In B. Butterworth (Ed.), *Language Production, 1.* London: Academic Press.

Stowe, L.A. (1986). Parsing WH-constructions: Evidence for on-line gap location. *Language and Cognitive Processes, 1*, 227-245.

Tannen, D. (1989). *Talking voices: repetition, dialogue and imagery in conversational discourse.* Cambridge: Cambridge University Press.

Vigliocco, G., Butterworth, B., & Semenza, C. (1995). Constructing subject-verb agreement in speech: the role of semantic and morphological factors. *Journal of Memory and Language, 34*, 186-215.

Vigliocco, G., Hartsuiker, R.J., Jarema, G., & Kolk, H.H.J. (1996). One or more labels on the bottles? Notional concord in Dutch and French. *Language and Cognitive Processes, 11*, 407-442.

Weiner, E., & Labov, W. (1983). Constraints on the agentless passive. *Journal of Linguistics, 19*, 29-58.

SUBJECT INDEX

STUDIES IN THEORETICAL PSYCHOLINGUISTICS

1. L. Solan: *Pronominal Reference.* Child Language and the Theory of Grammar. 1983 ISBN 90-277-1495-9
2. B. Lust (ed.): *Studies in the Acquisition of Anaphora.* Volume I: Defining the Constraints. 1986 ISBN 90-277-2121-1; Pb 90-277-2122-X
3. N. M. Hyams: *Language Acquisition and the Theory of Parameters.* 1986 ISBN 90-277-2218-8; Pb 90-277-2219-6
4. T. Roeper and E. Williams (eds.): *Parameter Setting.* 1987 ISBN 90-277-2315-X; Pb 90-277-2316-8
5. S. Flynn: *A Parameter-Setting Model of L2 Acquisition.* Experimental Studies in Anaphora. 1987 ISBN 90-277-2374-5; Pb 90-277-2375-3
6. B. Lust (ed.): *Studies in the Acquisition of Anaphora.* Volume II: Applying the Constraints. 1987 ISBN 1-55608-022-0; Pb 1-55608-023-9
7. G. N. Carlson and M. K. Tanenhaus (eds.): *Linguistic Structure in Language Processing.* 1989 ISBN 1-55608-074-3; Pb 1-55608-075-1
8. S. Flynn and W. O'Neil (eds.): *Linguistic Theory in Second Language Acquisition.* 1988 ISBN 1-55608-084-0; Pb 1-55608-085-9
9. R. J. Matthews and W. Demopoulos (eds.): *Learnability and Linguistic Theory.* 1989 ISBN 0-7923-0247-8; Pb 0-7923-0558-2
10. L. Frazier and J. de Villiers (eds.): *Language Processing and Language Acquisition.* 1990 ISBN 0-7923-0659-7; Pb 0-7923-0660-0
11. J.A. Padilla: *On the Definition of Binding Domains in Spanish.* Evidence from Child Language. 1990 ISBN 0-7923-0744-5
12. M. de Vincenzi: *Syntactic Parsing Strategies in Italian.* The Minimal Chain Principle. 1991 ISBN 0-7923-1274-0; Pb 0-7923-1275-9
13. D.C. Lillo-Martin: *Universal Grammar and American Sign Language.* Setting the Null Argument Parameters. 1991 ISBN 0-7923-1419-0
14. A.E. Pierce: *Language Acquisition and Syntactic Theory.* A Comparative Analysis of French and English Child Grammars. 1992 ISBN 0-7923-1553-7
15. H. Goodluck and M. Rochemont (eds.): *Island Constraints.* Theory, Acquisition and Processing. 1992 ISBN 0-7923-1689-4
16. J.M. Meisel (ed.): *The Acquisition of Verb Placement.* Functional Categories and V2 Phenomena in Language Acquisition. 1992 ISBN 0-7923-1906-0
17. E.C. Klein: *Toward Second Language Acquisition.* A Study of Null-Prep. 1993 ISBN 0-7923-2463-3

STUDIES IN THEORETICAL PSYCHOLINGUISTICS

18. J.L. Packard: *A Linguistic Investigation of Aphasic Chinese Speech.* 1993
ISBN 0-7923-2466-8
19. J. Archibald: *Language Learnability and L2 Phonology:* The Acquisition of Metrical Parameters. 1993 ISBN 0-7923-2486-2
20. M.W. Crocker: *Computational Psycholinguistics.* An Interdisciplinary Approach to the Study of Language. 1996 ISBN 0-7923-3802-2; Pb 0-7923-3806-5
21. J.D. Fodor and F. Ferreira (eds.): *Reanalysis in Sentence Processing.* 1998
ISBN 0-7923-5099-5
22. L. Frazier: *On Sentence Interpretation.* 1999 ISBN 0-7923-5508-3
23. B. Hemforth and L. Konieczny (eds.): *German Sentence Processing.* 2000
ISBN 0-7923-6104-0
24. M. De Vincenzi and V. Lombardo (eds.): *Cross-linguistic Perspectives on Language Processing.* 2000 ISBN 0-7923-6146-6

KLUWER ACADEMIC PUBLISHERS – DORDRECHT / BOSTON / LONDON